Y0-BER-696

# THE COLLEGE DROPOUT

# THE COLLEGE DROPOUT AND THE UTILIZATION OF TALENT

EDITED BY

LAWRENCE A. PERVIN, PH.D.

LOUIS E. REIK, M.D.

WILLARD DALRYMPLE, M.D.



PRINCETON, NEW JERSEY
PRINCETON UNIVERSITY PRESS
1966

Library of Congress Card No. 66-11976
Printed in the United States of America
by Princeton University Press
Princeton, New Jersey

# *FOREWORD*

THE PRINCETON UNIVERSITY CONFERENCES are a series devoted to discussion of significant issues for the academic and non-academic communities. This volume has emerged from a Princeton University Conference held in October 1964 and organized by Princeton's University Health Services. The conference—like the volume, entitled "The College Dropout and the Utilization of Talent"—enlisted not only most of the authors represented here but also other men and women from the academic, medical, and business worlds who were interested in this topic. From their interest and participation as well as that of our contributors has come much of our stimulus.

This plurality of experiences and approaches to our topic prevents the book from being devoted solely to a psychiatric, an administrative, or any other exclusive consideration of the issues involved in dropping out of college and in utilizing talent. Instead we have tried to organize an inclusive discussion of issues, facts, causes, and solutions (both actual and potential).

The college president or dean responsible for formulating his institution's response to the challenges of the dropout phenomenon, for example, will find a multitude of pertinent facts and opinions presented herein. He will not find, however, one answer or group of answers to "the problem." Its many aspects forbid such dogmatism. The contributors and the editors have sought to reveal the diversity of causes, effects, and possible answers which exists. Our aim has been to raise the sophistication of our society's consideration of this complex topic and not to convert individuals to a single point of view. Thus the reader will find it a frequent conclusion that dropping out is as beneficial to one student as it may be unfortunate for another, and will note that the utilization of talent proceeds from a complex interaction of many facets of the individual's mind and the institution's nature.

In their work the editors have enjoyed enthusiastic cooperation from the contributors, to whom they acknowledge grateful thanks. They also thank especially four other contributors to the conference whose ideas have spread to various parts of the volume: Arthur B. Bronwell, Dean of Engineering, University of Connecticut; Donald S. Bridgman, formerly of the American Telephone and Telegraph Company; Robert E. Iffert, United States Office of Education; and Joshua A. Fishman, Dean, Graduate School of Education, Yeshiva University. On the Princeton scene, two men have made particular contributions: Charles Taggert, then director of the Princeton University Conference Office, who organized the logistics of the conference superbly, and David Harrop of Princeton University Press, who gave encouragement and useful advice on the manuscript. Many other friends have contributed a share as well.

Finally, we extend to our readers our hopes that they be as educated by their reading as we have been by our writing and editorial work.

FOR THE EDITORS,

Willard Dalrymple, M.D.
Director, University Health Services
Princeton University

Princeton, New Jersey
August 1965

## CONTENTS

# PART I

# RESEARCH AND ADMINISTRATION

# *INTRODUCTION*

## THE DROPOUT IN CONFLICT WITH SOCIETY

THE EDITORS

THE MATTER OF dropping out of college, with its widespread ramifications in the educational and social realms, transcends the merely personal psychology of the individual. It is a phenomenon that highlights the ancient struggle between the environment and the individual, each striving to modify the other in ways as complex as life itself, until a better balance is achieved. This book, by focusing in its first section on social or environmental factors related to dropping out and in its second on the inner life of the dropout himself, attempts to avoid an attitude that favors either society or the dropout, *but seeks rather to invite study of the highly emotional interaction between the two.* If examination of this interaction discloses elements of ignorance or extremism on both sides, more rooted in emotionalism than in calm objectivity, perhaps the dropout may be less widely included among the failures, delinquents, and other undesirables. The sensitivity of students to the value system of a society that condemns dropping out is hinted at, even if half-facetiously, in the remark of one student: "If you quit school after your bachelor's degree, you're a dropout."

### *Dropouts and Educational Issues*

The eighteen-year-old daughter of a utilities executive decides that college is incompatible with marriage and drops out in her freshman year. . . .

The nineteen-year-old son of a middle-class businessman finds himself without a vocational goal and bored. He drops out in his sophomore year to enter military service. . . .

The twenty-year-old son of a steelworker, a lad with an I.Q. of 152, suffers a schizophrenic illness in his junior year. He is able to return to college two years later, shifting from a major in mathematics to one in psychology. . . .

The nineteen-year-old daughter of an accountant who has wished since high school that she had had the courage to try a career of free-lance writing leaves a small liberal arts college to live in Greenwich Village and work seriously on a novel she has had in mind for three years. . . .

An eighteen-year-old National Merit Scholar is required to withdraw from an outstanding metropolitan university for plagiarism. . . .

A junior at a leading engineering college has always been known to be brilliant in mathematics and theoretical physics. He has never attained outstanding marks in college, nor has he sustained creative work of any kind; at the end of the junior year he fails. . . .

To these fictional but representative capsule narratives most readers can add their own examples. Though the strands are so dissimilar, American education binds them all together into the rope called "dropouts." What is the significance of these events to the individuals and their families, to the colleges, and to society and the nation? What complicated personal and institutional factors led up to them? What are the issues raised? The investigation of these questions forms the subject matter of this book.

Clearly the investigation must cover considerable ground, and the problems involved lead into many of the great contemporary issues of higher education. Indeed, the fact that there are great issues today which demand a central place in the public attention accounts for the rise in interest in the college dropout. With typical commitment, the American people are convinced both of the desirability of education and of its perfectibility. While their commitment does not carry over into agreement on specific issues or methods, it does lead to general impatience with whatever stands in the way of progress and perfection. If a college education is desirable, society asks, why should any young person not seek to attain it in the appointed time? Society's immediate reactions are that the dropout has sacrificed his own future, squandered his institution's resources, and indeed detracted from the national interest itself.

Are these reactions justified? This volume urges a dispassionate point of view, and though few definitive answers to broad problems will be offered herein, the reader will find many suggestions that cases and problems differ, and that dropping out of college is not necessarily undesirable or wasteful. For some, leaving college—usually temporarily, but on occasion permanently—may be more educational than staying. In a majority of the examples given at the start of this introduction, it is possible that the student advanced more rapidly toward maturity, including educational maturity, by leaving college than if he had been required or enabled to continue. In many cases, the student's intellectual efficiency in learning has dissipated; he has "lost motivation"; he has "run out of gas"; he has suffered any of numerous emotional disturbances or distortions. The dean, the faculty adviser, the counselor, the psychiatrist know empirically that time away from college may help his efficiency.

And yet a nagging thought urges itself: if educators were more knowledgeable, more effective, better at preparing themselves and their students, could this event have been avoided? Here the trap may be the traditional inclination to think of education as preparation for life, although, as Dr. Kubie suggests, it may be equally true that life is a preparation for education.

"Education as preparation for life" regards education as the acquisition of tools and the skill to use them. Once accomplished, it provides the thoroughly educated young person with competence to deal with life's problems and to be a contributing member of society, earning a higher income in so doing. The faster, the better; so runs the theory. But "life as a preparation for education" regards a varied experience as valuable for learning. Not only does motivation often improve following a period of living away from the academic scene, but also comprehension, sense of proportion, and the ability to deal with content and methods meaningfully.

In this connection, there is a surprising and striking contrast between the concern of the older generation about college dropouts and the limited attention it pays to the desirability of submitting to recurring periods of formal education throughout life, particularly for those in professional fields where the rapid accumulation of new knowledge and change would suggest periodic reexamination of professional competency. Are there parallels here between the prolonged educational ordeal for the younger generation in the civilized world and the various initiation rites of primitive peoples? In both cases, once having passed through the ordeal and having been granted the privileges of adulthood, the initiated and the community are apt to assume that their education is complete.

But the issues raised by the dropout are much broader than the timing of education. As the colleges admit increasingly higher proportions of academically gifted students, both students and colleges are showing a growing preoccupation with matters having to do with the optimal utilization of talent. Is higher education's traditional insistence on disciplined conformity to a prescribed curriculum harmful to the creative few, though perhaps beneficial to the many? Are the students who wish to drop out because they believe that college stifles their creative impulses necessarily those with true creative potential? Or are they those who imagine, as many adolescents seem to do, that the informal life of Bohemia is a necessary condition and stimulus for creativity? How can students with a sustaining and sustained drive toward creativity be distinguished from those with a record of high academic achievement and occasional flashes of brilliance who are, nevertheless, basically hampered by inner conflict and so find it impossible to organize their energies in disciplined and creative ways?

And, then, what about the "match" between student and college? How often is dropping out the result of a mismatch? Should the aim be to evolve educational institutions of various kinds, each of which selects and admits only students with conforming expectations and needs? Or is there virtue in mixing the types of students and even the types of intellectual and sociological characteristics at any one institution?

Other issues raised by the dropout question are highly practical. What is the responsibility of society in training certain classes of professionals? The large supply of medical school applicants not only ensures enough manpower to fill available places in medical schools, but also means that selection is so rigorous and motivation so excellent that dropouts are relatively rare—less than 10 percent of any one class in recent years. The issue then becomes: who has the responsibility to provide the new facilities to educate the added doctors needed by the nation? At the other extreme is the plight of engineering education. There are too few young people interested in engineering, and of those who enter engineering schools far too many drop out before the completion of their course—over one-third in recent years. Whose responsibility is it to develop new methods to decrease the number of dropouts and to increase the number of applicants?

Some of these issues will be dealt with directly in this volume; others will be left to the reader to develop. The findings and hypotheses reported will all have relevance and significance beyond the immediate problems of the dropout, applying in addition to some of the fundamental questions facing our educational system.

### *Definitions and Assessments*

In this volume, the term "college dropout" refers to any student who leaves college for any period of time, regardless of reason, and thus does not obtain his degree at the same time as the class with which he originally enrolled. The definition is perhaps excessively broad, in that it includes transfer students with non-transfer students and fails to distinguish between students dropping out for differing reasons, such as academic, health, personal, disciplinary, and other cases. At the same time, the definition may be too narrow, since it fails to indicate the limits of the general problem of society's failure to utilize all talent effectively—disregarding, for example, the talented individuals who never attend college at all as well as those who graduate on schedule but whose intellectual and psychological growth in college is far below their capacity.

At any rate, college dropouts as defined above actually outnumber non-dropouts. Only about 40 percent of the nation's students graduate at the date scheduled for the class of their matriculation. The table below shows the variation from college to college in those graduating on schedule:

| | |
|---|---|
| University of Georgia | 35% |
| University of Iowa | 37% |
| University of Wisconsin | 38% |
| Pennsylvania State University | 43% |
| City University of New York | 45% |
| Hollins College | 53% |
| Princeton University | 80% |

Summerskill's review of the literature (1962) reports variation in these rates from 12 to 82 percent. Despite changes in colleges, students, curriculum, tuition fees, scholarship aid, and teaching methods, the national dropout rate appears to have been relatively constant since World War II.

Not only do the dropout rates vary from college to college, but also the year of withdrawal and the stated reasons for dropping out. Half of all withdrawals throughout the United States occur by the end of freshman year. At the University of Iowa, over 74 percent of the withdrawals take place before the beginning of the sophomore year. At some other colleges, such as Princeton and Harvard, dropouts are more evenly distributed over the four years.

To some extent, these differences in rates and patterns result from differences in selection and economic background. State institutions which must by law accept all or a majority of the state's high-school graduates on application usually have a high, early dropout rate. Moreover, many of these students do not have the financial reserves with which to meet personal or family reverses.

But there is reason to suspect that other factors, such as motivation, are of considerable importance, apart from the variables of selection and economic background of students. At another state institution, the University of California, for example, only the top 15 percent of high-school graduates are eligible for admission, yet 45 percent of the students withdraw before completing the requirements for a degree. At Pennsylvania State University in 1958, over 74 percent of the freshman class came from the top two-fifths of their high-school class, yet over 50 percent of the class did not graduate in four years, and in spite of a considerable increase in admission selectivity over the previous decade, the withdrawal rate showed little change. The most prestigious colleges nowadays admit only students believed capable of completing their college work; nevertheless, they continue to have dropouts. Even among such a select group as winners of Merit awards, from 10 to 15 percent become dropouts from college.[1]

These variations in patterns and rates of withdrawal, together with evidence of the importance of motivational factors, suggest the need for extensive, systematic research in this area. As Dr. Kubie suggests, the learning process and disruptions in it constitute a significant and complex area. Only research on all phases of the problem from a variety of points of view can hope to result in clarification of the relevant problems. This means that we need demographic studies, sociological studies of institutions, psychological studies of individual students to determine who drops out under what circumstances, and studies of individual students in interaction with different aspects of the college environment. The essays in this volume represent the findings of current research in this area and suggest avenues of research for the future.

### *The Dropout and Society's Value System*

When a student leaves college before graduating, he evokes a variety of responses from the social milieu, from his college, from his parents, and from himself. These responses may to some degree be appropriate and reasonable, but they are often strongly colored by the kind of emotional excess that an individual's deviation from some widely accepted and institutionalized value system is apt to evoke. The danger is that there then follows a shift in emphasis away from the event of dropping out itself—the rationale for which remains unexamined because the act is judged in advance to be rebellious or perverse—to a tangential debate between those who uphold and those who seem to threaten conventional standards. Experience with dropouts themselves, the majority of whom seem immersed in a struggle to find solutions for private troubles and personal aspirations, suggests that they are far from soliciting such a debate, for it only compounds their difficulties.

1 A. W. Astin, "Personal and environmental factors associated with college dropouts among high aptitude students," *Journal of Educational Psychology*, 1964, 55, pp. 219-227.

## *The Dropout in Conflict with Society*

In the state of present knowledge, it is of course difficult to demonstrate conclusively to what extent society, whether at the national level or otherwise, is guilty of premature judgments and emotionalism when it looks at the college dropout. There are, however, hints that the guilt is there. The dropout is often referred to as a drain on national resources. He is presumed to represent wasted talent, so that a dropout rate of 50 percent is taken to mean the loss to the national economy and welfare of 50 percent of the most talented population, which then becomes a cause for national concern.

As applied to engineering, this concern becomes particularly acute. The proportion of students completing their bachelor's degree to students matriculating in engineering is particularly small: 36 percent for state universities—as low as 20 percent in some—and 55 percent for private colleges. These figures led the members of a committee on engineering student attrition to conclude:

> We are living in an age of swiftly evolving technologies, as well as of a rapidly rising scale of technological needs. Our burgeoning population, the growing emphasis upon research to unlock the new sciences and to develop the new technologies, the mounting needs of industry, and the astronomical needs of our defense and space technology programs are all geared to a much higher order of science and technology in the years ahead. The increasing sophistication of technology in itself is demanding not only a higher level of scientific and technological competence to bring about innovation, but also a much larger total engineering manpower pool to translate innovations into technological progress.
>
> Competition with Europe, Russia, and Japan will continue to mount at an accelerating pace, jeopardizing large sectors of American industry. A recent report of the Engineers Joint Council has made it abundantly evident that the diversion of scientific and engineering manpower resources to the military and space programs has seriously retarded technological growth in many areas vital to our industrial economy and public needs.

> Beyond our own needs, there is our growing moral commitment to the free world to assist newly emerging nations in their educational and technological growth.
>
> From a purely competitive point of view, it is a virtual certainty that within a decade, Russia will have an engineering manpower pool exceeding our own by a numerical amount equal to our engineering manpower pool today. During the next decade, Russia will graduate about 1,350,000 engineers, as against an estimated 435,000 in the United States. Today, both nations have approximately equal engineering manpower pools. With Russia able to deploy her technological manpower to suit her aggressive political ambitions, this could be a decisive force in the struggle between Communism and the free world.
>
> In the face of growing need, the year-by-year decline in engineering enrollments and graduations poses a severe threat to our nation's wholesome industrial and economic growth, as well as to its influence as a stabilizing force in the free world.[2]

In this case, society concentrates on the need for specially trained manpower to meet certain needs, particularly in competition with foreign countries, and neglects the status of the individual in the educational system and even the possibility of other sources of such manpower.

The questions raised by this engineering report can be generalized as follows: Should the attitude expressed in it apply to fields of less critical national interest? Does the report realistically represent the problem? How does one measure the loss of talent either to the engineering profession or to society as a whole? Realistic answers to such questions can be given more confidently when more information is available about why these students drop out, what happens to them afterward, and what alternative means exist for increasing the supply of engineering manpower.

The engineering report stresses national concerns. What is the overall federal responsibility in the college dropout prob-

[2] "Engineering student attrition," New York: Engineering Manpower Commission, 1963.

lem? What type of investment might the federal government be willing to make to deal with it?

Federal concern to date has focused primarily on the high-school dropout. Even here, an eminent economist, Burton Weisbrod, after a benefit-cost analysis of an attempt to reduce the high-school dropout rate, concluded that the experimental attempt was successful in many ways but was not profitable on a purely economic basis. While the preventive program kept some students from dropping out of high school, few monetary returns could be proved. Furthermore, "the data suggests that waiting until students are 16 years old to cope with the dropout hazard may be too late. Prevention seems to be difficult at that stage, even when extensive counseling and work-study programs are tried; attitudes and motivations may be too solidified."[3]

These conclusions seem relevant to the college dropout problem as well as to the high-school dropout. At the very least, proposals for extensive programs to prevent dropping out need critical consideration and evaluation by pilot projects before adoption.

The United States is not alone in its concern about college dropouts. In Costa Rica, they are one of the major research interests of the colleges; and at the University of Costa Rica each person leaving the university is interviewed by a social worker.[4] In England, where only the intellectual cream has been admitted to the universities and 75 percent of the students are grant-aided, 20 percent leave college without a degree. Malleson notes the increasing interest in the college dropout at British universities as pressure upon university places increases. But the quotation that follows raises the question whether in England, also, the dropout is too readily consigned to the category of failure and waste, and whether the assumption is too easily made that whatever time he spends in the university is worthless if he does not go on to qualify for a degree: "Since they all stay at least one year at $1,200 per head,

[3] B. A. Weisbrod, "Preventing high school Dropouts—a Benefit cost analysis," The Brookings Institution, November 1963.

[4] M. L. Coronado, "Costa Rica," in D. Funkenstein (ed.), *The student and mental health,* New York: World Federation for Mental Health, 1959.

the cost of failure to the British community is about twenty million dollars a year."[5]

In the Philippines, the community's extremely liberal attitude toward admission to college is in sharp contrast to the severe selectivity that prevails in England, where only one out of 640 can be accepted. "To most [Philippine] parents, a high school diploma is a sure passport to the university, hence many students are actually enrolled in universities who have neither the inclination nor the aptitude for higher education. The solution appears to be simply one of selection and screening of students who enter the universities."[6] Contrast this proposal with Malleson's disillusionment regarding careful screening as a device to solve the dropout situation in England: "It is our view that improved selection, even if proven methods are available, could hardly make a very great difference. . . . In our view any substantial reductions in the failure rates must be brought about by modifications in university practice and by improved techniques of managing the difficulties, both academic and personal, that individual students will inevitably meet during their course. Further research in this field can lead in two directions, to the university on the one hand and the student on the other, for it is in their mutual interaction that failure is born."[7]

Next, what response does the dropout receive from his college? How does the problem which he embodies relate to the college's own value system?

At a recent conference on the college dropout sponsored by the United States Office of Education, a preeminent item of discussion was the philosophy of education relating to dropouts. The following questions were raised: What percentage of entering and transfer students "must" be failed? Is the first semester of a student's college career a "trial" period? Is the college dropout really viewed as a problem or a responsibility by a sizable percentage of faculty and administration? Knoell,

[5] N. Malleson, "Great Britain," in *ibid.*, p. 48.

[6] E. Aldaba-Lim, "Philippines," in *ibid.*, p. 59.

[7] N. Malleson, "Student performance at University College, London, 1948-1951," *Universities Quarterly*, May 1958, pp. 288-319.

in her review of the dropout literature, raised the questions: Can the college afford to admit students whose objectives can be met with less than a four-year program? Does the faculty feel that a certain percentage of dismissals or probationary cases is healthy? Does the college regard the freshman year as a screening device, at least in part?[8]

Just as the college dropout can be viewed nationally from an economic perspective, so can he be viewed by the college in terms of the economic implications for facilities, faculties, and students. Robert Iffert, a pioneer in research on the college dropout, has analyzed some of these implications. He notes that a reduced enrollment leads to inefficient use of dormitories, laboratories, libraries, and other facilities. "On the other hand, the practice of overloading facilities with first-time students on the assumption that dropouts will bring enrollment and capacity into line is educationally irresponsible. Admission of replacements in the academic year will help utilization indices, but may seriously complicate programming and scheduling in smaller institutions."[9]

Iffert further notes that the withdrawal rate has implications for college faculties. A high dropout rate must inevitably have an effect upon faculty morale, particularly in relation to teaching introductory freshman courses. It seems likely that there is a circular effect here, with freshman students becoming disenchanted with faculty members who have become disenchanted with the high proportion of student withdrawals. Finally, the student who attends college briefly and obtains little has lost the money used to support this period at school, plus the income he might otherwise have made. Iffert concludes that "no adequate cost figures are available with which to estimate the aggregate cost of unused higher education facilities resulting from student dropout. Responsible administration dictates that these costs be determined institution by

[8] Dorothy Knoell, "Needed research on college dropouts," in J. R. Montgomery (ed.), *Proceedings of the research conference on college dropouts* (Cooperative Research Project No. F-065), Knoxville, Tenn.: University of Tennessee, 1964, pp. 54-83.

[9] R. E. Iffert, "Institutional implications—facilities, faculties, students," paper presented at the Princeton University Conference, October 8, 1964.

institution and that they be related to the costs of preventive measures such as increased faculty salaries."[10]

If the college sees itself as a place where all high-school graduates have an opportunity to experiment with higher education, then a high dropout rate may not detract from its mission. If it sees itself as a place where values and ideals are formed, then the success of the college depends upon the assimilation of those values and ideals by the students, a process that may or may not be related to the dropout rate. If the college's goal is the training of students in certain vocational skills, particularly if these skills are considered equivalent to a bachelor's degree, then a high dropout rate would clearly mean that the college was not effectively attaining its objective.

Obviously, colleges differ in their missions. Therefore, while the dropout phenomenon has ramifications common to all colleges, its significance varies from college to college. Furthermore, the relative amount of approval or disapproval of dropping out also varies. One dean of a liberal arts college has said, "My particular interest in the college dropout problem is simply related to the fact that if you lose 6 or 7 percent of a highly selected group, you want to be very certain you lose them for good reasons." Many of the contributions to this volume will be devoted to what these "good reasons" are, judged on various levels of practical and psychological sophistication. Administratively, of course, each college must decide for itself what represents a reasonable dropout rate and what constitutes a good reason for dropping out. The data and arguments presented here can only be background material for such decisions. And, of course, beyond the educational philosophies at play, the college must analyze the effect of the dropout rate on its own efficiency. What is the effect on the utilization of its physical plant, on student and faculty morale, and on the ratio of lower-level to higher-level courses, for example?

*The Parents' Point of View.* While government and college

[10] *Ibid.* For a review of studies of institutional efforts to help college dropouts, see the appendix to this volume: "Programs and selected publications relating to college dropouts," by Montgomery and Hills.

administrations ponder dropout rates in general, parents react to individual dropouts. Rationality and objectivity become even more difficult to achieve. Not only are the parents' affection and concern for their child immediately involved, but his dropping out of college also touches upon their own aspirations and upon their own uncertainties as to their role as parents. If the parental conclusion is that dropping out is a failure, then it may lead to the further conclusion that the parents have failed as parents. If the departure from college is attributed to psychopathology, this may also imply failure to the parents—failure to give the child something he needed or failure to help him in time of need. On the other hand, if dropping out expresses courage to pursue one's own goals, then the parents may feel proud that they have helped to give their child certain strengths which allow for individuality.

As Levenson points out in Chapter 9, parents interpret dropping out according to their own life experiences. For many, the child's admission to college, particularly a select college, represents a fulfilled dream and the fruition of years of struggle and hope. Any interruption of the smooth course of this dream shatters the image of hope created during the worthwhile years of effort. For example, the parents of a freshman who was having psychotic delusions and hallucinations struggled to keep their son in college. When the university insisted that he withdraw to receive psychiatric help, the parents sought to take him home for a week, after which they hoped he would be able to return. Another student who had reached the decision to drop out told of the struggle with his parents. They called him names, interpreted his behavior as an expression of hostility toward them, and said: "This will cost you $150,000. You'll kick yourself in the pants ten years from now. You're lazy and a coward. Don't expect to be able to bury your head in the ground."

These reactions are extreme but consistent with the attitudes of a substantial group of parents of dropouts. But they are not the only attitude parents express toward dropping out. Some are indifferent. Some, viewing it as wise, encourage it. Others see it as the only choice, and many view it with mixed feelings. Some parental attitudes are helpful to the student;

others are destructive. Some are realistic; others, unrealistic. One of the functions of this volume, especially in the chapters by Ford and Pervin, is to help parents and others have more realistic attitudes toward dropping out of college and to enable them to be more sophisticated and effective in their attempts to assist young people in their search for valid educational goals.

*The Attitude of the Student.* Not the least important is the attitude of the dropout toward himself and his own action, which must take into account the reaction of society, college, and family toward what he does. Indeed, he may have many attitudes toward dropping out, both at any one time and at different times. Previous to becoming a dropout, he may feel quite differently than immediately afterward. His feelings a number of years later may change still further. Pervin's chapter on long-term follow-up studies of dropouts documents some of these changes in attitudes.

Students' attitudes toward withdrawal are rarely independent of parental feelings. The interaction between student and parental attitudes is complex, involving rebellion, passivity, identification, counter-identification, and other dynamic processes discussed in Chapter 5.

Not only the event of dropping out but also the expressed reasons may be influenced by factors of which the dropout is not fully aware. One student wanted to leave college but could not decide to take the positive step of doing so. His partly unconscious strategy was to perform so poorly in his academic work that he would be required to leave. Obviously, disciplinary withdrawals, particularly when out of character, may have strong unconscious determinants, as in the case of a student whose brother, with whom he had long been in rivalry, had recently attracted parental attention by leaving college to live a bohemian life. It was in this setting that the student stole an item from a college-owned store in obvious fashion.

The social setting and size of the dropout rate similarly may influence withdrawals. The student at a large state institution with a high dropout rate may find it possible to be relatively comfortable about dropping out. In sharp contrast is the student who is the first representative of his home town at a prestigious college. Dropping out may mean to him that he has let down not only himself but his family and home town in a particularly conspicuous manner.

Over the years, predominant conventional wisdom has frowned on dropping out. This negative attitude has been summarized by Reik as follows: "To the colleges, dropping out appears equivalent to a kind of death, if only an intellectual one. Dropouts are referred to in academic circles as 'casualties' or 'non-survivors.' The dropout rate is called the 'mortality' rate."[11] These negative attitudes have not only had the effect of placing the dropout under increased pressure but have also often determined policies, particularly those concerning readmission and even concerning transfer students.

As this volume indicates, the tide seems to be turning in this value system—turning, at least, to the point where there are beginning signs of realization that individual dropouts need from society the forbearance and understanding that can come from a careful hearing in an atmosphere as free as possible from prejudice. The pioneering long-term follow-up studies of the fate of dropouts referred to in this volume have led to the discovery that many of them are not permanent dropouts, and that leaving college for a period, voluntarily or even involuntarily, may be useful to individual and society. R. Sargent Shriver, former director of the Peace Corps, has aptly summarized this more hopeful attitude: "If the college sophomore wants to drop out of school, let him. Let the bored or the confused or the burned-out undergraduates have a short, meaningful interlude—a sojourn in reality—for a year or two years, so that he can come back revitalized, committed, concerned enough to finish both college and graduate work."[12]

[11] L. E. Reik, "The dropout problem," *The Nation*, May 19, 1962, pp. 442-446.

[12] R. S. Shriver, *Wesleyan University News*, 1964, 2, p. 1.

## *Conflicting Values of Society and the Dropout Concerning the Utilization of Talent*

When a Merit Scholar or an apparently gifted student decides to leave college—an event that is less uncommon than many parents realize—society is apt to be puzzled and uncomprehending, if not alarmed. Its concern with the apparent failure to utilize talent leaves out of account, however, two considerations that seem very important from the dropout's point of view. First, many college dropouts challenge conventional standards of talent. And, second, many of these young people are struggling to free themselves from bonds and shackles preventing the free and effective use of their talents.

As the Harvard psychologists Bruner[13] and McClelland[14] point out, a new kind of meritocracy has developed with heavy emphasis on academic excellence as measured by grades, skill in taking examinations, and finding solutions to problems set by others. Yet, Holland and Astin[15] find that grades often have little relationship to such desirable attributes as leadership, vocational achievement, creativity in science and the arts. McClelland asks, "What of the little boy who doesn't make it academically? Is he a failure? Can he feel that he can contribute importantly to society if he does not make the academic grade? Overstressing academic merit can discourage young people with types of talent that are very important for our society and can create in them a discontent and sense of frustration that lasts a lifetime."[16]

Some of the dropouts seem to be rebelling against and challenging this meritocracy, and at the same time show certain of the attributes of creative people noted by MacKinnon: a lack of interest in small details and facts for their own sake, a freedom from conventional constraints and inhibitions, less

13 J. Bruner, *The process of education,* Cambridge: Harvard University Press, 1960.

14 D. C. McClelland, "Encouraging excellence," *Daedalus,* Fall 1961, pp. 711-724.

15 J. L. Holland and A. W. Astin, "The prediction of the academic, artistic, and social achievement of undergraduates of superior scholastic aptitude," *Journal of Educational Psychology,* 1962, 53, pp. 132-143.

16 McClelland, *op.cit.,* p. 714.

inclination to strive for achievement in settings where conforming behavior is expected and rewarded, independence of thought and action leading to unwillingness to accept the interpretations and values of their teachers.[17] In short, these students, as MacKinnon observes, are not always to their professors' liking.

It is interesting that many of the issues that are of concern to college students and which sometimes lead to their dropping out are relevant to characteristics of creative people. Consider the following characteristics of such people as noted by MacKinnon and how frequently dropouts are seen to be struggling to define themselves in these terms: some signs of psychopathology but clear evidence of adequate control mechanisms; openness to feelings and emotions, including the feminine side of one's nature; ability to admit complexity and disorder without becoming anxious about the resulting chaos; flexibility and spontaneity; tolerance for the tension of holding opposing values; openness to ideals and freedom to explore them; freedom to rebel as opposed to fear of doing so or compulsive need to do so. In one way or another, dropouts not infrequently complain that their college environment is not assisting them in acquiring these characteristics, but that college may do so at some other place or at some future time.

The question of how students become blocked or freed to use their talents involves the study of intra-psychic conflict as well as conflict in the social sphere. Part II of this book deals at greater length with the problem of the utilization of talent—a subject that is, of course, closely bound up with dropping out and has important psychological facets. Admittedly, the two spheres, psychological and social, are mere abstractions, and no one can say where one begins and the other leaves off. But for practical purposes, particularly in the case of the gifted dropout where the interaction between society and the individual shows clear signs of needing improvement, it is well to examine this interaction with care in the hope that the way will open up for mutually beneficial new solutions. But these

[17] D. W. MacKinnon, "Nature and nurture of creative talent," *American Psychologist*, 1962, 17, pp. 484-495.

solutions will probably always have to take into account the unique needs of individual students, rather than rely on general formulae, however admirable in principle the latter may seem. Perhaps the only general proposition that society and the dropout can both accept—especially at a time when mass methods and sentiments have an increasingly powerful appeal—is one that seeks to preserve the individual and to prevent him from becoming lost in the crowd.

# CHAPTER 1

## THE ONTOGENY OF THE DROPOUT PROBLEM*

LAWRENCE S. KUBIE, M.D.

AS WE CONSIDER the ontogeny of the dropout, it is illuminating to recall St. Augustine's comment that the innocence of childhood has more to do with the weakness of their limbs than with the purity of their hearts. It may be equally true that it is the weakness of their limbs which keeps the very young from becoming dropouts. Would not many a kindergarten child drop out if he were powerful enough to exercise his will? And in the primary and elementary schools, would not the truant be a dropout if he could get away with it? Parental and social pressures, the law, the courts, and the truant officer deprive him of this option. Youth cannot become a dropout until he is old enough so that the law will no longer oppose him, old enough also to stand up against the pressure of parental authority. This point is made seriously and not as a jest, to remind us that there is what might be called a "latent dropout potential" in every student population which long antedates its appearance in manifest form in high school, college, or later life. It follows that if we are to study the origins and development of the dropout problem, we must begin our study in early childhood.

I thought of this as I listened to the rebellious mutterings of a brilliant fourteen-year-old. He has an academic rating that never drops below 95. Yet he said: "I hate school. I would leave it today if I could get away with it. They have no sense of humor. They are regimented and inflexible. And it is all competition. They kill my interest in everything I really care about." And this in one of our better schools.

Another aspect of the dropout problem has to do with a basic change in our culture. There was a time when it was

* With the permission of the publishers, an editorial on this topic, adapted from this article, appears in Vol. 141 (No. 4) of the *Journal of Nervous and Mental Disease*.

taken for granted that as soon as a child was big enough and strong enough to work, he was expected to do productive chores for the family. These chores would be of one kind on a farm and of another kind in a family store or shoemaker's shop. Every family was a producing unit, not just a consuming unit. Today's adolescents, young and old, have lost the productive functions which were an important part of the experience of growth only a few decades ago. These functions gave youth an opportunity to identify with his home and with the adults in his world. The jobs he did led to the jobs they did. This is no longer true. Now youth can identify with adults only as consumers; and as consumers the model we set for our children is not admirable. In this role man is rarely at his best, whether in the home or out of it.

Instead of responsible sharing in the productive activities of the adult world, youth now goes through long years of preparation for a future that seems to him so far off as to be both unreal and uncertain. For us to assume that under these conditions it is more healthy for him to be submissive than to be rebellious is to assume something that we have no right to take for granted. The youth who conforms is convenient for us, because he causes no trouble and enables us to hold up our heads among our neighbors. Yet this does not mean that conformity is necessarily healthy for him. Nor does the fact that youth is rewarded for conforming and penalized for rebelling mean that conforming is always healthier than rebelling. Actually the decisive question is not whether youth conforms or rebels, but whether he is in the grip of psychological processes which make his conduct obligatory, repetitive, unlearning, and insatiable. This would be the hallmark of neurotic conformity or of neurotic rebellion equally. In other words, when the tendency either to conform or to rebel becomes an involuntary expression of processes which are predominantly unconscious rather than conscious and preconscious, then these processes predetermine its automatic repetition; and the resultant pattern becomes rigid, repetitive, insatiable, and involuntary. The youth can no longer learn from experience, from trial and error, from rewards or punishment, from success or failure, from reason or exhortation. He can no longer respond to changes in his own conscious purposes.

Applied to the dropout problem, this principle indicates the necessity for extensive studies of individual dropouts to compare with equally intensive studies of an adequate, representative sample of those who do not drop out. Superficial assembly-line studies are likely to lump together processes which are essentially different, even when the final step is to drop out of school or college. Although the view from the top will be the same, there are many ways of climbing a mountain. It is the way up that counts. It is the approach to dropping out that differentiates one process from another, determining when the dropout is an expression of something wrong in our educational system or when it results from disturbances within the individual. Therefore I repeat that if we want to understand this phenomenon, we must undertake intensive comparative studies of statistically adequate representative samples of dropouts and non-dropouts alike.

In this country the attitude toward dropouts is quite different from the attitude which until recently has existed in Britain and in all European countries. Particularly on the Continent the dropout has been taken for granted. It is well that here we care and worry about him, both for the sake of the man and so as to secure the fullest possible use of our educational facilities. Under the European system many students enrolled and then moved to other fields or to other universities. The rate is said to vary from 50 to 60 or sometimes 75 percent. Under such a system the "dropout" is taken for granted. It would be illuminating to find out why the attitude of some of the major European universities toward this wasteful process has begun to shift in the last decade. We should watch to see whether it will move gradually to an attitude closer to our own.

Another way to illuminate the dropout problem would be to compare its incidence in different schools and different disciplines, and then to seek the reasons for these differences. Why, for instance, is the dropout rate so high in engineering, even among those who are doing well? And why is it so low in medicine? Why does legal education come in between?

I state these questions as though the subsumed facts are based on precise statistical studies. Unfortunately, this is not the case. They are based on the long experience of many educators in these three fields and on some preliminary statistical inquiries; but these have not been carried out with the precision which such studies require. Furthermore, the issue of the student's maturity before he launches his training makes it relevant to ask whether the dropout rate is as high among those who go into engineering only after college as among those who go to engineering school directly from high school. Is the younger or older group more likely to change course in midstream?

This brings us to the next question—namely, whether or not the incidence of the problem is increasing in relation to the student population. Actually we do not know. We know that there are many more adolescents today. Not only are more born, but because of the improvements in medicine more of these survive. Furthermore, we are drawing into the educational system a larger percentage of our young people, and we hold them there longer. Under these circumstances it is inevitable that more will drop out; but we do not know whether there is an increase in relation either to total numbers or to duration of education. I would guess that there is some increase, but we do not know the facts because the statistics on the present have not been corrected for these two concurrent variables, and also because accurate statistics on the past are not available.

What we can say, however, is that as the educational process lengthens, the price that is paid for the dropout increases, in the cost both to the student and to our educational system as a whole. Back-tracking is a costly matter, both for the individual and also for the institution. When *A* uses up a place in a medical school or engineering school and then either fails or voluntarily drops out, *A* has cost that discipline not one but two possible scholars or practitioners: i.e., himself and *B*, who would have been there in *A*'s place if *A* had not been there; and *B* might not have become a dropout.

At high-school and college levels much research is needed in order to establish correlations between the incidence of dropouts and variations in economic, educational, cultural, racial, and national backgrounds at all age and educational levels, in all special fields of work, and so forth. Subsequently correlations with the lost potential creativity of those who drop out must also be sought. To study this problem will require a rare combination of honesty and humility. If we are to study what it is in our methods of education which contributes to the occurrence of dropouts, we must study not only the dropout himself as an individual, but also ourselves as individuals. Yet we cannot avoid being biased judges as we consider ourselves. We were not dropouts and we have a secret pride over the fact that we are among those who submitted to the grind and who survived it. Yet can any one of us say what part of our potentially creative capacities survived the grind? Or what part was destroyed? If our own unacknowledged, unrecognized, and well-hidden conflicts helped us to survive the course, can we avoid having an ax to grind for our own way of growing up—i.e., for our own personality quirks? Can we judge fairly those others who drop out? Are we not asking ourselves to be the investigators, the subjects of the investigations, the defending attorneys, and the judge all at once? This is impossible unless we plan carefully to correct for these biased sources of error.

At the same time, while we study the dropouts, it would be well to recall that with the lengthening of the duration of the educational process we also pay a higher price for submissive conformity. There are some educators who feel that our process of selecting students and of educating them sets a high premium on those who are neurotogenically submissive and therefore non-creative and non-productive. We lose many of the potentially most creative minds not through academic failures, but through those who drop out in spite of the fact that they are succeeding scholastically, or even excelling. To this we may add the potentially able students who disappear because of academic difficulties which also result from neurotogenic conflicts. These impressions have formed over many years, but like all such impressions require precise and detailed documentation. In the meantime, however, the conviction that many of the best minds drop out is widespread among educators in every field.

In most considerations of this problem there are disagreements and also uncertainties as to precisely what we mean by a "dropout." Some writers seem to assume that anyone who changes his mind about what he wants to study should for that reason be looked upon as a dropout from the field he abandons. One man went to college expecting to become a lawyer, and majored in government and economics. In his junior year he made up his mind to study medicine. Thirty years later his son went to college expecting to study medicine, but ended up by saying that he had become equally interested in law and government. So he studied economics and became a lawyer. Another man with a degree in naval architecture and marine engineering ended up in education, politics, and writing columns for a country newspaper. The son of an eminent psychiatrist finished his legal training and even had his law degree before he decided that what he really wanted to do was to study medicine and become a psychiatrist. Are all of those to be regarded as dropouts?

Such changes are only rarely the result of a discrepancy between the demands of the discipline and the native aptitudes of the student. Nor do they always result from clashing interests and tastes. More often they depend upon the length of time it takes for resolutions or changes to occur in the ambivalent feelings which sons and daughters regularly have about their elders, whether eminent or obscure, living or dead, present or absent. In one such instance the son had first expressed his defiance by studying a discipline which his father scorned. Then as he worked out of that in therapy he decided that he had been cutting off his nose to spite his face, that he had in fact been turning his back on the field in which he was most interested and for which he was most gifted.

Evidently the course of education should include an unlearning as well as a learning process. For the student of our educational system, the important question is not whether an individual changes fields (although this, of course, is wasteful of time and educational facilities), but to what extent our educational processes help him to resolve these ambivalent identifications early enough in his student years to minimize wasteful late changes. Or, alternatively, to what extent does our educational system entrench the student in his conflicting identifications?

I have already alluded to a question more than once: is the dropout always "sicker"—i.e., more "neurotic"—than the student who stays the course? In considering this we must make an essential distinction between the illness of an individual (i.e., the intrinsic process of illness) and the illness of a *life*.[1]

A neurosis may in its essence be only a minor deviation from normal development. Yet its symptoms may launch a chain reaction of profoundly destructive secondary consequences for a whole life. What may result is a familiar paradox: a man whose illness is minor and easily alterable, but whose life is destroyed. We see this clearly in some alcoholics. There are alcoholics in whom the underlying basis of the alcoholism is a profound disorder, or even a masked psychosis. But alcoholism may also arise out of a simple anxiety neurosis or a simple chronic depression.

Conversely, we may see people who are deeply sick in subtle ways, yet whose illness tends to energize them to productive activities which are so richly rewarded that for many years their lives will be protected from the consequences of their

[1] The same distinction applies in all fields of organic medicine. An individual may suffer an attack of poliomyelitis. When the attack is over, the virus may be not only inactivated but eliminated; yet the man may be left with all four limbs totally paralyzed. From that moment on his life is a sick life, even though we can no longer say that he is suffering from an active sickness. This distinction is equally important in psychiatry and especially in its relation to education. Therefore this is a distinction of which we cannot afford to lose sight. I stress this because it is rarely recognized even by our psychiatric colleagues.

illnesses. This occurs frequently among creative people in every scientific discipline and in every profession, as well as in music, art, literature, and the like. It may also occur in the business world.

Because the consequences of being a dropout—for no matter how sound and healthy a reason—can be destructive to a student's future life, the secondary and tertiary results may lead him to illness. The observer tends to project this retroactively and to conclude that dropping out itself must always result from illness.

I have already pointed out that there are dropouts from successful careers in life just as there are dropouts among successful students. Failure is not the only experience which leads to that deep inner dissatisfaction and impatience which cause men to change their paths in the midst of their journeys through life.

In this group of successful dropouts there are two fundamentally different kinds. There are dropouts of the corpus—i.e., when the body disappears, carrying with it a spirit which survives. Among these some are trying to salvage their own creative potential by leaving school. But there are also the dropouts of the spirit. These are the students who somehow manage to survive the course with passing grades (occasionally even with high marks), but at the sacrifice of their entire creative potential. This is a familiar problem. One later manifestation of it is that diagnostic category which I have called "the campus hero": the man who in school or college has succeeded scholastically, academically, socially, athletically (i.e., in all curricular and extracurricular activities) but who has used his success to hide his unsolved inner problems. Unfortunately these usually catch up with him in the end, often in the forties, fifties, or sixties. Then when he breaks, we find that his success was a salve to cover over and hide a wound, to make it so painless for the time being that he was not forced to do anything about it until years later.

Let me summarize these evidences of flaws in our educational processes. There are many, but from among them I will pick out those which are most relevant to the dropout of the spirit as well as of the body:

(1) The discrepancies between promise on early test scores and early excellent performance on the one hand, and ultimate achievement on the other hand.

(2) The dropouts among successes.

(3) Survival, but with destroyed creative talent.

(4) The breakdowns of successes which occur all along the line.

There are no easy solutions to be found for these many interdependent problems, either by changes in techniques or by methods of screening or of educating. This is clear from the many efforts that have been made. If the problems had been easy to solve, solutions would have been found long since. Yet, in part at least, our failure to find any answers has been due to our complacent failure to recognize the existence of the problems. Instead we have shied away from them, in part because their existence challenges us to face the complex interdependence between education and psychotherapy, between the learning processes and the lessons learned from the early use of psychotherapy for preventive purposes. This is one aspect of what has been called the "X" factor in education.

The dropout problem also challenges us to reexamine our concepts of readiness for education: a readiness which depends in part at least upon emotional maturation. Any effort to do anything about this will introduce at least three innovations into the educational process.

(1) We may have to find ways to use living as a preparation for schooling—i.e., as a way of maturing the student to a point at which he can profit from education. Perhaps in place of the responsible chores of a pioneer society, a Peace Corps type of activity interpolated into the sequences of school and college and graduate years would help. Or perhaps all schools could be reorganized along the lines of the George Junior Republic in Freeville, New York. This is the exact reverse of what we have taken for granted in the past: namely, that school is a preparation for life.

(2) We may also have to develop new methods by which to assess the child's emotional readiness for schooling even before we admit him to kindergarten, and then reassess that

same child every autumn before he starts his next school year.

(3) More speculatively, this could mean that we would launch each year with a screening period during which group methods of exploring inner problems would be used both for diagnostic and for preliminary psychotherapeutic purposes—i.e., as an antechamber to definitive therapy.

(4) A further extension of this approach would call for such group experiences to involve not only the schoolchild but also his family in family-group therapy and parent groups, teacher groups, and finally teacher-parent groups. The vision of a society struggling toward a new maturity through its school system is exciting. Beyond it we face the question: where are we to find the trained personnel to conduct such groups? I have the temerity to believe that I know the answer to that critical question, but its discussion would lead us into other areas.

Let me then repeat that school readiness is dependent on emotional maturation. Its relation to educability is another aspect of what I have called the "X" factor in education. We know that some people unwittingly seek erudition as a substitute for growing up. Furthermore some seem to succeed in this strange endeavor, even to the extent of achieving the stereotyped image of the absent-minded professor, who in spite of specialized erudition remains humanly an infant. Others find themselves incapable even of elementary learning until they have broken away from infancy to attain some measure of maturity. These phenomena have been known for generations, but they have never been studied. Yet it is essential to find out how to facilitate affective maturation as a preparation for education, and how to prevent the educational process itself from entrenching the affective retardation which in the end produces the professorial infant. These questions are relevant to the dropout problem, to the problem of creativity, and to the destructive impact of the educational process on the creative potential. There seems to be a somewhat unexpected link between the dropout problem and the problems of talent and creativity: which is why this is a book both on the dropout problem and on the salvaging, preservation, protection, and encouragement of talent.

I will illustrate the problem with a brief case history of a man in his late thirties. His I.Q. was somewhere around 150. He was the oldest in his family. At four years of age he was sent to a private kindergarten just around the corner; but because of certain disturbing experiences in his first years merely to go this far from home precipitated him into a profound and immobilizing depression, infused at the same time with terror and rage, as is usually true in the acute affective upsets of early childhood. Nothing was done about this except ineffectual exhortation, punishment, and bribery. Every autumn thereafter he would return to school full of high hopes and sincere resolve; but each time the echo of the initial separation from home triggered off an automatic recapitulation of that first paralyzing depression. Only his exceptionally high endowments carried him through one of our most difficult preparatory schools and halfway through college before he became frankly ill. Thereafter, his life became sicker than he himself ever became, a process which in the end cost him his very life. Our whole educational system had failed in not demanding that the family provide adequate treatment before allowing him to continue in school. It had failed by not responding adequately to the transparent warning signals of his initial upset.

All of this has less to do with procedures and techniques of the educational process *per se* than with what we might call the readying of the would-be student for education. We may have to acknowledge that education does not usually prepare us for life; but that many of us have to live longer and more wisely and fully and undergo some form of spontaneous or guided therapeutic experience in order to make ourselves emotionally ready to be educated. Perhaps much of the problem of the dropout arises out of our effort to educate those who are not yet sufficiently mature to be educable. This is another challenge which may require that eternal vigilance on which all freedom depends. Indeed, the challenge may have to be faced resolutely over and over again throughout our learning years, and throughout our teaching years as well.

As I have already said, such cases as that described above constitute a failure of our educational system on every front and at every level. Do we need to accept this as being the best we can do? What will happen if we reexamine the tacit assumption that the educational milieu must be highly competitive, while at the same time demanding actively gregarious socializing? Can this be right for all youngsters? And what of the concept that education consists primarily of grill and drill on a conscious level? Does this not neglect the fact that most effective learning is done without effort, on an asymbolic, imageless (i.e., "preconscious") level, without repeated exposure, little drill and less grilling, and with little conscious participation except for the final important tasks of communicating, ruminating, and testing? What if from primary school through college and professional school the dominant use of drill and grill simply entrenches the student's neurosis?

We are paying a high price for our failure to look closely at these problems. We have always known that there is a purely accidental relationship between erudition and maturity, or between erudition and wisdom. Is it not time to consider how to produce the maturity and the wisdom which will make true erudition possible?

Finally, dropout confronts us with another unsolved cultural problem: the problem of youthful impatience. We have been human beings for many generations, living repeatedly through the experience of being little and then of growing up. Yet generation succeeds generation without ever becoming reconciled to this fact. The child rarely believes that he will ever be "big." Therefore he is obsessed by size.

One result here is that buildings and cars are too big, as in Rome pictures and statues are too big. Everything has to be big as a protest against the smallness of childhood; since the child persists in us as the inner rings of a tree persist throughout the rest of that tree's life. How is it that we have never learned how to reconcile children to being children, a reconciliation which they can achieve only when it is based on an inborn confidence that they too will grow up, a confidence which can take root only through strong positive identifications with adult figures around them? Education complicates this problem in many ways, but especially by placing premature emphasis on verbal and other symbolic skills instead of on performance skills. Is this because words do not require strength, size, or physical dexterity? Certainly the precocious child can exploit an early expertness in using words as a consolation for smallness and to develop a secret illusion of size.

At the kindergarten level it is known and acknowledged that we destroy the free, joyous, spontaneous creative imagination of the small child. At the other pole, the head of one of our greatest engineering schools wrote me: "We probably have the ablest student body in the world; rarely any one with less than straight A's. Yet we have learned that it is not enough to survive the course, even with top honors. There are too many breakdowns and too many dropouts among the ablest; and these occur all along the line from start to finish and even after. What is more important is the fact that the relation between mere academic survival or high academic honors and subsequent creativity is purely accidental."

I submit that these facts confront us with a basic failure of education to solve its own problems, and that the reasons for this must be studied before anyone rushes in with pet solutions. We must explore the nature of these failures and diagnose the malady, before we prescribe for it. Neither traditional nor so-called progressive education has solved it. Furthermore, such studies must be carried out in many settings and by multidisciplined teams. This will require the conjoined efforts of neurophysiologists, neurobiochemists, geneticists, pediatricians, sociologists, cultural anthropologists, psychiatric social workers, clinical psychologists, psychiatrists, psychoanalysts, educators, and cooperating parents. In itself this implies the need for an Institute for Basic Research on the Educational Process, to develop new diagnostic and predictive techniques, to set standards for mature research elsewhere.

One of the central problems of the educational process is the subtle way in which even under optimal circumstances education reinforces and entrenches the ubiquitous, masked neurotic process, while at the same time the educational process itself can be totally stalled by hidden but already entrenched neurotic difficulties. Both destructive interactions occur frequently even in highly endowed students. This is one of the great unsolved problems of human culture; and it demands intensive investigation.

# CHAPTER 2

## THE LATER ACADEMIC, VOCATIONAL, AND PERSONAL SUCCESS OF COLLEGE DROPOUTS

LAWRENCE A. PERVIN

BECAUSE COLLEGES MUST select among qualified applicants, and business and the nation need talented individuals of proven ability and accomplishment, the dropout from college is often looked upon as an unfortunate problem. This view is well described by Reik: "Dropouts are referred to in academic circles as 'casualties' or 'non-survivors.' The dropout rate is called the 'mortality' rate. Under these conditions it is natural for college authorities to discourage dropping out, even though the student may benefit by leaving school for a time."[1]

Approximately one-half of the students who enter college will become, for one reason or another, dropouts. Yet, we know remarkably little about the effects of withdrawal upon the student or about his later performance in the academic, vocational, and personal realms. While the phenomenon of the dropout *per se* has received a fair amount of research investigation, there have been extremely few follow-up studies. The problem is hardly mentioned in either of two recent reviews of the literature on the college dropout by Knoell[2] and by Summerskill.[3]

The lack of long-term follow-up studies of college dropouts represents a significant gap in our knowledge, since we cannot evaluate the extent of the problem until we know more about what later happens to the dropout. The question may be

1 L. E. Reik, "The dropout problem," *The Nation*, May 19, 1962, pp. 442-446.

2 Dorothy M. Knoell, "Institutional research on retention and withdrawal," in Hall Sprague (ed.), *Research on college students*, Boulder, Colo., Western Interstate Commission for Higher Education, 1960, pp. 41-65.

3 J. Summerskill, "Dropouts from college," in N. Sanford (ed.), *The American college*, New York: Wiley, 1962, pp. 627-657.

phrased as follows: what is the effect of dropping out of college upon the student, and what can be said about his later academic, personal, and vocational success? This chapter attempts to approach an answer to this question by reporting the results of two follow-up studies of college dropouts, one done at Princeton University and the other at the University of Illinois.

### *The Princeton Study*[4]

The study of Princeton dropouts by Pervin began with the felt need for long-term follow-up studies concerning the fate of dropouts in later life. For the study, a dropout was defined as a student who officially left the college at some point prior to graduation and thus did not receive his degree by the end of eight semesters or four years after entering Princeton. This definition included students who transferred to other colleges and students who left Princeton but later returned to obtain a degree.

The Princeton classes of 1940, 1951, and 1960 (i.e., those entering in 1936, 1947, and 1956) were chosen for investigation because they were relatively unaffected by economic depression or war. Since the three classes span a period of twenty years, they provide the basis for an analysis of changes over time.

The names and present addresses of all dropouts were supplied by Princeton's Bureau of Alumni Records. Information concerning the date of and reason for withdrawal were obtained for each dropout. A control group of non-dropouts was obtained by taking the name of the non-dropout following that of the dropout on the alumni roster.

Every dropout from the Princeton classes of '40, '51, and '60 was sent a questionnaire. This questionnaire covered four areas: (1) reason for withdrawal and services consulted prior to withdrawal; (2) immediate and long-term effects of withdrawal; (3) later academic performance and reasons for later academic failure or success; and (4) later personal and vocational success, physical and emotional health. Each control non-

[4] This study was carried out by the author under contract S-029-64 with the Office of Education, U.S. Department of Health, Education and Welfare.

dropout was sent a similar questionnaire which omitted questions relevant to dropping out. Second, third, and fourth letters, together with additional copies of the questionnaire, were sent to all non-respondents. Responses were received from 57 percent of the dropouts and 77 percent of the non-dropouts. In each of the three classes, a greater proportion of non-dropouts than dropouts responded to the questionnaire.

Before turning to the responses to the questionnaires, we can look at some data concerning dropouts obtained from the alumni records. These data indicate that the percentage of students withdrawing from Princeton has *not* changed since the class of '40. Between 15 and 20 percent of the students entering Princeton drop out at some time. While approximately the same percentage of students have dropped out of each of the three classes, their reasons for doing so have changed considerably. Currently there are more students dropping out for *non-required* reasons (personal and health) as opposed to *required* reasons (academic and disciplinary). Whereas in the class of '40, 74 percent of the dropouts did so for required reasons (67 percent for academic reasons), in the classes of '51 and '60 only about one-half dropped out for required reasons (about 45 percent for academic reasons). The great shift is in the decrease of academic dropouts and increase of dropouts for personal reasons.

*Reported Reasons for Leaving.* The dropouts were asked to describe their reasons for dropping out of Princeton. Most respondents gave the same reasons for withdrawal as were listed on the administrative card. The same types of reasons for leaving Princeton show up in each of the three classes. Almost no one claims a lack of ability, which fits with the views in the Admissions Office that every student admitted to Princeton has the ability to succeed.[5] The problems of poor

[5] The administrative records of the dropouts and non-dropouts were used for comparison of their intellectual abilities. This was determined from their scholastic aptitude test (SAT) scores, predicted grade averages (based on rank in high school), and their first semester grades. In general, more able students are coming to Princeton, or at least SAT scores are going up. The dropouts generally did less well than the non-dropouts on the verbal and math SAT, on predicted grade average, and first semes-

motivation and immaturity are consistently noted as contributing to withdrawal. In most cases poor motivation was attributed to a general lack of interest ("Just didn't want to study"), boredom, apathy, dislike of the curriculum, getting nothing out of college, a lack of goals or choice of major.[6]

---

ter grades. While some of these differences were statistically significant, the differences between the two groups on these variables have been decreasing. In the class of '60, the differences between dropouts and non-dropouts were quite small and in one case—verbal SAT—the dropouts had a slightly higher mean score. Apparently academic ability alone does not play a significant part in determining who drops out of Princeton; it cannot be used effectively in attempts at prediction and this has become increasingly true with recent classes.

[6] The expression of concern about the lack of goals and uncertainty as to major and career choice confirms the finding of the National Merit Scholarship group (A. W. Astin, "Personal and environmental factors associated with college dropouts among high aptitude students," *Journal of Educational Psychology*, 1964, 55, pp. 219-227) that uncertainty about what to study is the most frequent reason talented students give for dropping out of college. This is particularly interesting in that most dropouts in this study reported that they were somewhat certain or very certain of their choice of major and vocational goal when they entered Princeton. In the class of '40, about one-half of the dropouts reported some certainty or great certainty about major or vocational goal and about two-thirds of the dropouts from the class of '60 reported some or great certainty. These percentages were very similar to those reported by non-dropouts.

Either time has distorted the memory of the dropouts or, more likely, many who came to Princeton thinking that they were clear about their future found that they had somewhat unrealistic expectations, which resulted in some disruption of their functioning. The finding of D. L. Thistlewaite ("College press and change in study plans of talented students," *Journal of Educational Psychology*, 1960, 51, pp. 222-234) that many students who drop out of a field do so because their expectations of certain career fields proved to be incompatible with reality tends to support this latter explanation.

Inaccurate expectations also play a part in leading some students to transfer from Princeton after they find that it is not what they had expected it to be like and in causing discouragement in some who expected to continue to be at the top of their class. In a recent study by the author, 86 percent of Princeton freshmen reported that they expected to be in the top half of their class upon graduation and 76 percent reported the top half of the class as the minimum level that they would find acceptable to themselves. Similarly, at the University of Chicago, A. Berger ("The unexpected findings: A study of the expectations of college students," unpublished manuscript, Chicago: National Opinion Research Center, 1963) found that 86 percent of the entering class expected to have a first-year grade average of "B" or better and 67 percent expected to make Dean's List. In fact, only 20 percent of them would actually succeed in making Dean's List.

While the problem of lack of motivation and immaturity appeared in each of the three classes, some differences in reasons for dropping out could be noted. In the class of '40, respondents reported an interest in making money, getting started in life's work, a feeling that college was unrelated to and probably unnecessary for success in life. In contrast to this, respondents from the classes of '51 and '60 report concern with a lack of goals, indecision about a choice of major, a lack of preparation for college and difficulty in making the transition from high school to college, and discontent with Princeton leading to transfer. Whereas a portion of the '40 dropout population knew where it was going and felt that college was not necessary, a portion of the '51 and '60 populations did not know where it was going but felt that college was necessary.

*The Withdrawal Process.* The respondents in this study indicated whether they had considered withdrawal from Princeton prior to dropping out (dropouts) or prior to graduation (non-dropouts). More students are now more seriously considering withdrawal than in the past; that is, while the dropout rate has not changed, more students are considering it as a possibility. For example, whereas for the class of '40 only 13 percent of the non-dropouts reported having considered withdrawal prior to graduation, 44 percent of the class of '60 non-dropouts did so. This change over time is true for both dropouts and non-dropouts, though it is particularly true for the latter. In sum, dropping out appears increasingly as a serious possibility in the minds of Princeton undergraduates.

Since a high percentage of non-dropouts consider withdrawal prior to graduation, two questions may be asked: Are there differences in the factors causing dropouts and non-dropouts to consider withdrawal? Are there differences in the factors which cause non-dropouts who consider withdrawal to remain in college in contrast to the dropouts who actually leave? Since both dropouts and non-dropouts often consider withdrawal, different forces may be pushing the two groups toward or away from leaving college.

The replies gave little indication of a difference between

dropouts and non-dropouts in causes of consideration of withdrawal. The predominant reason for both groups was disappointing grades. The second most frequent reason was dissatisfaction with the University, either owing to some academic aspects of the college (curriculum, faculty, etc.) or to some social aspects. Like the dropouts, the non-dropouts also reported a lack of direction as a significant factor.

In reporting why they had stayed in college after considering withdrawal, dropouts gave the following major reasons:

(1) Desire not to hurt the family and fear of family reaction.

(2) Desire to avoid the shame and guilt associated with withdrawal—a sense of pride, a fear of disgrace, a wish to avoid failure.

(3) The lack of acceptable alternatives to being at college, or at this particular college.

(4) Desire to stay and continue having a good time in spite of poor grades and aimlessness.

(5) Overt psychodynamic reasons, such as the wish to be asked to leave rather than leave voluntarily.

Non-dropouts reported two major reasons for staying after considering withdrawal which understandably do not show up in the reports of dropouts—grades improved, and a goal or vocational aim was found. Unfortunately, there was little in the reports to suggest just why these students were able to improve their grades or find a goal, in contrast to the experiences of those in the dropout group. Some reports suggested a quality of persistence or extra incentive in the face of adversity, but this was only hinted at. Beyond these two factors, non-dropouts reported considerations for staying similar to those of the dropouts—they experienced parental pressure to stay and considered withdrawal to be cowardly: "Desire not to quit or take the easy way out." "I consider withdrawal an act of cowardice." "Dropping out meant a loss of self-respect."

Reports of close and casual friendships at Princeton indicated that dropouts tended to have fewer close friends. A lack in this area was particularly characteristic of those dropping out voluntarily or for non-required reasons. It is likely that friends and social ties serve to discourage voluntary withdrawal and perhaps serve to motivate academic performance. On the other hand, perhaps the same factors which led these students to choose to drop out also led to their sense of alienation from other students at the college.[7]

*Later Academic Performance.* When students drop out of college, they may or may not have plans for continuation of their formal education. The replies from our respondents indicated that there has been a clear change over time in dropout expectations concerning further education at the time of withdrawal. Whereas in the class of '40 approximately one-half of the respondents reported such plans, in the classes of '51 and '60 over 90 percent did so. Furthermore, more dropouts from the classes of '51 and '60 reported plans to return to Princeton than did dropouts from the class of '40. These findings are consistent for both required and non-required withdrawals.

While these were their reported plans, how many of these dropouts actually did go on for further education, and how many of them went on to obtain an undergraduate degree? The data indicating the percentage of dropouts returning to college and the percentage obtaining the baccalaureate degree are presented in Table 1. The later academic performance of the dropouts, particularly that of the dropouts from the class of '60, is quite impressive. The percentage of dropouts returning to college has been increasing and proportionately more of these students are successful in obtaining the baccalaureate degree. The percent obtaining the baccalaureate degree might have been higher for the classes of '40 and '51 had not the Second World War and Korean War interfered with the return of some dropouts.

7 Some research being conducted by the author and Donald Rubin suggests that students who see themselves as quite different from the college and from other students there tend to be dissatisfied with the non-academic aspects of college life and consider dropping out for non-academic reasons. These data suggest that some students fit in better at some colleges than at others and that the degree of fit is significantly related to satisfaction with and consideration of withdrawal from a college.

TABLE 1. LATER ACADEMIC PERFORMANCE OF PRINCETON DROPOUTS AND NON-DROPOUTS

| | PRINCETON CLASS | | |
|---|---|---|---|
| | *1940* | *1951* | *1960* |
| *Dropouts* | | | |
| Percent dropouts returning to college | .57 | .82 | .97 |
| Percent of returning dropouts to obtain B.A. degree | .53 | .74 | .88 |
| Percent of total dropouts to obtain B.A. degree | .30 | .64 | .85 |
| Percent of B.A. dropouts to go on for further education | .50 | .43 | .58 |
| Percent of dropouts to go on for further education who obtain advanced degree | .75 | .78 | .93 |
| Percent B.A. dropouts to obtain advanced degree | .50 | .33 | .56 |
| *Non-dropouts* | | | |
| Percent non-dropouts to go on for further education | .73 | .76 | .84 |
| Percent non-dropouts to go on for further education who obtain advanced degree | .79 | .77 | .91 |
| Percent B.A. non-dropouts to obtain advanced degree | .56 | .59 | .77 |

The data for the dropouts from the class of '60 are particularly noteworthy. Since 88 percent of the returnees completed their undergraduate work, a returning dropout had a better chance of obtaining a baccalaureate degree than the average freshman had of obtaining the degree without becoming a dropout! Data comparing required and non-required withdrawals have not been reported in Table 1, but these data indicate that there is no consistent difference between these two groups for any of the three college classes; that is, both required and non-required withdrawals show a high probability of academic success upon return to college.

The data in Table 1 indicate that there is a considerable increase in the percentage of the entering class that obtains the baccalaureate degree beyond the percent doing so in four years at Princeton. Other data indicated that for the classes of '40, '51, and '60, respectively, approximately 85 percent, 90 percent, and 95 percent of the entering class eventually obtained the baccalaureate degree at Princeton or elsewhere. Not only are more Princeton dropouts returning to college, but proportionately more are returning to Princeton. Whereas in the class of '40 only about 10 percent of the dropouts who returned to college returned to Princeton, about 30 percent of the returning dropouts from the classes of '51 and '60 did so. At least for the more recent classes of '51 and '60, there appears to be a greater tendency for non-required withdrawals than for required withdrawals to return to Princeton.

Often education does not stop with the undergraduate degree and the progress of dropouts toward more advanced degrees is also indicated in Table 1. Here the performance of dropouts can be compared with that of non-dropouts. In each of the classes, approximately 50 percent of the dropouts continued their education toward an advanced degree. While this proportion is not quite as high as that for non-dropouts (from 75 to 80 percent of the non-dropouts go on for further education), *the dropouts who do go on are as successful in obtaining the advanced degree as are the non-dropouts.* More non-required withdrawals than required withdrawals go on for an advanced degree and a higher percentage of those who go on are successful in obtaining the degree. If the three classes are compared, both dropouts and non-dropouts show an increasing degree of success in obtaining the advanced degree. Whereas in the class of '40 approximately 75 percent of those who went on for further education beyond the baccalaureate degree obtained a higher degree, by the class of '60 the percentage was above 90. The data for the class of '60 are particularly striking—*85 percent of the dropouts obtain a baccalaureate degree, 93 percent of those who go on for an advanced degree are successful in obtaining this degree, and eventually 56 percent of the original dropouts obtain a more advanced degree.*

*Later Vocational Performance.* What can be said about the later performance of these talented dropouts in the vocational realm? The questionnaire inquired into the first and present jobs, salaries, additional incomes, history of increases in earnings, number of jobs, weeks of unemployment, and job satisfaction.

The mean and median current salaries of dropouts and non-dropouts are presented in Table 2. These data indicate

TABLE 2. MEAN, MEDIAN, AND RANGE OF CURRENT SALARIES FOR PRINCETON DROPOUTS AND NON-DROPOUTS
(in thousands of dollars)

| | *1940* | | *1951* | | *1960* | |
|---|---|---|---|---|---|---|
| | *Dropout* | *Non-dropout* | *Dropout* | *Non-dropout* | *Dropout* | *Non-dropout* |
| Current mean salary | 21.4 | 22.7 | 13.7 | 15.1 | 5.8 | 7.0 |
| Current median salary | 15.0 | 20.0 | 12.0 | 14.0 | 6.0 | 7.0 |
| Current salary range | 5.0=100+ | 6.0=75.0 | 5.0=40.0 | 2.0=50.0 | 1.0=10.0 | 1.0=15.0 |

that non-dropouts do make more money than the dropouts. A difference of approximately $1,500 between the dropout and non-dropout mean salaries consistently shows up in each of the three classes. The discrepancy in mean incomes does not get larger for the earlier classes, though it may be that a degree is more important today and the difference between dropout and non-dropout salaries for the classes of '51 and '60 will increase with time. The evidence indicates an overall greater earning power for non-dropouts, but the salary ranges indicate considerable overlap between dropouts and non-dropouts.

While these data would tend to indicate a certain economic value in having a degree, a comparison of dropout salaries by No Degree, Degree, and Beyond Degree categories raises some puzzling questions. The No Degree dropouts are *not* consistently at a disadvantage. In fact, in the classes of '51 and '60, they have higher mean and median incomes than either the Degree or Beyond Degree dropouts.[8] *In sum, while non-drop-*

[8] These differences between No Degree, Degree, and Beyond Degree dropouts may be due to the fact that No Degree dropouts go into business whereas many of the Degree and Beyond Degree dropouts go into teaching. A cross-classification of profession was not done on the three groups.

*outs appear to earn more than the dropouts, this can not easily be attributed to the lack of a degree on the part of the dropouts.*[9]

Other data related to the vocational realm may be noted briefly. In general, dropouts tended to have a greater number of jobs and more weeks of unemployment. However, the mean number of weeks of total unemployment was never very considerable, the highest being 9.6 for the class of '51 dropouts. Aside from differences in actual earnings, there appears to be no difference between dropouts and non-dropouts in how quickly they have increased their earning abilities. Finally, there was no difference between dropouts and non-dropouts in the amount of satisfaction with their work that they reported.

*Later Personal Success.* While it is easier to obtain some measure of academic and vocational success than of personal success, the questionnaire attempted to obtain some global indications of success in this area. One area inquired into was marital history. There is little difference between dropouts and non-dropouts from the classes of '40 and '51 in percent married. Approximately 90 percent of the respondents in both categories reported being married. In the class of '60, a greater proportion of non-dropouts reported being married (66 percent for non-dropouts, 52 percent for dropouts).

[9] It should be clear that some caution must be exercised in drawing conclusions from these data. The number of individuals included is not very large and as the groups are divided into more complex categories, such as No Degree, Degree, and Beyond Degree, the number of cases in each category decreases considerably. Furthermore, the data are based upon returns from 45 to 85 percent of the populations and there may be some bias in them; that is, perhaps only economically successful individuals respond to the questionnaires. On the other hand, this bias might operate for both dropouts and non-dropouts. Also, there was no consistent trend for higher or lower salaries to be reported on first, second, third, or final returns to the questionnaires. Finally, we are dealing with a somewhat select population which is not representative of the general population. Both dropout and non-dropout earnings are considerably above the earnings listed by the national census for part-college, college, and beyond-college individuals. While the possibility of bias remains, the data clearly indicate that many of these individuals find themselves unable to use their talents in the academic world but prosper in the business world.

While differences in percent currently married are not striking, differences in percent divorced are quite striking. *In every one of the three classes, more of the dropouts than non-dropouts reported having had a previous marriage terminated by divorce.* Whereas for dropouts from the classes of '40, '51, and '60 the percents reporting a past divorce are 35, 11, and 7, respectively, the comparative percents for non-dropouts are 16, 5, and 2 respectively.[10] A similarly high divorce rate showed up in an earlier study of dropouts from the class of '41, where 27 percent of the respondents reported past divorces.

*Effects of Withdrawal.* The data on later academic, vocational, and personal success provide some objective criteria for evaluating the later success of dropouts. However, these data do not describe how the individuals themselves perceive the effects of withdrawal. The questionnaire inquired into perceptions of the immediate and long-term effects of withdrawal upon the dropouts. These were open-ended questions and the responses were categorized into four groups: Positive Effect, Negative Effect, Mixed Effect, and No Effect. Sample descriptions of immediate effects of dropping out are as follows:

*Positive Effects*—"Glad to be out and doing constructive work." "Happy not to be involved in college life any more and to get started in business." "Relieved to be out of a difficult situation and to have the opportunity to recover, return, and make a fresh start." The word "relief" consistently came up in relation to dropping out.

*Negative Effects*—"Very sorry." "I was in a state of shock. I felt the bottom had dropped out of everything." "Guilt and depression." Responses here ranged from some regret, to a sense of guilt and depression, to considerable damage to the self-esteem and the need for hospitalization.

*Mixed Effects*—"Shock, but determination to return and do better." "Shame and felt relieved." "Freedom for a more constructive life and guilt over disappointing the family."

*No Effects*—"The effects were small and easily passed off." "Too busy to give the matter much thought."

[10] The difference in divorce rates is significant at the .05 level of confidence only for the class of '40.

In general, the most frequent immediate response was a sense of relief, a feeling of guilt and shame, or a combination of the two.

Examples of the long-term effects of dropping out are as follows:

*Positive Effects*—"Became more self-reliant." "For me it was one of the most important, informative, and educational periods in my life. When I returned to school, I knew what I wanted." "The effect was crucial. During my first three years at Princeton, I never felt a whole person, one who could identify himself with himself and have individual meaning. With time off, I found the pleasures and challenges available to an interested, seeking mind. I gained self-satisfaction, maturity, and a broadening of perspective."

*Negative Effects*—"Loss of status." "There are few who know that I did not graduate. Consciously and unconsciously I've been battling it ever since." "The biggest mistake in my life. Very few days passed without my thoughts drifting back to those days prior to leaving Princeton. I have had dreams of being enrolled again in the University on so many nightly occasions that it is impossible to count them."

*Mixed Effects*—"I have regretted that it was necessary to leave but feel that it worked out well." "It was a failure but it also contributed to the success I have achieved."

*No Effects*—"None." "Nice to graduate but not necessary. I got a lot out of Princeton in my three years."

These are the kinds of effects the dropouts report. As can be seen, they are quite varied and range from extreme positive effects, to extreme negative effects, to no effects. Data on the frequency of each of these kinds of immediate and long-term effects are reported in Table 3. When the data are looked at historically, dropouts from the more recent classes of '51 and '60 are seen to be more affected by dropping out, or at least more often recall having been so, than dropouts from the class of '40. Whereas in the class of '40 almost one-half of the respondents reported no immediate effects and two-thirds reported no long-term effects, the comparative figures for the

TABLE 3. IMMEDIATE AND LONG-TERM EFFECTS OF WITHDRAWAL (in per cent)

| | IMMEDIATE | | | | LONG-TERM | | | |
|---|---|---|---|---|---|---|---|---|
| | *Positive* | *Negative* | *Mixed* | *None* | *Positive* | *Negative* | *Mixed* | *None* |
| *1940* | .15 | .30 | .07 | .48 | .10 | .20 | .04 | .66 |
| *1951* | .32 | .44 | .07 | .17 | .36 | .25 | .11 | .27 |
| *1960* | .35 | .37 | .15 | .13 | .60 | .17 | .08 | .15 |

classes of '51 and '60 are about 15 percent and 20 percent, respectively.

If we look at the immediate effects of withdrawal, we note that the more recent classes report more positive effects than the class of '40, even when the differences in percents reporting some effects are taken into consideration. In the class of '40, 15 percent reported positive effects and 30 percent reported negative effects, a 1:2 ratio, but in the class of '60, 35 percent reported positive effects and 37 percent reported negative effects, just about a 1:1 ratio. Thus, over time more immediate effects are being reported as a result of dropping out and more positive effects are being reported, so that by the class of '60 positive and negative effects are reported with equal frequency.

When we turn to long-term effects of withdrawal, we find that fewer members of the classes of '51 and '60 report no long-term effects of withdrawal. In terms of effects reported, there are some interesting changes over the three classes. For the class of '40, 10 percent reported long-term positive effects and 20 percent negative effects—once more, a 1:2 ratio. In the class of '60, 60 percent reported long-term positive effects and 17 percent reported negative effects—approximately a 3:1 ratio. The class of '51 falls midway between these two classes. There was little change in the percent reporting long-term negative effects, this figure always being around 20 percent. However, the percent reporting positive effects has increased sharply. The big change over the three classes is the decrease in reports of no effects and corresponding increase in reports of positive effects. The increase in percent reporting long-term positive effects is characteristic of both required and non-required withdrawals.

When immediate and long-term effects for each of the classes are compared, all groups report some decrease in effects or increase in no effects over time. In the class of '40, both positive and negative effects decrease over time, with a corresponding increase in no effects. In the class of '51, it is only the negative effects that show a decrease in time with a corresponding increase in no effects. Finally, for the class of '60, there is a shift from immediate negative effects to long-term positive effects with *no* increase in no effects. This holds true for *both* required and non-required withdrawals. *In sum, by the class of '60, more students indicate immediate positive effects of withdrawal, more indicate long-term positive effects, and more change from reports of immediate negative effects to reports of long-term positive effects.*[11]

*Summary.* The findings reported in this study may be summarized as follows:

(1) There is *no* evidence that the percentage of students withdrawing from Princeton has been increasing. However, the data do suggest that current students more often drop out for personal reasons than for academic reasons. Also, dropping out appears to be a much more serious consideration in the lives of current undergraduates than was true in the past.

(2) Academic ability alone appears to play a minor role in determining which Princeton students drop out and cannot be used effectively in attempts at prediction. We need to know

[11] These data may be somewhat biased. The discrepancy between dropout and non-dropout returns suggested that shame about having withdrawn might have prevented some dropouts from responding to the questionnaire. On the other hand, the data are quite consistent and the percent returns for dropouts from the classes of '51 and '60 did reach 78 percent and 66 percent respectively. While complete data on all classes might alter the findings some, it is unlikely that they would change the overall picture. At a minimum it is clear that many students experience relief upon dropping out and later find it to have been a valuable experience, while many others recover from the initial shock to find more rewarding kinds of experiences.

more about motivational factors in relation to academic performance and dropping out. Two areas which would appear to be worthy of investigation are the effects of frustrated expectations on students, and the question of student-college fit leading to satisfaction or dissatisfaction with one's college.

(3) A considerable number of dropouts return to college and go on to obtain a baccalaureate degree. The percent returning to Princeton or to some other college and the percent going on to obtain the baccalaureate degree have been increasing.

(4) As for earnings, non-dropouts appear to earn more money than dropouts. However, the non-degree dropouts do not appear to have suffered greatly in the economic realm. Their mean and median incomes compare favorably with the national data for part-college and whole-college males. The range of dropout incomes is not very different from that of non-dropouts, and they report as much job satisfaction.

(5) While differences in percent married are not striking, dropouts report a far higher divorce rate than non-dropouts.

(6) In terms of dropout evaluations of the immediate and long-term effects of withdrawal, individuals increasingly report immediate and long-term positive effects. While individual responses are quite varied, 50 percent of the respondents from the class of '60 dropouts reported some or only immediate positive effects and 68 percent reported some or only long-term positive effects.

### *The Illinois Study*

The data presented here were gathered in 1962 by Bruce K. Eckland as part of a study designed to trace the academic and social careers of male students who entered the University of Illinois as freshmen in 1952. Information was obtained from the University's records, from a mail questionnaire to the former students which yielded a 94 percent response, and from 104 colleges and universities that supplied the records required to verify the students' reports of transfer and graduation elsewhere. In this study a person who transferred to another college or university without an interruption was not designated as a dropout. The following summary of Eckland's work is based upon excerpts from a series of recently published papers.[12]

*Those Who Came Back.* Whereas 586 of the 1,180 respondents received a bachelor's degree from the University of Illinois or elsewhere following a period of continuous attendance—i.e., no academic interruptions of one or more semesters—594, or 50.3 percent, dropped out of school. In this study, 417, or 70.2 percent of the 594 dropouts, came back to college sometime during the ten years following matriculation. Furthermore, 54.9 percent of those who came back went on to graduate. This brings the total graduation rate of all respondents to 69.1 percent.

Even after ten years it appears that some dropouts still are potential graduates. The academic careers of the entering students can be followed through the data presented in Table 4. If all non-graduates attending college who were in senior standing are classified as potential graduates, the eventual total of all graduates rises to 74.2 percent. The data in Table 4 indicate that a relatively large number of graduates received their degrees from institutions other than the University of Illinois.

To summarize briefly, out of every ten male freshmen who entered college ten years ago at the University of Illinois, four graduated from the University in continuous progression, one graduated elsewhere in continuous progression, and five dropped out. Of the five dropouts, three later came back to college with one graduating at Illinois, one graduating elsewhere, and the third failing for a second time. Overall, seven graduated and three did not. Clearly eight semesters in four years is not the usual progression to graduation.

12 See his "College dropouts who came back," *Harvard Educational Review,* 1964, 34, pp. 402-420; "Social class and college graduation: Some misconceptions corrected," *American Journal of Sociology,* 1964, 70, pp. 36-50; "A source of error in college attrition studies," *Sociology of Education,* 1964, 38, pp. 60-72; "Academic ability, higher education and occupational mobility," *American Sociological Review,* 1965 (in press). I am grateful to him for permission to include his material and for his critical reading of this manuscript.

TABLE 4. DISTRIBUTION OF 1952 MALE FRESHMEN BY GRADUATION STATUS AND DEGREE-GRANTING INSTITUTION[a]

| | GRADUATES | | | | | | | |
|---|---|---|---|---|---|---|---|---|
| | *University of Illinois* | | *Transfer Institution* | | NON-GRADUATES | | TOTALS | |
| GRADUATION STATUS | *(no.)* | *(%)* | *(no.)* | *(%)* | *(no.)* | *(%)* | *(no.)* | *(%)* |
| Graduated in class of June 1956 or before | 336 | 28.5 | 46 | 3.9 | | | 382 | 32.4 |
| All others who graduated in continuous attendance | 154 | 13.1 | 50 | 4.2 | | | 204 | 17.3 |
| Dropouts who came back and *later graduated* | 135 | 11.4 | 94 | 8.0 | | | 229 | 19.4 |
| Dropouts who came back and are *potential graduates* | | | | | 60 | 5.1 | 60 | 5.1 |
| Dropouts who came back but whose *graduation appears unlikely* | | | | | 128 | 10.8 | 128 | 10.8 |
| Dropouts who *never came back* | | | | | 177 | 15.0 | 177 | 15.0 |
| TOTALS | 625 | 53.0 | 190 | 16.1 | 365 | 30.9 | 1,180 | 100.0 |

[a] Bruce K. Eckland, "College dropouts who came back," *Harvard Educational Review* 1964, 34, p. 405.

*Correlates of Return to College.* A number of variables were investigated for their possible relationship to returning to college and later graduation. How is the time of leaving related to returning to college and later graduating? The data (Table 5) indicated that the dropout's chance of returning progressively increased with the amount of time he spent in college before leaving, and, if he returned, his chance of graduating also increased with the length of prior attendance. Although the data indicate that more dropouts who left college with longer periods of attendance already behind them later returned and graduated, it must be emphasized that there was a better than 50-50 chance that even the very early dropout (one semester) would come back and, if he returned, about a 50-50 chance that he would eventually attain a degree.

TABLE 5. RELATIONSHIP BETWEEN LENGTH OF ATTENDANCE BEFORE LEAVING COLLEGE, LENGTH OF ABSENCE, AND RETURN TO COLLEGE AND LATER GRADUATION[a]

| | *Percent of Dropouts Who Came Back* | | *Percent of Returnees Who Ever Graduate*[c] | |
|---|---|---|---|---|
| Totals | 702 | (594)[b] | 69.3 | (417) |
| A. *Returning to College and Later Graduation by Number of Consecutive Semesters Enrolled Before Leaving* | | | | |
| One semester | 57.3 | (131) | 50.7 | ( 75) |
| Two semesters | 66.1 | (118) | 70.5 | ( 78) |
| Three or four semesters | 74.9 | (167) | 71.2 | (125) |
| Five or more semesters | 78.1 | (178) | 77.0 | (139) |
| B. *Graduation of Dropouts Who Returned by Duration of Non-Attendance Period* | | | | |
| One year | | | 65.8 | (149) |
| Two years | | | 77.6 | ( 85) |
| Three years | | | 76.0 | ( 83) |
| Four years | | | 61.2 | ( 49) |
| Five or more years | | | 62.7 | ( 51) |

[a] Bruce K. Eckland, "College dropouts who came back," *Harvard Educational Review*, 1964, 34, p. 410.

[b] Figures in parentheses indicate the number of subjects in each subgroup upon which the percentages are based.

[c] "Ever graduate" refers to both the 229 dropouts who have graduated and the 60 dropouts who are potential graduates (i.e., those who recently were still enrolled in college and who had attended over five semesters).

How is the duration of the non-attendance period related to late graduation? Dropouts who were out of college four or more years had about the same success upon return as those who were absent only a year. Between these extremes, however, the data in Table 5 suggest that there is an optimum duration of about two or three years' absence, which may be related to a period of active duty in the military service, judging from the experience of many of the dropouts who left college in the early 1950's and later returned to school.

The relationship of many of the variables in the dropout phenomenon was found to differ, depending upon whether the criterion was graduation without having dropped out or total graduation (including dropouts who returned to college and obtained a degree); that is, some variables predict who will drop out but do not predict which of the dropouts will be successful upon return to college, whereas other variables are related to success upon the readmission of a dropout to college but not to the initial withdrawal. For example, high-school percentile rank appears to predict the permanency of the dropout status only about half as well as it predicts whether or not a student will leave college in the first place.

Some variables actually reverse the direction of the relationship, depending upon which criterion is used. For example, while suburban community background is directly related to dropping out of college, it is inversely related to remaining out of college. Similarly, students who reside in a fraternity and whose parents pay most of their college expenses are much less likely than others to become a dropout. However, the dropout who is most likely to return and graduate is the one who did not reside in a fraternity and whose parents contributed very little to the cost of college.

Finally, is there a relationship between reported reason for withdrawal, later return to college, and subsequent graduation? Although the temporary and permanent dropouts did not appear to differ substantially in terms of the percentages reporting various reasons for withdrawal, when the reasons for leaving college were ranked by the percentage who never graduate among those reporting them, some clear differences emerged. Dropouts did not frequently cite marriage, lack of interest, or job opportunities as reasons for leaving, but those who did were not apt to return and graduate. In contrast, students who claimed to quit for lack of goals, military service, or personal adjustment problems (statements usually expressing immaturity or discontent) were quite likely to attain a college degree at some later date. Academic and financial problems, although often cited by dropouts, ranked neither very high nor very low in terms of staying power, for about half of those reporting these reasons eventually returned to graduate.

*Occupational Achievement.* Past studies have indicated a relationship between education and occupational achievement. However, Eckland notes that these studies have not provided evidence of the separate effects of ability and education upon mobility. He asks: Is the high correlation found between education and occupation largely incidental to the ability of the students who succeeded in the school system, or is formal education, independent of ability, really the crucial variable?

The data in this study were used to relate the effects of three independent variables—i.e., academic ability, class origins, and college graduation—to occupational achievement. Ability was defined by the rank of each student in his high-school graduating class. Social class origin was determined by using Duncan's Index of Socio-economic Status[13] as applied to father's occupation. Later occupational achievement of the students was also determined by Duncan's index, here applied to the student's present occupation.

Data on the correlations of each of the independent variables with the other independent variables and with the dependent variable are presented in Figure 1. In addition, the separate effects of each of the independent variables upon occupational achievement were investigated by means of partial associations. Eckland's analysis indicated that very little of the effect of education (college graduation) upon occupational achievement could be accounted for by the influence of ability and class origin on graduation. Ability alone had an important influence on college graduation, but its direct or independent effect upon occupational achievement was insignificant. When social class was related to occupational achievement, independent of ability and education, its effect also was found to be small. When, however, the graduates were differentiated from the dropouts, the data indicated that while social class was not related to the occupational achievement of the graduates, it was to the achievement of the dropouts; that is, whereas the graduates' achievements after leaving college was not altered by social class, the dropouts' was.

In sum, some degree of success is almost guaranteed by the attainment of a college diploma, quite independent of either

[13] A. J. Reiss, O. D. Duncan, P. K. Hatt, and C. C. North, *Occupations and social status,* New York: Free Press of Glencoe, 1961.

FIGURE 1. INTERCORRELATION OF INDEPENDENT VARIABLES (CLASS ORIGIN, ACADEMIC ABILITY, COLLEGE GRADUATION) WITH ONE ANOTHER AND WITH OCCUPATIONAL ACHIEVEMENT[a]

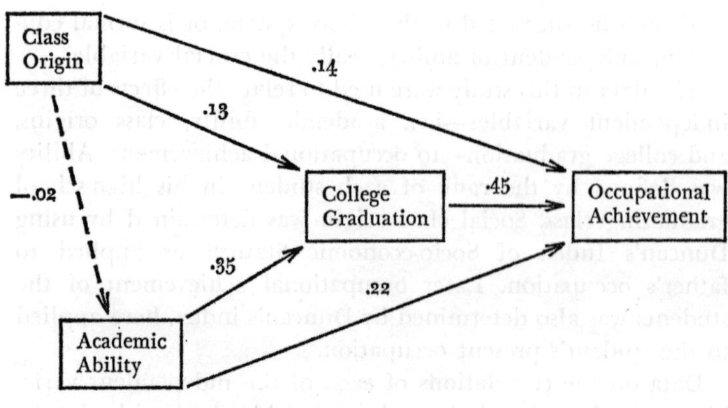


[a] Bruce K. Eckland, "Academic ability, higher education and occupational mobility," *American Sociological Review* (in press).

the student's academic ability or class background. Without a diploma, the occupational achievement of the college dropout was not altered by academic ability, but was significantly affected by his class origin.

### *The Significance of Follow-up Studies of College Dropouts*

The results of these studies suggest that we may be in need of a reassessment of the nature of the dropout "problem." Current interest in the phenomenon has developed with the increased emphasis upon higher education for the masses, and with the extreme competition for admission to the elite colleges. The current attitude appears to be that dropping out of college is bad, and that the situation is worse now than it has been in the past. Research indicates that the dropout rate at most colleges has not changed over the past twenty-five years.

However, the Princeton data suggest that there may have been a change in the nature of the dropouts. At Princeton there has been a decrease in students dropping out for academic reasons and an increase in students dropping out for personal reasons. These changes may reflect changes in the ability of Princeton students, changes in the problems today's students face and how these problems become manifest, changes in student attitudes toward dropping out, or changes in administrative policy. From the data in this study it is impossible to determine which of these possible factors is most influential in this change.

What is clear, however, is that while the dropout rate is not changing, a higher proportion of students are now giving serious consideration to dropping out of college, at least temporarily. This may reflect greater acceptance of dropping out as opposed to viewing it as a failure, greater student unrest, or more familial and college support for a period of delay before completion of college and continuation on to the greater responsibilities of graduate school or business. Awareness of these changes over time may be helpful to us in determining the most significant stresses leading to dropping out of college.

The data on the later academic success of college dropouts suggest that we have been overestimating the negative implications of a national 50 percent dropout rate.[14] For many students, dropping out is a temporary phenomenon and another step in the process of obtaining a degree. While the percentage of students successfully completing the degree in four years is higher at Princeton than at Illinois, and the percentage of dropouts returning to college to obtain a college degree is higher, both universities show the same pattern of a considerable increase in the total number of students who eventually obtain the college degree over the number obtaining the degree in four years at the same institution (Table 6). Similar data have been reported by Max[15] at the City University of New York,

14 There is some evidence that we have also been overestimating the high-school dropout rate. See N. Young, letter to the editor, *Harvard Educational Review*, 1964, 34, pp. 580-582.

15 Pearl Max, "College dropouts—a broader base for inquiry," unpublished manuscript, City University of New York, 1964.

TABLE 6. COMPARISON OF LATER ACADEMIC PERFORMANCE OF PRINCETON AND ILLINOIS DROPOUTS

| | *Princeton 1951* | *Illinois 1956* |
|---|---|---|
| Percent of entering class graduating in four years from same institution | .82 | .29 |
| Percent of dropouts to return to college | .82 | .70 |
| Percent of returnees to obtain B.A. degree | .74 | .55 |
| Percent of total class to obtain B.A. degree | .94 | .70 |
| Percent of non-dropouts to go on for advanced degree | .76 | .55 |
| Percent of dropouts to go on for advanced degree | .43 | .37 |
| Percent of non-dropouts to go on for further education who obtain advanced degree | .77 | .76 |
| Percent of B.A. dropouts to go on for further education who obtain advanced degree | .78 | .66 |

where 45 percent of the entering students graduate in four years, 63 percent graduate within seven years from the college of original enrollment, and 70 percent eventually graduate from one college or another.

It may be of some interest to note that this pattern of successful return to college after dropping out is also found among college students in England.[16] In a follow-up study of dropouts from two British universities, it was found that over half of the failing students tried again and over 70 percent of these were successful upon their return to college. The conclusion drawn from that study is similar to the one drawn from the Princeton and Illinois studies: "Even if our respondents have been more successful than the non-respondents, we can have some justification in saying that those students who initially failed to qualify do not constitute a group of permanent educational failures."

The Princeton data on the later vocational performance of dropouts indicated that dropping out is not indicative of fail-

[16] M. Kendall, "Those who failed: Part 1," *Universities Quarterly*, 1964, 18, pp. 398-406; "Part 2," *ibid.*, 1964, 19, pp. 69-77.

ure throughout life. Similarly, in another study, Harrison found that students who left Yale for emotional reasons tended to improve and later make satisfactory adjustments in life.[17] The findings in the Illinois study suggest that a college degree is of greater importance to later occupational achievement than was suggested by the Princeton data. This difference may be due to different measures of vocational success or to differences in the populations investigated. The Illinois finding that social class was a significant factor in the occupational achievement of dropouts would suggest that the lack of a degree was not as critical to Princeton dropouts because more came from middle- and upper-class families. On the other hand, the correlations in the Illinois study indicated that later vocational success or occupational achievement is largely a function of factors other than college graduation or social class.[18] Once more it is interesting to note that in the study of dropouts from English colleges, it was found that while non-dropouts earned more money than did dropouts, the dropouts who returned to obtain a degree were earning less money than the permanent dropouts.

These studies show that many dropouts make satisfactory academic, vocational, and personal adjustments in later life. While the Princeton data suggest that withdrawal is more often than not a profitable experience for students leaving for personal or health (non-required) reasons, other studies are necessary to define further the characteristics of the student for whom withdrawal will be a profitable experience. Also, further studies are necessary to define which types of experiences are most profitable for dropouts during the interim between leaving and returning to college. The significance of this phase in the academic career of some students has been

17 R. W. Harrison, "Leaving college because of emotional problems," in B. M. Wedge (ed.), *Psychosocial problems of college men*, New Haven: Yale University Press, 1958.

18 The multiple regression of all these variables with occupational achievement was .43, accounting for less than 20 percent of the total variance. While college graduation is clearly a factor in later occupational achievement, and social class is clearly a factor in the occupational achievement of dropouts, in both cases the overwhelming proportion of the variance remains to be accounted for.

noted by Riesman: "If a student doesn't choose to go to college but lands there, his decision to drop out and enter the Army may represent a stage of growth. He may want to see something of 'life' as an alternative to the university. But then he may find that life did not live up to its billing or that he doesn't want to be a GI for the rest of his career, and so he may decide to return and get his degree with a more committed sense of why he is there."[19]

Finally, research is needed on the factors which will enable administrators and clinicians to determine the readiness of a student to return to college after he has dropped out. The Illinois data suggest that many of the variables predicting who will drop out may not be predictive of which of the returning dropouts will be successful upon readmission. The chapter by Peszke and Arnstein in this volume represents a contribution to this area of research.

Colleges have a responsibility to their dropouts: to help make sure that dropping out becomes a profitable rather than a traumatic experience for the student. This may involve help in finding another college to transfer to, or in suggesting steps to ensure a successful return to the original college. In a more basic way, it involves the college's interest in the student's situation and in his future.

While studies must be made to determine how representative the findings reported here are of other institutions, the data strongly suggest that deans and university counselors are justified in regarding dropping out as a potentially profitable experience in the education of some students. As one professor described it, dropping out may be an inefficient but effective means of obtaining a college education.

[19] D. Riesman, letter to the editor, *Harvard Educational Review*, 1964, 34, pp. 582-584.

# *CHAPTER 3*

# A CRITICAL REVIEW OF RESEARCH ON THE COLLEGE DROPOUT

DOROTHY M. KNOELL

College dropout studies may soon rival college prediction studies in sheer numbers, but there appears to be little advancement of knowledge in either field by the accretion of discrete, routine studies of the type now being made in countless colleges and universities. Lacking and sorely needed are, first, a useful basic design for student follow-up studies which could be adopted by institutions with little research capability and, perhaps more important, a comprehensive model for the flow of students in higher education—from high school to college, between and among colleges, from level to level, and with lapses in enrollment which are permanent for some. Attrition is but one aspect of the more general phenomenon of college attendance—the decision to go to college (or not to go), the choice of institution (two- or four-year, public or private, in the home community or away), the selection of a major, and then, periodically, the urge to drop out or to transfer to another institution. As attrition is but one aspect of college attendance and flow, so is the student but one factor in the model for the flow. Other factors of equal importance are the collegiate institution and the system of higher education of which the institution is a part. Attrition may then be viewed as one type of resultant of the interaction of student, institution, and system variables.

Research to date on the college dropout has tended to be microcosmic in nature, rather than macrocosmic as implied in the suggested model for the flow of students in higher education. Periodic reviews or critiques of research on attrition have reflected this characterization. There are grounds for expecting a shift toward a more macrocosmic approach in a number of longitudinal studies now nearing completion. However, until they can be properly reviewed, it will not be known how close they come to fulfilling the need to study attrition in the context of a comprehensive model for student flow. Reference is made throughout this volume to noteworthy dropout studies with particular emphases. Little would appear to be gained from still another systematic review of existing literature. The previous reviews have demonstrated clearly the stability of certain findings concerning attrition over time, while pointing up major gaps both in the findings and in the research design.

This chapter will draw upon the literature on attrition in assessing the current status of research in the field, examining certain operating assumptions, formulating certain assertions to guide future research, and identifying certain promising studies which are in various stages of completion.

## *Reviews of the Literature*

The status of research on the college dropout was reviewed and assessed by Knoell in 1960[1] and Summerskill in 1962.[2] In the summer of 1964 a research conference on college dropouts was held with support from the U.S. Office of Education, the proceedings of which include a more comprehensive assessment than was possible in either review.[3] The earlier review by Knoell focused on the methodology of research on attrition, while pointing out what appeared to be promising leads from what were then current explorations of non-intellective variables as they related to performance in college. Four major types of studies were analyzed and examples of them were given: (1) the census study, which serves primarily to establish base-line data for particular institutions or states; (2) the "autopsy study," which attempts to identify the reasons for attrition by asking the dropouts questions at the time they withdraw; (3) the case study approach, often used by admissions officers and others whose concerns are decisions about

[1] Dorothy M. Knoell, "Institutional research on retention and withdrawal," in Hall Sprague (ed.), *Research on college students*, Boulder, Colo.: Western Interstate Commission for Higher Education, 1960, pp. 41-65.

[2] J. Summerskill, "Dropouts from college," in N. Sanford (ed.), *The American college*, New York: Wiley, 1962, pp. 627-657.

[3] J. R. Montgomery, *Proceedings of the research conference on college dropouts* (Cooperative Research Project No. F-065), Knoxville, Tenn.: University of Tennessee, 1964.

students, rather than research; and (4) prediction, in which admission variables are related to success and failure in college, including dropout. The lack of experimentation with action research programs to reduce the incidence of attrition was noted, together with the need for analysis of institutional or organizational characteristics which might affect attrition rates.

Summerskill reviewed research on the various factors which are usually associated with attrition, as well as studies producing attrition rates. The major factors with which he dealt are biological and social, academic, motivation, adjustment, illness and injury, and finances. Conflicting evidence was obtained from various studies of a number of the factors, sometimes as a result of poor control of related variables, other times because of a very fundamental lack of insight into the psychology of the college student, and finally because of a confusion of causes and outcomes in interpreting data. Academic factors, e.g., high-school preparation and performance in college; motivation, including both lack of it and changes or conflict in it; and finances emerge most clearly from the literature as important determiners of attrition. Illness and injury account for a small but reliable portion of attrition. However, evidence concerning the roles of social factors (such as socio-economic variables and home-town location and size) and personal-social adjustment is still inconclusive. In a summary statement concerning directions for future research, Summerskill emphasizes the need for basic research on student motivation in specified college environments.

The research conference on college dropouts exhibited certain concerns which have been underrepresented in the research literature. Among them are the effects of changes in institutional policies and procedures on attrition rates, techniques for the early identification of potential dropouts, programs for reducing attrition in certain subgroups of students, and the need for post-dropout study and action programs. However, one of the major recommendations for research which emerged from the conference was that a new national census-type study be undertaken soon, in a sense replicating Iffert's study in the early 1950's, which has served as a bench mark for so long.[4] Advances in computer technology since 1950 have been such that it is now possible to collect and analyze comprehensive follow-up data fairly routinely and with little expenditure of staff time, once a basic design has been developed. Iffert's study yields not only normative data on attrition, for comparison with rates obtained in new census studies, but also extensive material relating to student characteristics, reasons for going to college, financial resources, ratings of college facilities and services, and extracurricular activities and interests. Thus the conference on college dropouts recognized the need for both census-type studies on an up-dated, continuing basis and for some vast changes in approach to the study and remedy of the attrition problem.

### *Stability of Findings*

Summerskill makes the point that research on college dropouts has a history of at least forty years and that the attrition rate has not changed appreciably during this period.[5] Collegiate institutions have lost and continue to lose about half their undergraduate students in the four years after freshman admission, despite changes in student characteristics, programs offered, standards enforced, and services rendered. A total of about 60 percent graduate from some institution, at varying times—approximately 40 percent four years after entering a particular institution and an additional 20 percent at a later time and/or elsewhere. The gross statistics on graduation and attrition conceal a very high degree of variability among collegiate institutions—public and private, colleges and universities, under different types of control, and in different states and regions.

Stability in the gross attrition rates over an extended period of time should give little cause for complacency, if one considers the changes in both society and higher education which have taken place in recent decades. One might hypothesize that attrition rates for individual institutions have varied

[4] R. E. Iffert, *Retention and withdrawal of college students*, Bulletin No. 1, U.S. Department of Health, Education and Welfare, Washington, D.C.: U.S. Government Printing Office, 1957.

[5] Summerskill, *op.cit.*, p. 630.

markedly over time and that only the gross rates have remained stable. However, there is little evidence to support such a contention and it behooves the researcher to explore other explanatory factors. A few of the changes in higher education which might be expected to bring about significant changes in the phenomenon of attrition, if not in the actual rate, are:

(1) The steady increase in the number and percentage of our youth who are going to college as a result both of increased opportunity for higher education and of greater value placed on it by our present-day society. This increase in college-going will undoubtedly produce greater heterogeneity in the college freshman class with respect to academic and specialized talents, family backgrounds, vocational and other interests, motivation, values, and other characteristics which may be related to attrition.

(2) The phenomenal growth of the community junior college and a concomitant increase in the percentage of new freshmen who will take their lower-division work in a two-year institution. There has been little speculation and almost no research on the question of the long-term effects on attrition and the production of baccalaureate degrees of: (a) the dramatic increase in opportunity for low-cost education in the students' home communities; and (b) the diversion of students from four- to two-year colleges by raising admission requirements, increasing tuition and fees, and restricting enrollments by other means in the four-year institutions.

(3) The development of attractive one- and two-year vocational programs in the junior colleges which lead to immediate employment, rather than transfer to four-year institutions, and the failure of researchers to take account of students in these terminal programs in dropout studies.

(4) Improvements in the quality of the entering college freshmen. State institutions with open-door admission policies are now becoming more selective, both by restricting admission to applicants who appear to have a reasonable probability of success and by doing a better job of informing the high schools about the kinds of students who will succeed in

their programs. At the same time the instruction in the high schools is both accelerating and improving, with the result that some new college students enter with much of their freshman year's work already completed.

(5) Greater diversification of opportunity in both two- and four-year colleges in the various states, as teachers' colleges become multipurpose institutions, as state scholarship and other aid programs are expanded, and as more communities develop local opportunities for education beyond the high school. Youth may even become confused by the plethora of educational opportunities available after high school. The bases for initial choice of college are clear neither to the researcher nor (probably) to the high-school seniors and their parents who make the choices.

(6) Greater mobility of college students—from two- to four-year colleges, between four-year colleges in the same and different states, to overseas campuses (or to travel abroad for a brief period), into the Peace Corps, or to work in social action programs—some as temporary dropouts and others permanently.

(7) Greatly increased competition for admission to the "preferred" colleges. Fears on the part of parents and high-school students about gaining admission to any college, enrollment pressures resulting from the expected increase in the volume of youth wanting to attend college, and, in some instances, rapid and uncontrolled growth in previously small institutions with a concomitant lack of regard for student welfare.

Societal changes which might be expected to have the greatest impact on attrition in college are the increasing social unrest among college-age youth and the greater questioning of traditional values. The stigma which was formerly attached to early marriage, dropout from school and college, lack of church affiliation, and other deviations from expected patterns of behavior associated with social class membership have now diminished and in some instances vanished. At the same time an atmosphere of economic prosperity and "cold war" peace prevails which contrasts quite vividly with the 1950's, when Iffert's monumental attrition study was undertaken. Other changes could be enumerated but those which have been noted are believed to give strong support to the contention that a new, many-pronged attack on attrition research is presently needed as part of the study of the flow of students in higher education.

The assumption that a relatively stable rate of attrition over time implies a static set of circumstances in higher education and society at large is believed to be but one of a number of questionable operating assumptions which have tended to confuse the design of past studies and the interpretation of their findings. Other questionable assumptions which appear to apply to a considerable body of research on attrition are:

(1) Every student who enters a four-year college (or a transfer program in a two-year college) has both the ability and the motivation to complete a baccalaureate degree program. In the case of the four-year college, the further assumption is made that he will earn a degree from the institution in which he matriculated as a freshman and will remain in continuous attendance while doing so.

(2) Every student who fails to enroll in each successive semester after admission and until graduation is a dropout and, in the eyes of the college, a failure.

(3) Attrition is unrelated to academic ability and achievement, since as many "good" students drop out as "poor" and since academic difficulties account for only one-third of the dropouts.

(4) Attrition is necessarily harmful to the student and a loss to the college.

(5) Student characteristics which are related to attrition are static, education does not change them and, in fact, has little to do with them, and no new behavior will manifest itself during college which may be related to the act of dropping out.

## *Proposed New Focus for Research*

If we assume that the need for a new national census study is self-evident, attention might be more properly turned to other areas of needed research which emerge from the critique of the past and the analysis of present trends. The focus of one such set of studies would be on the student, a second on environmental press, and a third on action programs. A moratorium might well be declared on what have been called "autopsy studies," in which dropouts are queried about their reasons for withdrawing. Research resources thus saved could be channeled into evaluative studies of the educational, vocational, and personal outcomes attained by students who fail to complete degree programs. The need is particularly critical in the junior colleges, where attrition is exceedingly high after only one year and where a large proportion of the students in transfer programs do not enter four-year institutions. One very important aspect of such an evaluative approach is an assessment of the long-term effects of failure among college students. Knowledge of this kind might be useful in deciding how much freedom should be given to college students at various points when choices must be made, some of which will lead almost inevitably to failure.

A second proposal for the diversion of present research efforts involves a lessening of attention to follow-up studies of marginal or probationary students admitted by the college and a concomitant increase in research on the so-called sporadic attenders. This group includes part-time students, temporary dropouts, delayed college attenders, and enrollees in extension, night, and non-resident programs—i.e., those who do not fit the stereotype of the full-time resident student whose entire life falls under the influence of the college until or unless he drops out before graduation. The sporadic attenders are expected to increase markedly in number, particularly as college-going rates include more children from families with no tradition of college attendance. Knowledge of their progress in degree programs, including their problems and frustrations, should provide one basis for improving services for these students, such as financial aid, vocational counseling and placement, and testing of skills and knowledge acquired outside the classroom. Research should be designed to accompany the College Entrance Examination Board's recently proposed program of college-level examinations, particularly to evaluate its usefulness in working with the so-called unaffiliated students.

The third new focus in student follow-up studies should be on the mobility aspect of the dropout phenomenon. The recent study of male undergraduates at the University of Illinois which produced the finding that as many as 70 percent received a baccalaureate degree within a ten-year period after freshman admission should provide an incentive for other institutions to make a very thorough canvass of dropouts who may have transferred elsewhere.[6] Increases both in the proportion of students attending a two-year college for their lower-division work and in the volume of transfer between four-year colleges appear to mandate a sharper focus on student mobility as part of the phenomenon of attrition. Cooperation among institutions on a regional and perhaps on a national scale will be necessary in order to obtain reliable feedback on mobility over time. Evaluation should be as much the concern in this type of study as in studies of dropouts who do not transfer. The most efficient pattern of college attendance is one of full-time enrollment in one institution for four continuous years, or until the degree is granted. However, as this pattern ceases to be the norm in the total flow of college students through the system, the evaluation of alternative patterns involving mobility among institutions takes on added importance. An assessment of reasons for transfer and gains to the student by doing so may replace many current efforts to assess reasons for dropping out.

The second set of studies which is proposed involves the college environmental press as a factor in student attrition. Several instruments for assessing press have now been refined sufficiently for them to be useful in attrition studies, including Pace's College and University Environment Scales (CUES) and Astin's Environmental Assessment Technique (EAT). The fact of diversity in higher education is now so well established that it has almost become a cliché. However, progress has been rather slow in describing the diversity along dimensions other than academic. Astin's recently published study,

[6] B. K. Eckland and Anita C. Smith, *A follow-up survey of male members of the freshman class of the University of Illinois in September 1952*, Office of Instructional Research, Report No. 105, Urbana, Ill.: University of Illinois, 1963.

*Who goes where to college,*[7] represents a considerable contribution to our understanding of diversity, on the basis of which individual colleges and universities can assess their own characteristics more effectively. Students enter college with certain skills, abilities, achievements, interests, values, motivations, dispositions, and resources. While the first three factors tend to set an upper limit on their performance in college, the effective utilization of their talents depends in large part upon the remaining factors. Both students and collegiate institutions have certain academic and non-intellective characteristics. Research to date has made it possible to do a fairly good job of matching students and colleges on the various academic dimensions. However, study of the interaction of students and institutions with respect to non-intellective characteristics remains a major challenge in any program of research on attrition. The student's perceptions of the college of his choice may be in error, his interests and motivation may change as he matures in college, and his values may be seriously challenged while in the college environment. Studies of these phenomena are by no means uncommon, but there has been comparatively little effort devoted to date to relating them to the attrition problem. The lack of a comprehensive model for studying the factors which affect the flow of students may again be a major limitation in current research undertakings.

The third area of study which is proposed involves experimental or action programs for reducing attrition in particular institutions. One might conclude from the literature that the "doers" often have little orientation to research or that successful programs are so time-consuming that staff members involved in them are unable to prepare reports for publication. Two types of programs are envisioned: (a) action programs designed to identify potential dropouts and to intercept this occurrence by various techniques whenever it is feasible to do so; and (b) actions designed to have some desirable effect on the entire student body or some major portion of it, without particular reference to dropouts but with the general intent of reducing attrition. Research during normal college

[7] A. W. Astin, *Who goes where to college,* Chicago: Science Research Associates, 1965.

operations often cannot include the various controls which are necessary in a true experiment. Therefore, there is need for good base-line data in order to find out whether change in rates or types of attrition has taken place as a result of particular action programs. Such programs may involve changes in policies or standards, as well as student services in counseling, placement, and other personnel areas. Considerable discussion was devoted at the Research Conference on College Dropouts to programs and techniques for reducing attrition, which tended to take the form of an information exchange rather than a reporting of research findings. It is possible that the addition of a research person to the team of student personnel workers (or others) involved in action programs would ensure the systematic reporting of procedures and findings in the literature.

### *Assertions as Guides in Further Research*

Certain assertions about the nature of attrition and probable conditions under which it takes place can be made, based on the existing research literature, which might serve as an elementary framework for the design of some needed research. Such a framework is not a substitute for the comprehensive model for the flow of students which has been proposed, but should be compatible with it. The list is by no means exhaustive and certain of the assertions may need to be modified on the basis of further discussion and research.

(1) High-school graduates enter college with a vast range of goals, interests, motivations, and values. Some come with specific educational and vocational goals which they established many years earlier—e.g., medicine and teaching. Others seek only general education with no particular commitment to working for a degree. Still others, particularly in junior college, enter with no real goals and sometimes with little motivation for further education. For some, college attendance represents either an avoidance of some other activity, such as employment at low pay, or the marking of time after high school until marriage or military service. Attrition may be expected among students with various types of motivation (or without any) but for various reasons.

(a) Students with specific interests and strong motivations may make unwise choices, in terms of their academic potential or their understanding of the demands of their chosen field. Unless they are able to modify their goals while in college they will become early candidates for attrition.

(b) Students with only very general goals may withdraw after they complete only one or two years of college, unless they are stimulated to pursue knowledge for its own sake or to develop some specific goals which may be achieved in baccalaureate degree programs.

(c) Students who attend college for lack of a more attractive opportunity after high school may drop out quite early with only a flimsy excuse, after having accomplished little but the passing of time, unless they develop interests and motivation which will keep them in college.

(2) Decisions of individual students to withdraw and institutional rates of attrition both are a function of the interaction of student input (ability, interests, age, sex, motivation), the curriculum, methods of instruction, grading and retention standards, intellectual and other climates, student personnel services, activities, and, finally, outside impinging forces such as family, national crises, and accidents. Programs designed to change one or more of these factors should result in a change in the volume and nature of attrition in particular situations.

(3) Some characteristics of entering students are fixed or static, but others can and should change as a consequence of education and/or maturation. Some rather obvious examples of static traits are age at the time of matriculation, sex, race, family origins, prior educational achievement, and native ability. Examples of characteristics which might change during college are subject-matter and other interests, values, insights into self, strength of motivation, socialization, and habits. Institutional objectives might be restated in behavioral terms so as to include some of these desired changes, in a way which would permit their periodic assessment in connection with attrition research.

(4) The decision to withdraw or persist is not always within the province of the students who are dropouts. Perhaps no more than half the dropouts have real freedom of choice. For

example, academic dismissal is the direct cause of many lower-division dropouts from public institutions. Other forced withdrawals include disciplinary suspensions, illness or accident which incapacitates the student at least temporarily, loss of financial support for college, and military service. It might be argued that the causes are multiple even in these instances, in that the student may fail because of financial distress or poor social adjustment. However, for purposes of research it appears useful to dichotomize withdrawal action as forced or voluntary, in terms of the student's opportunity to make a real choice about persistence.

(5) Although the factors related to attrition are usually multiple, a single incident may serve as a trigger for the dropout action. Most students begin to think about dropping out long before they actually do so. As they progress through their four-year programs, the probability of their persistence and eventual graduation increases as the factors of poor grades, financial problems, lack of motivation, and poor adjustment diminish in importance.

(6) A clear distinction should be made in research among dropouts who transfer to other colleges (particularly those who transfer from junior colleges), those who withdraw with a definite plan to return after a brief absence, and those who appear to be leaving for good. The volume of transfer between colleges seems to be large at the present time and growing, although documentation is lacking. Incidence of temporary withdrawal is also increasing, particularly among students in the elite colleges who have few financial or academic difficulties. While it might be argued that the only really permanent dropouts are the deceased, there is reason to believe that some workable definition can be arrived at which will serve to distinguish between the true dropout and those with reasonable expectations of returning to college.

### *Studies Not Previously Reviewed*

A number of longitudinal studies of students which are being conducted at the Center for the Study of Higher Education should yield insights into attrition among different kinds of students and in different types of colleges.[8] Attrition has not been a major focus of investigation in any of the studies, but it would obviously be impossible to ignore attrition while studying the flow of students in higher education and the impact of college on them. The two most important longitudinal projects which have been conducted at the Center involve (1) about 10,000 high-school graduates in a sample of 16 communities in nine states, which began in the spring of 1959;[9] and (2) college freshmen who entered a sample of eight colleges in the fall of 1958, including both public and private institutions of various types.[10] Still another longitudinal study which is nearly complete involves winners of scholarships or certificates of merit from the National Merit Scholarship Corporation in 1956.[11] The focus has been on the psychological development of the students, rather than on their academic performance in college, but the findings should have considerable relevance to research on attrition. A fourth longitudinal study, which was started in 1961, was concerned with a large sample of junior college students who transferred to 41 colleges and universities in 10 states.[12] While attrition during and after junior college was not within the scope of the study, the several thousand students who dropped out after transfer were the subject of much attention in the study.

Finally, two new studies of student characteristics have been undertaken quite recently at the Center. The first is a com-

8 See the *Annual Report* of the Center for the Study of Higher Education, University of California, Berkeley, for periodic reports of various studies in progress.

9 *Characteristics and background of high school graduates and their subsequent personal and educational development* (Cooperative Research Project No. 1328) and *Factors associated with various patterns of college attendance* (Cooperative Research Project No. 2790), J. W. Trent and L. L. Medsker, co-investigators.

10 *Differential recruitment and institutional impact in selected institutions,* a longitudinal study supported by a grant from the Carnegie Corporation, conducted by a research team including Paul Heist, Burton Clark, Martin Trow, Harry Webster, George Yong, and T. R. McConnell.

11 *Persistence and achievement of academically superior students,* a study under the direction of Fred T. Tyler.

12 Dorothy M. Knoell and L. L. Medsker, *From junior to senior college: A national study of the transfer student.* Washington, D.C.: American Council on Education, 1965.

munity college study supported by the Carnegie Corporation, one phase of which involves a follow-up study of students who entered a sample of more than 50 two-year colleges in 21 states. The second, which will be supported by a grant from the College Entrance Examination Board, will follow a large sample of ninth-grade students through high school and into college, in order to investigate planning, decision-making, choices, and achievement in relation to college attendance.

Tentative findings from the ongoing study of high-school graduates in 16 communities[13] show that two students in 10 who entered college right after high school transferred at least once during the four-year follow-up period and that five students in 10 were no longer enrolled in *any* college after four years. The assumption was made that all junior college students in transfer programs would in fact transfer to and persist in four-year colleges, which may tend to inflate the attrition figures. However, the implication is clear that these students were mobile after high school—in and out of college and between institutions. A grant was also secured to study the factors associated with various patterns of college attendance in this group, including delayed entry into college, temporary and permanent dropout, transfer, and delayed graduation. Data will be used which were collected during the students' senior year in high school and later in the follow-up period, including a biographical questionnaire, attitude surveys, ability test data, transcripts, and interviews. Special attention will be given to able high-school graduates who did not attend college, as well as to students with various patterns of attendance. An attempt will be made to relate the various college attendance patterns to a wide range of personal and academic characteristics of the students, their family backgrounds, economic status, and vocational experiences after high school.

Institutions in the eight-college longitudinal study are Reed, Antioch, Swarthmore, St. Olaf, San Francisco State, the University of the Pacific, the University of Portland, and the University of California at Berkeley.[14] The focus has been on the intellectual development of the students attending these vari-

[13] Trent and Medsker, *op.cit.*

[14] Heist *et al., op.cit.*

ous institutions. Analyses have been made of differential recruitment to the several institutions and particularly of changes in the characteristics of their students during the undergraduate years. While no final report has yet been published, some of the preliminary findings show: (1) a very high loss from higher education of the academically talented, creative women who are attracted to the "elite" colleges but who do not seem to find satisfaction in the regular programs offered by them; (2) the likelihood that certain types of potential dropouts could be predicted well in advance from personality and other measures obtained at the time of admission, particularly in the case of the unique and relatively small liberal arts colleges; and (3) the seeming inability of youth in their late teens (particularly women) to make rational decisions about college attendance when alternatives to persistence are presented. Extensive interviewing and visitation have taken place throughout the study, as well as data collection involving both personality and biographical measures.

The main focus of the transfer student study[15] was the analysis of the performance (including attrition) of more than 8,000 students from junior colleges, all of whom might have been regarded as dropouts when they left the two-year institutions. Attrition after the students transferred as juniors was found to be nearly 30 percent. A large number of the dropouts appear to have made unrealistic choices of a four-year college, considering the level of their achievement in junior college and the size of the drop in grade-point average they might have expected to experience after transfer. However, many dropouts with upper-division standing transferred to other four-year colleges and were in most cases making satisfactory progress toward their degrees when the study ended. Both financial and motivational factors loomed large in the decision of many of the students to drop out after transfer. One conclusion to be drawn from the transfer study findings is that decisions about college attendance, persistence, withdrawal, transfer, reentry, and graduate work are made by people of all ages, in various phases of their lives and careers.

[15] Knoell and Medsker, *op.cit.*

A substudy of the transfer student project involved the collection of extensive data on the volume and sources of all new undergraduate transfer students in 1963, together with policies governing transfer, expectations about their future accommodation, and opinions about their success. The findings are quite clear that both volume and sources of transfer students vary widely among different types of colleges and among the states, at least partly as a function of the junior college enrollment and the diversification of educational opportunities offered in particular states. The statistics showed that about half the new undergraduate students in many large colleges and universities are transfers or dropouts from other colleges, particularly in the public institutions. The most prevalent pattern observed might be described as vertical transfer upward to the major state universities by students who left two- and four-year colleges which did not offer baccalaureate degree programs in particular fields. Although junior colleges were not among the respondents, a certain amount of vertical transfer downward could also be expected by students from major state universities and private institutions who failed academically, who were unable to adjust socially to large universities, or whose financial resources ran out.

One of the most serious gaps in our knowledge of dropouts as a potential loss of talent is in the area of the junior college. It is fairly well established that a large percentage of the high-school graduates who enter two-year colleges fail to complete certificate or associate degree programs. There is also reason to believe that many who enter with the intent to transfer do not do so. Neither our statistics nor our insights into the phenomenon of the junior college dropout are now adequate to the task of assessing this loss of talent. While now somewhat dated, the most reliable national data are still those obtained by Medsker in another Center study which was published in 1960[16] Data were collected for more than 17,000 students in a sample of 63 two-year colleges. He found that only one in three

[16] L. L. Medsker, *The junior college: Progress and prospect*, New York: McGraw-Hill Book Company, 1960. As was noted above, the study is now being repeated under a new grant, one part of which involves longitudinal study of students.

entering students transferred to a four-year college, that about one in three received an associate degree from the two-year college, and that slightly more than half the graduates transferred. Inferences concerning loss of talent might be drawn from the companion finding that more than two-thirds of the entering students enrolled in transfer programs and thus presumably expected to transfer to four-year colleges, although only one-third did so. An assessment of either personal or societal loss owing to this type of attrition cannot be made without further knowledge of the academic potential of the students who failed to complete their programs or to transfer (or both), of changes in their goals and values as they progressed through junior college, and of their family backgrounds and economic resources for higher education beyond the junior college. On the surface, the difference between the two-thirds who intended to transfer and the one-third who actually did so appears to be a serious loss—to the students who were frustrated in their degree aspirations and to society. However, no conclusion should be drawn without considerably more research on the accomplishments of the non-transfers in junior college and afterward, to find out whether they became college dropouts in the sense of a loss to society, or whether they were in fact terminal students who gained useful skills and general education while in college. From these and other studies of student characteristics relating to college choice, one gains the impression that the factors determining who goes to which college and for how long (before dropout or transfer) are still very heavily weighted by the economics of the situation.

The concept of attrition as mobility would be quite pointless if it were possible to achieve the best of all possible worlds in higher education, in which every capable student would (1) enter the right college (for him) as a freshman and (2) be fully subsidized until he had achieved the highest level of education from which he could profit. Neither condition appears to be within our reach, nor do we believe it to be entirely desirable to limit the students' choices severely. For these and other reasons it is proposed that attention be given to student mobility as one aspect of attrition in a comprehensive model for the flow of students from high school to college and through degree programs, while continuing to work on the twin problems of maximizing our utilization of talent among our college-age youth and evaluating the outcomes for those who do not complete programs.

# *CHAPTER 4*

## COLLEGE DROPOUTS: SUCCESSES OR FAILURES?

DONALD H. FORD & HUGH B. URBAN

THE TITLE OF THIS book, *The College Dropout and the Utilization of Talent,* is intriguingly non-committal. It identifies two terms and implies a relationship between them, but the nature of that relationship is left ambiguous. On the one hand, one may infer that college dropouts represent a loss of potential talent to our society, and therefore a phenomenon to be changed. However, one can as readily consider the possibility that students are moving toward more effective use of their talents when they drop out, and thus represent a benefit to our society rather than a loss. Although the term "college dropout" has become a bad word in the popular press and the American home town, we should take care not to let that social phenomenon cloud our view of the matter. The possibilities of both loss and benefit should be considered.

Throughout this chapter we will argue that college dropouts may be considered someone's failure whenever they represent an instance in which a youngster with aptitudes, interests, personal characteristics, and career objectives appropriately developed in a college environment fails to complete his course of study, and for one reason or another is forced to lapse into a life-pattern which is less appropriate, less satisfying, and which, for him, represents a poor second choice. For this kind of student, dropping out of college represents a waste of talent, time, and money both for him and for the university.

We will also argue that attendance at a university or college is an appropriate way for some, but not all, people to develop themselves and their careers. Across the land we have hundreds of young men and women who are coaxed and wheedled into going away to college—youngsters who are not academically oriented; who do not learn well under the circumstances provided by the typical university, with its highly formalized system of abstract instruction, course requirements, credit structures, and the like; or whose career aspirations actually call for an entirely different kind of background than that provided by our colleges and universities. For students such as these, the decision to leave college may represent a constructive act, a step toward a more productive, meaningful life. The error will have occurred in the selection of a college education in the first place.

In portions of this chapter we will present some data acknowledging the customs of careful scholarship. We will be freely speculative, also recognizing this to be somewhat more risky—but fun.

### *The Reduction of College Dropouts*

*Any university that chooses to do so can make a major reduction in the proportion of its students who drop out, unless that proportion is already quite small.* Knowledge and techniques are now available to make a sizable dent in the problem if we decide to stop wringing our hands, get out of our arm chairs, and do something about it. Let us elaborate on that assertion. We will use the efforts of one state university with which we are most familiar, The Pennsylvania State University, to illustrate how the problem of dropouts may be attacked. Illustrations could be drawn from other universities as well.

*Some Empirical Findings.* One of the first things a university must do is to acquire some base rates of information about its own individual situation. It must arrange for a steady flow of data and research concerning the admission, academic performance, and related characteristics of its students. Careful study of both graduates and dropouts is essential. It is only by such feedback that a university can evaluate its efforts and discover those aspects of its operation which need to be improved. During the last eight years, Penn State has accelerated its efforts along this line. Jefferson D. Ashby, Associate Director of the Division of Counseling, recently completed a thorough follow-up of over 2,500 students admitted to The

Pennsylvania State University as baccalaureate degree freshmen in the fall semester, 1955. That class was selected partially because in 1956 a series of new efforts to improve our situation was initiated, even though some effective procedures had been undertaken during the preceding decade. At the time Ashby conducted his study, it had been eight years since the 1955 freshman class entered Penn State.

Of 2,516 freshmen in that class, 60 percent have earned a degree from Penn State, 15 percent were dismissed for poor scholarship, and the remaining 25 percent voluntarily interrupted their studies without completing their degree at Penn State. Before we talk about the 40 percent who did not complete their degree at Penn State, let us provoke your imagination with a little information about those who did graduate.

Penn State has ten colleges and some of the 1955 class graduated in each of the colleges. All the students completed a standard test of scholastic ability as entering freshmen. The average score for the student in this class who graduated from one of our colleges was over one standard deviation lower than the average score of the group graduating in another of our colleges. The averages for the remaining colleges were distributed between those two poles. In less statistical terms, this means that the typical graduate from this class in the one college had less scholastic aptitude than 85 percent of classmates who graduated in another college in the same university.

A typical faculty reaction in an American university to such a statistic would be "That college must have awfully low standards to graduate such dumb kids." There is no doubt that the lower students were less clever with words and less facile with abstract theory. It doesn't follow, however, that they were too dumb to deserve graduation. They had a reasonable level of competence with abstract symbols, and their programs of study required other abilities that were not measured by the standard scholastic aptitude test. This fact illustrates the notion that the situational contexts within which students may be asked to perform may be quite different, even within the same university.

It is also interesting to look at graduation rates for this class in relationship to the frequency with which they changed colleges within Penn State before finally graduating or leaving. This does not include such changes in major as from electrical engineering to mechanical engineering. Of the students who made no change but stayed in the college they chose as entering freshmen, 62 percent earned degrees from Penn State. Comparable graduation percentages for other groups are: one change—40 percent; two changes—78 percent; and three or more changes—91 percent. Moreover, students who made two, three, or more changes had higher scholastic aptitude scores than those who made no change or one change. Is it possible that a highly flexible university structure within which students can make one commitment and then another until they hit pay dirt is the most conducive to the graduation of bright students? Incidentally, about half of our students who do graduate in four years do so in exactly the same major they chose as freshmen, and half in a different major.

Let us return to the 40 percent of the class who did not earn a degree from Penn State. What happened to them? Why did they drop out? Before we look at the group statistically, let us tell you about a few of the individuals to help make the statistics human. One young man who now has a B.S. in economics said, "I wasn't mentally prepared for college, in the sense that I had no definite goals or real incentive to study—therefore, I just hung around. I just didn't try." One boy transferred to another school in order "to be closer to home and my girl friend."

A young man who is now a dentist stated, "My major reason for leaving Penn State was an emotional immaturity." Another boy dropped out for academic reasons, but eventually graduated from another college with honors. He wrote, "My advice to those students who are considering dropping out of school: if your goals are hazy, go out into the world and see how other people are living. Live among them, experience the things they experience. Then give careful consideration to the path you want your life to follow. And if you still have the ambition and the means to secure a college education, by all means pursue this course."

An honors high-school graduate and freshman scholarship holder who has not finished a degree wrote, "The only goal

I had in mind was to be an Air Force pilot—somehow everything else seemed secondary. When the goal of being a pilot fell through due to a loss of hearing, I began to look for a job. I found a rather good job. It has been a very rewarding one, as I have had two raises and three promotions in two and a half years. I have been told in my evaluations that I have a real ability and a lot of drive. Why now and not at State? As I look back after three years, two things come as most important. One, I never had a bad grade in a class where the professor had a real desire to teach. On the other hand, I had a lot of graduate students as instructors who were no more qualified to teach than I am, who literally didn't give a damn."

A navy lieutenant now doing graduate work in naval engineering dropped out because of low grades and lack of direction. He wrote, "My year at Penn State was an enjoyable one. To say the least, it brought out my own deficiencies, which I have for the most part been able to remedy." Did the decision to drop out of college represent a success or a failure for these people?

There were about 1,000 such dropouts whom Ashby attempted to contact. He was successful in obtaining follow-up information on about 73 percent. Of these 730 students, 35 percent reported they had obtained a college degree of some kind. Approximately 1.7 percent more reported they had completed some other kind of educational program, such as nursing. Another 12 percent reported they were actively enrolled, working toward a degree. Six of the class are known to be dead. Thus, approximately 50 percent of the dropouts have completed or are completing an educational program of some kind. Even if we assume that none of the 270 dropout students Ashby could not contact have obtained any kind of a degree, we still find that 70.5 percent of the 1955 freshmen have already completed some kind of college degree or certificated training. Some of these now actively working toward degrees will receive them. (The questionnaires and telephone conversations make us confident of this.) It seems reasonable to conclude that at least three out of four members of the class entering in 1955 have earned or will earn some kind of degree or certificate.

What about the one in four, the 25 percent, who probably will not complete a degree of any kind? Do they represent a loss of talent to our society? A good many of this group appear to be enjoying successful, productive careers and personal lives without a college degree. Some are clearly dissatisfied and disappointed that they could not finish.

In general, Ashby's study suggests that the efforts made at Penn State in the decade after 1945 produced some results, since the success rate for the 1955 group appears to exceed that of the typical land grant university. More can probably be done.

*A Rationale.* Before proceeding to discuss some approaches to the problem of dropouts, it will be useful to remind ourselves of a few generalizations about human behavior and how it works. We need a conceptual framework within which to order our thinking about the problem. We can start with a generally accepted axiom in psychology that a person's behavior at any moment is a function of the habitual responses he brings to that moment and the characteristics of the situation in which he is responding.

*The Response Pattern.* Each person acquires, in the course of his development, thousands of different behavior patterns in relation to all kinds of situations. Thus, he learns a set of things to say and do when meeting a new person, how to solve an algebraic problem, how to respond when being reprimanded, how to relate to the opposite sex, habits of thought, how to control his emotions, self-evaluations, and so forth. These patterns are in turn composed of many different kinds of responses. Each involves its own characteristic set of thoughts, feelings, acts, imagery, and physiological accompaniments, all intertwined in complex ways.

The intricacy involved in this complex patterning of behavior makes for an impressive degree of variability and modifiability in the way a person responds to each kind of situation. A response pattern is always learned at first in a particular kind of situation. For example, a boy may have learned to respond to his father's anger with thoughts like "He's going to give me hell and I won't even have a chance to explain." In addition, he may experience emotions of fear, resentment, or both, a knot in the stomach—perhaps accompanied by slight feelings of nausea—and the motoric act of escaping from this upsetting circumstance by going to his room. Such a pattern may remain specific to the situation in which it was learned, or may become general to several situations which have something in common. For example, the boy may come to respond to other males in positions of authority, such as teachers, coaches, or employers, in the same way—even when they aren't angry.

Many people in both their personal and professional lives tend to overemphasize this generality. There is a tendency to think of people as generally cynical, aggressive, wise, and so forth. If a man goofs off on one job, there is a tendency to assume that he must be a lazy worker on all jobs. If a student fails one semester, teachers sometimes infer that he is a poor or "unmotivated" student in general. People sometimes reach these same erroneous, overgeneralized conclusions about themselves.

The fact is that seldom, if ever, does a pattern become completely general to all situations. This is true even for the most deteriorated psychotic. The same person can be highly motivated under one set of circumstances and lackadaisical under another. To be accurate, one must specify that the person typically becomes angry, begins to loaf, or has difficulty learning when certain situations occur but not in others. This degree of accuracy is particularly important when one is attempting to develop or modify human behavior, as do universities.

The modifiability of human behavior is as impressive as its variability. Efficient modification of behavior is possible partly because each complex response pattern is composed of a network of different kinds of responses. To modify the operation of a pattern, one often needs to change only a crucial portion rather than the entire pattern. For example, an antagonistic, cynical, rebellious, irresponsible student may become a conscientious, creative, independent-minded student if one can identify and modify the mistaken ideas about adult authority which help trigger off the entire pattern.

We may expect, then, that each student comes to the university with a repertoire of habitual response patterns, some of which are situation-specific, and some of which are more generalized. Some of the patterns may enable the student to be effective in the situation, while others may interfere.

*The Situation.* Now for the other part of the formula. Behavior is also a function of the situations under which it occurs. We emphasize this because much of the research and theorizing about human behavior in the last couple of decades has tended to emphasize the consistency of behavior across situations rather than the variability of behavior from one situation to another. The fact is that an individual's behavior is highly variable, and this is due in considerable degree to the continually changing environment to which he responds. It is often possible to modify the way a person is behaving by changing the situational context to which he is responding.

Every college boy knows that he stands a good chance of changing the behavior of an angry girl friend toward him if he sweet-talks her, buys her a present, entertains her, and in other ways displays his high regard for her. Parents often discover that their children behave quite differently in the presence of guests than in the privacy of the family circle. Nations find that economic cooperation, or the presence of warships or missiles armed with nuclear warheads, may change the behavior of a belligerent neighbor. Today's most influential theories of learning assume that the situational consequences of a behavior sequence are major factors in producing learning. In fact, the entire enterprise of formal education assumes that it is possible to affect what a person will learn by exposing him to systematically organized and specially selected patterns of situational events (lectures, discussion classes, reading assignments, laboratory work, and so forth).

One of the most crucial kinds of situational event for a person is the behavior of other people. The social environment seems to be the most powerful force in human learning. In particular, the way other people evaluate a person appears to have special power in influencing particular acts, and what is learned. (School grades are acts of evaluation.) One might expect, then, that the situational context provided by a particular university would be very influential in what and how well a student learns. For example, the differences between Vassar College in New York and Parsons College in Iowa are extensive, though the fact that both are called colleges might tend to obscure these differences. The differences within a college, even from one professor to another, are also very great. The kind of situational context a college or university provides each student is a powerful factor in determining whether the student will perform successfully and to his own satisfaction.

*Approaches to the Problem of Dropouts.* This sketch of a few aspects of human behavior includes three general ingredients which can be applied to thinking about students in a university setting. These are (1) the many habitual response patterns which each student brings, including both their subjective and their overt components; (2) the varied situational contexts which the university provides; and (3) the kinds of interactions that will result when a student with his varied response patterns exposes himself to one or another of the university's situational contexts.

The value of representing the general issue in this way is that it immediately suggests several foci of attack on the problem of college dropouts. First, we can seek the best match possible between a student's habitual response patterns, and the various contexts provided by the university. Second, once the student has been admitted, the university can direct its efforts toward helping the student modify those aspects of his behavior which may interfere with his most effective functioning in that particular setting. This may range from dealing with an inadequate grasp of basic mathematics, to helping modify damaging habits of self-evaluation. It presumes someone can identify which patterns need changing, and in what direction. Third, we can change the situation so the student can perform more successfully with his existing response repertoire. This might be thought of as a problem of university organization, curriculum and course planning, teaching procedures, housing arrangements, and the like.

Now, we will indicate a few possible lines of attack by describing some of the efforts being made at The Pennsylvania State University.

*Seeking the Best Match Possible.* A number of years ago a continuing research program was developed to identify the student response patterns which best matched the educational environments provided by the University. Largely on the basis of this research, and partly because of increased demands for admission, the criteria used for selecting students for admission have been gradually revised. A variety of direct and indirect measures of students' past behavior have been studied. Some selection factors have been discarded, such as the extent of a student's participation in high-school activities, because they seem to be irrelevant to the selection criteria. Some new ones have been added, such as the percent of students going on to college from the student's high school.

For each of the 19,000 students who applied for admission as freshmen in the summer and fall of 1964, a prediction of the performance level they could be expected to obtain was made for each college and for four general categories of study. Each student was admitted on the basis of one of these predictions.

There are value judgments involved in the selection of admissions criteria, however. For example, there is a very great likelihood that any student graduating from a high school from which 90 percent of the graduates go on to college will succeed in college. Suppose, though, that one admits only students graduating from high schools where large percentages go on to college. Can you visualize their socio-economic background? Their families' values? The social pressures upon them? Their social habits and expectations? In contrast, visualize the background of graduates of a high school from which only 5 to 10 percent go on to college. The first group might come from well-to-do suburbs of northern Philadelphia, while the second might come from one of Pennsylvania's depressed coal-mining towns. Whom do you want to educate? We honor these differences by using a variety of selection formulae.

The importance of this matching procedure may become more apparent from an example. A young man applies for admission to the University to study engineering. We have about twenty different engineering programs. From our research, we have learned that the basic interest patterns of the young men in the various engineering majors are very similar. However, we have also found that boys who succeed in the baccalaureate engineering programs must be more proficient in dealing with theoretical abstractions than those succeeding in our associate degree programs. Therefore, we make separate predictions for these two programs. There is some overlap, of course, but a boy's success or failure in preparing for an engineering career may be determined by getting him into the appropriate program.

However, effective matching cannot be accomplished solely by the University's matching the student to its program. One of the most important aspects of the matching process is the student's involvement in it. Consequently, Penn State has developed a post-admission, preregistration counseling program for students and their parents, which has as one of its objectives careful study and planning with the student and his parents, seeking the best match possible between the University's educational opportunities and the student's aspirations, talents, and other characteristics. This also enables us to help the parents learn to keep their aspirations out of the matching process.

The student may decide to change his plans as a result of this program. If so, the University will change its admission decision. About 20 percent of each entering class have been making changes from one college to another within the University before registering for their first classes. We continue to search for new prediction models, additional relevant factors, and new counseling procedures to help a student better match himself to the educational environments we provide. We have only scratched the surface of the possibilities.

All universities have a major problem with the criterion for prediction. Grades are a primary factor determining whether a student will stay in or drop out of college, even when the student's average meets graduation requirements. However, this is something of a will-o'-the-wisp criterion. If one studies grade distributions in a university over a period of years, an important phenomenon becomes obvious. The distribution of grades assigned by the total faculty within the university remains remarkably stable over periods of decades, independent of changing characteristics of students being admitted.

Again, we can use Penn State as an example by referring to Figure 1. This figure reveals that the percentage of A's, B's, C's, D's, and F's given to Penn State undergraduate students each year for a decade have remained practically constant, with a slight variation in 1961-1962, the causes of which are not particularly relevant to this discussion, but are interesting to speculate about.

FIGURE 1. THE TREND OF GRADE DISTRIBUTIONS,[a] APTITUDE TEST SCORES,[b] AND HIGH-SCHOOL RANK[c] FOR STUDENTS AT THE PENNSYLVANIA STATE UNIVERSITY OVER A TEN-YEAR PERIOD

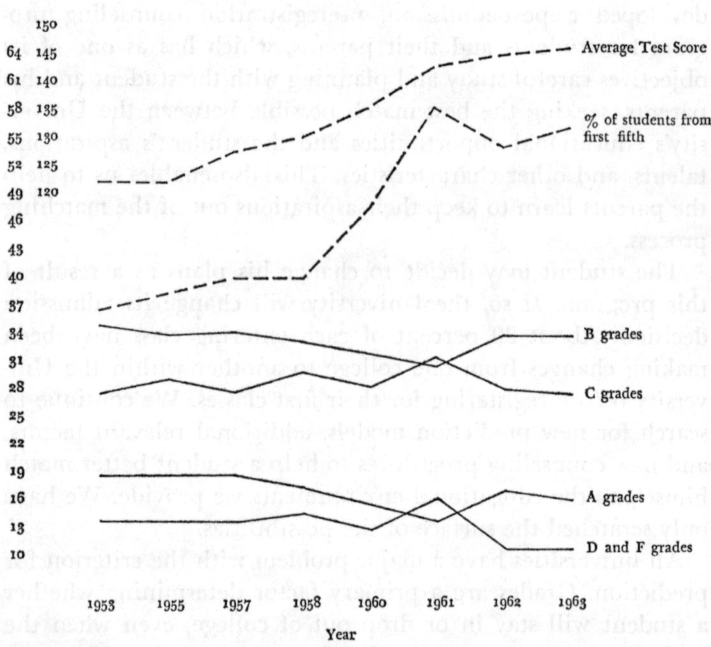


[a] Computed for all Penn State Students.
[b] Pennsylvania State University Aptitude Test.
[c] Computed for Penn State freshmen only.

Data from other universities reflect the same phenomenon. It is not solely American, either. The president of a university in Yugoslavia privately reported to us that he found the same phenomenon there. Figure 1 also shows the trend of two variables used by most universities as their best predictors of academic success: aptitude test scores and high-school grades. During the decade represented, the average aptitude test score of entering freshmen increased by over one standard deviation, and the proportion graduating in the top 20 percent of their high-school class increased from about 38 percent to about 61 percent. However, grades given by the faculty remained essentially the same, or got somewhat worse. Why didn't better students earn better grades?

In the absence of stable reference points for evaluating the performance of their students, faculty assign grades within the framework of students in class that term. Few faculty members use evaluation procedures which enable them to compare this year's students with those of last year or five years ago. Moreover, most examination procedures used by faculty are demonstrably unreliable as measurement devices. Those of us who teach seldom have the time to develop really adequate procedures for evaluating the performance of students. Even fewer of us have been trained in how to build a valid, reliable test. Students frequently recognize the inaccuracy of our measurement, and sometimes feel discouraged, disgusted, cynical, or helpless. Yet, give us a stable criterion in any university and we can promise a major reduction in dropouts by developing empirically validated admissions, teaching, and counseling procedures. Much more could be said about getting the proper match between student and learning situation, but perhaps we have said enough to illustrate how one can go about tackling some of the issues.

*Changing the Student's Response Repertoire.* Of course, a perfect match is never likely. Each of us usually has to change the ways we think and act in some respect to fit into important new environments. This can be easily observed in people who go to live for a period of time in a country quite different from their own.

It is possible to improve a student's likelihood of graduation by helping him change some of his behavior so that it better fits the demands of the situation in which he would like to succeed. A few simple examples will help make this clear. A bright youngster who was very successful in high school by studying one hour a day may need some help in learning to discipline himself to study the six or eight hours a day his college program requires. A student who has developed a facility for remembering broad generalizations but an habitual carelessness about details may need some help in changing his habits of thought to succeed in a chemistry curriculum. A student used to having his life structured and guided by his parents may need some help in acquiring the habits and attitudes necessary for effective self-direction.

Such changes take time and patience, however, and students sometimes get into deep academic hot water before the necessary changes begin to occur. It is at this point that a good many students transfer to a different university where they will not have the handicap of their previous poor record dragging them down, while they apply their newly developed behaviors to make a better record. It is unfortunate that most American universities lack effective policies for forgiving past academic sins when a student begins to show the behavior changes necessary to make him a better student.

At Penn State, we have developed a counseling program which has as one of its tasks helping students determine what changes they need to make in themselves and helping them produce those changes. We are trying to intertwine three traditions—the public health or preventive tradition, the clinical or remedial tradition, and the educational or constructive tradition which focuses on strengths rather than weaknesses, on accomplishment rather than problems. In addition to using a variety of counseling procedures, we have the authority to take a student out of the typical academic channels for a few terms to control his academic program while seeking to achieve the desired changes. Several thousand students have now graduated from Penn State who would have flunked out or dropped out had this program not been in existence.

Again, we should note that other procedures in the university are focused on this same objective, but we are only attempting to indicate the approach rather than make an exhaustive list of the possibilities.

*Changing the Situation to Fit the Student.* Sometimes it is more appropriate to modify the situation rather than the student's behavior in order to improve his chances for success. For example, when you were eighteen years old, would your learning performance have been affected by a roommate who was a borderline psychotic, a homosexual, a depressed person thinking of suicide, or a drunk—i.e., a person who was constantly upsetting you with bizarre, disgusting, or frightening behavior? A simple change of roommate might make a great deal of difference in whether or not you stayed in college. Changing a student from one learning setting to another within the university may mean the difference between success and failure. A girl failing in her chemistry major may shift to an art major and become an outstanding student.

We can return to the grade distributions mentioned earlier to illustrate this point in another way. Although the grade distributions of the total faculty are quite stable over time, there are wide differences among the faculty. For example, in one college at Penn State recently, one department gave only 5 percent A's, while another gave 40 percent A's in all courses taught that term. In a second college the spread between departments was from 6 percent to 60 percent. The F's given ranged from .2 percent to 7 percent in one college and from 0 percent to 8 percent in another. A student could markedly improve his chances of graduation by careful selection of courses from departments which have a high A, low F frequency of grades.

Institutional changes can be made which may affect many students. Unfortunately, faculty members characteristically assume a difficulty stems from the student, not from the situation. Curriculum organization, course content, and methods of teaching are all situational factors which might be modified to increase a student's chances of success. How many of us sat ten or twenty rows back and tried to see what was going on in a laboratory demonstration when we were in school? Now we use television instructional procedures so that each student may see such a demonstration as if he were at the professor's elbow. Our universities have been far too unimaginative in evolving their approaches to educating young people. Universities have taught their students essentially the same way for several hundred years. Our rituals change slowly, if at all. Perhaps the last great educational device invented was the laboratory, and that was some time ago.

*Results.* Do efforts like those we have been describing pay off in improved performance and graduation rates, even in a situation where nearly 75 percent of the students are already completing some kind of higher education? It will take several years before we will have adequate data to answer such a question. However, we already have some encouraging evidence. Figure 2 shows the total number of students dismissed from Penn State for poor scholarship each spring for the last seven years and the number who made the Dean's list, or honor roll, during that same period. Since this book is concerned with dropouts, the lower line representing dismissals is of particular interest. The continual decline in the number of students dismissed is especially gratifying when you realize that during this seven-year period Penn State enrollments were increasing at the rate of from 500 to 1,000 students a year. Thus, a graph in terms of proportions would be even more pronounced.

The major change in the spring of 1962 is interesting. It represents a basic situational modification at Penn State. In the summer of 1961, Penn State changed from an eighteen-week semester to a ten-week term calendar, and from a 50-minute to a 75-minute class period. This meant that students concentrated on three or four courses rather than six or eight at one time, and their vacations fell between terms rather than interrupting studies in the middle with lengthy vacations such as Christmas. It also meant that professors had to reorganize most of their courses to fit the new format. This in turn meant they had to revise their examinations. They had to slice their knowledge into fewer but larger chunks. We think these changes affected their attitudes toward students. There were other effects, but these examples illustrate the impact of a

FIGURE 2. THE NUMBER OF BACCALAUREATE DEGREE STUDENTS AT THE PENNSYLVANIA STATE UNIVERSITY WHO WERE PLACED ON DEAN'S LIST OR DISMISSED FOR POOR SCHOLARSHIP AT THE END OF THE SPRING TERM OVER A TEN-YEAR PERIOD

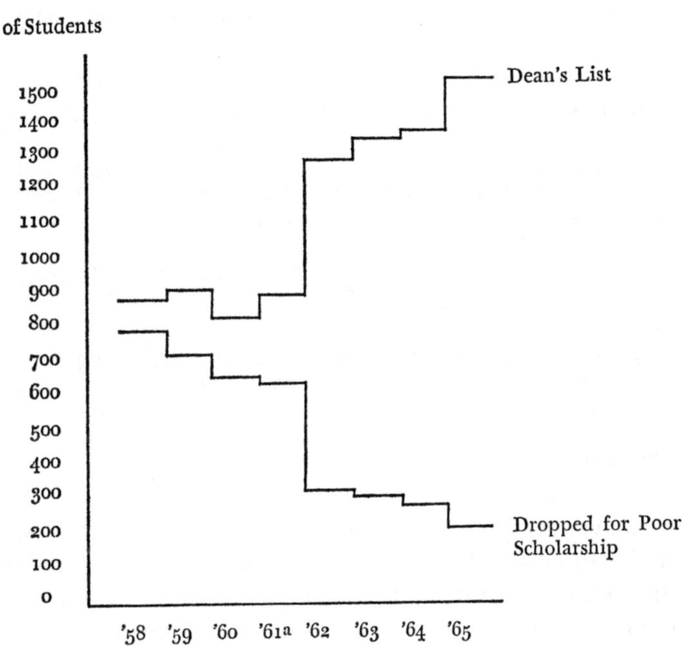


[a] The four-term plan began in 1961.

major change in some important situational variables in a university.

During the period represented in Figure 2 our new counseling program began to function fully, the administrative and curriculum structure of the University was reorganized, a new academic calendar was introduced, most individual courses were reorganized, an extensive program of research on instructional procedures was developed, new instructional procedures were adopted by departments, admissions policies were modified, better student personnel programs were evolved, and we believe subtle changes in the attitude of the faculty occurred.

Another view of what is happening to students in a university may be obtained by following a particular group of college students through several years of college study. One of the things such longitudinal studies can reveal is the point in time at which students drop out. Table 1 provides such data for

TABLE 1. PERCENTAGE OF BACCALAUREATE DEGREE STUDENTS AT THE PENNSYLVANIA STATE UNIVERSITY CONTINUING STUDIES FROM ONE TO THREE YEARS AFTER ADMISSION

| | *Fall 1952* | *Fall 1953* | *Fall 1954* | *Fall 1955* | *Fall 1956* | *Fall 1957* | *Fall 1958* | *Fall 1959* | *Fall 1960* | *Fall 1961* | *Fall 1962* | *Fall 1963* |
|---|---|---|---|---|---|---|---|---|---|---|---|---|
| *Freshmen Admitted* | 3607 | 3623 | 3688 | 3576 | 3938 | 4380 | 4313 | 4487 | 5123 | 4570 | 3804 | 4392 |
| PERCENTAGE REGISTERED | | | | | | | | | | | | |
| *After 1 year* | 69.1 | 72.6 | 76.2 | 73.5 | 73.9 | 68.5 | 71.9 | 73.1 | 76.2 | 81.4 | 81.9 | 85.2 |
| *After 2 years* | 58.5 | 57.8 | 54.8 | 57.6 | 60.5 | 56.4 | 59.1 | 62.1 | 65.4 | 68.6 | 71.6 | a |
| *After 3 years* | 48.7 | 48.1 | 48.3 | 52.8 | 54.0 | 49.8 | 54.4 | 57.1 | 58.6 | 63.0 | a | a |

a Information not available.

a twelve-year period; or, to put it another way, for twelve freshman classes. In 1952, 31 percent of the entering freshmen dropped out during the first year. Only 15 percent of the 1963 class dropped out during their first year. From 1952 through 1961, the dropout rate during the first three years declined from 51 percent to 27 percent. This decline occurred in the face of rising academic standards, as an example will illustrate. In 1952, freshman engineers started their mathematics sequence with a course which combined advanced algebra and trigometry. A few years later, the beginning math course was analytical geometry. Now freshman engineers begin with calculus. We should remind ourselves at this point that a significant number of the students we have labeled dropouts did not drop out of college permanently. Many transferred to other universities or temporarily interrupted their studies and returned at a later time to complete their degrees.

It is also pertinent to know how many of the students who dropped out were actually dismissed, and how many dropped out voluntarily for a variety of reasons. Table 2 reports data

TABLE 2. PERCENTAGE OF BACCALAUREATE DEGREE STUDENTS AT THE PENNSYLVANIA STATE UNIVERSITY DISMISSED FROM ONE TO THREE YEARS AFTER ADMISSION

| | *Fall 1952* | *Fall 1953* | *Fall 1954* | *Fall 1955* | *Fall 1956* | *Fall 1957* | *Fall 1958* | *Fall 1959* | *Fall 1960* | *Fall 1961* | *Fall 1962* | *Fall 1963* |
|---|---|---|---|---|---|---|---|---|---|---|---|---|
| *Freshmen Admitted* | 3607 | 3623 | 3688 | 3576 | 3938 | 4380 | 4313 | 4487 | 5123 | 4570 | 3804 | 4392 |
| PERCENTAGE DISMISSED | | | | | | | | | | | | |
| *After 1 year* | 6.7 | 5.6 | 5.2 | 6.5 | 4.9 | 10.0 | 9.2 | 8.2 | 7.7 | 3.2 | 3.5 | 2.9 |
| *After 2 years*[a] | 10.5 | 11.5 | 11.3 | 12.6 | 8.7 | 14.0 | 11.5 | 10.1 | 8.8 | 4.3 | 4.7 | |
| *After 3 years*[a] | 14.7 | 13.5 | 13.3 | 14.3 | 10.3 | 15.2 | 12.7 | 11.1 | 9.3 | 5.0 | | |

[a] Cumulative figures.

on dismissals. Nearly 7 percent of the 1952 freshman class were dismissed during their freshman year, while slightly less than 3 percent of the 1963 freshmen were dismissed. The total dismissals for the 1952 class during the first three years was nearly 15 percent and this figure declined to 5 percent for the first three years of the 1961 class. Clearly, there has been a sharp decline in the proportion of students being dismissed.

Table 3 summarizes the data on students who dropped out on their own initiative. The proportion dropping out during the first year was cut in half between 1952 and 1963. Considering the first three years as a whole, however, one sees that the decline has been much more moderate. The data also reveal that most of the voluntary dropping out takes place during the first two years. There are undoubtedly a variety of reasons for this, but we suspect two are more prominent. First, a sizable number of students start at one university and later transfer to another to finish their degree. Such transfers usually occur before the student enters his third year. Second, students without an academic commitment are unlikely to persist beyond a year or two at the most.

TABLE 3. PERCENTAGE OF BACCALAUREATE DEGREE STUDENTS AT THE PENNSYLVANIA STATE UNIVERSITY WHO VOLUNTARILY DROPPED OUT FROM ONE TO THREE YEARS AFTER ADMISSION

| | *Fall 1952* | *Fall 1953* | *Fall 1954* | *Fall 1955* | *Fall 1956* | *Fall 1957* | *Fall 1958* | *Fall 1959* | *Fall 1960* | *Fall 1961* | *Fall 1962* | *Fall 1963* |
|---|---|---|---|---|---|---|---|---|---|---|---|---|
| *Freshmen Admitted* | 3607 | 3623 | 3688 | 3576 | 3938 | 4380 | 4313 | 4487 | 5123 | 4570 | 3804 | 4392 |
| PERCENTAGE DROPPING OUT | | | | | | | | | | | | |
| *After 1 year* | 23.0 | 21.3 | 18.5 | 20.0 | 21.2 | 21.5 | 18.9 | 18.7 | 15.8 | 15.4 | 14.6 | 11.9 |
| *After 2 years*[b] | 29.8 | 31.1 | 33.0 | 29.8 | 30.8 | 31.5 | 29.3 | 27.7 | 25.8 | 27.0 | 23.7 | a |
| *After 3 years*[b] | 34.9 | 36.3 | 35.3 | 32.0 | 34.8 | 34.5 | 31.9 | 30.4 | 29.6 | 29.9 | a | a |

[a] Information not available.
[b] Cumulative figures.

It is also instructive to determine what proportion of students in each freshman class actually completes a degree at the university where they started. Table 4 presents such information for Penn State students. Approximately 48 percent of the 1952 freshmen obtained a Penn State degree in five years, while nearly 55 percent of the 1959 freshmen did so. Of course, this does not represent the total who eventually obtain their degrees at Penn State. It will be recalled that in the

TABLE 4. PERCENTAGE OF BACCALAUREATE DEGREE STUDENTS AT THE PENNSYLVANIA STATE UNIVERSITY GRADUATED FROM THREE TO FIVE YEARS AFTER ADMISSION

| | *Fall 1952* | *Fall 1953* | *Fall 1954* | *Fall 1955* | *Fall 1956* | *Fall 1957* | *Fall 1958* | *Fall 1959* | *Fall 1960* |
|---|---|---|---|---|---|---|---|---|---|
| *Freshmen Admitted* | 3607 | 3623 | 3688 | 3576 | 3938 | 4380 | 4313 | 4487 | 5123 |
| PERCENTAGE GRADUATED | | | | | | | | | |
| *After 3 years* | .7 | .8 | 1.1 | .9 | .9 | .5 | 1.0 | 1.4 | 2.5 |
| *After 4 years*[b] | 39.8 | 40.6 | 42.3 | 43.0 | 44.2 | 39.5 | 44.5 | 46.3 | 48.0 |
| *After 5 years*[b] | 47.6 | 47.8 | 49.2 | 50.4 | 51.7 | 47.3 | 51.9 | 54.8 | a |

[a] Information not available.
[b] Cumulative figures.

Ashby study reported earlier, 60 percent of the 1955 class had obtained their degree after eight years, whereas only 50 percent had obtained their Penn State degree after five years.

One further point may be noted in all four tables by inspection of the data for the class of 1957. For this particular class, the proportion of students continuing declined, the percentage dismissed or dropping out increased, and the proportion graduating declined. What caused this sudden change? In 1957, the faculty decided "standards" should be raised. In American universities, raising standards often takes the form of more demanding "flunk rules." New "flunk rules" were established at Penn State in 1957. The results are apparent, but were temporary. From that point on, there has been steady improvement in retention and graduation rates.

All of these data support the view that we have made significant progress in improving retention and graduation rates at Penn State. Academic dismissals have declined to the point where they are presently a minor problem, involving only about 200 students out of a class of approximately 4,500. We plan further studies to gain more information about the students who withdraw voluntarily (presently about 30 percent). What proportion transfer to other colleges and universities? How many leave to get married or take a good job? How many would be wiser to remain and complete their degree? We are confident that some should, but others should not.

May we repeat our initial assertion? Any university that chooses to do so can make a major reduction in the proportion of its students who drop out, unless that proportion is already quite small, if it is willing to make the effort in terms of people, time, money, and institutional changes. It has been the purpose of our presentation up to this point to make that assertion plausible.

### *The Constructive Implications of College Dropouts*

We have been talking about what colleges and universities can do individually. We can also concern ourselves with what colleges can do collectively. Our college dropouts are trying to tell us something. Our total educational system is inadequate—there are some gaps in it. We as educators have oversold the concept of a college education, representing it as the single preferred method of becoming educated. We have encouraged our fellow citizens to believe this, and we have failed to foster alternative avenues of career and educational development throughout our society. It is *not* true that any youngster with a high IQ who doesn't go to college represents a loss of talent to our society. Universities *aren't* the only place where people can learn things. A college education isn't the only avenue to a personally meaningful and socially productive life.

Some youngsters find this out and have the courage to fly in the face of prevailing social attitudes. Two examples from Ashby's follow-up study will illustrate this point. The father of a boy who dropped out because he wanted a practical rather than a theoretical or liberal education wrote, "He is mechanically minded, and could not see the coordination between what he wanted to do and general education. He is doing OK, owns $30,000 in farm machinery and about all paid for. A part interest in a truck. He operates three farms and is repairman for a contractor. Is married and has two fine boys." A young woman who has not completed a degree wrote, "I only left because of my strong desire to be successful in my field of art; and to guarantee this success one must spend a few years struggling as an apprentice with a salary of little merit. After three years I found that the struggling was worth it financially and now I am successful, married, and have two babies."

Look around. There are many capable, successful people in our country who do not have a college degree. That doesn't mean they are uneducated. It does demonstrate that there are other, and perhaps better, ways of learning many things than going to college.

One might argue that such people have only learned a specialty; they are not educated. We in higher education have a tendency to be a bit snobbish about our product. Perhaps it is time we take a hard look at some of our dogma. We doubt that the golden world we are striving to create will be built solely, or perhaps even primarily, on the foundation of college-educated people *as we know them today*. There are many people without a college education who are decent, just, wise, and able to accept and act on new ideas.

The destructive impact on some individuals of the growing glorification of the college degree should not be minimized. May we quote from a memo from our friend and colleague, John Walmer, who is a university psychiatrist at Penn State:

> There seems to be a common denominator of fear at a far deeper level in the students I am seeing at Penn State. This common denominator is an attitude about education which equates education with a ruthless god with arbitrary powers of salvation and destruction. This attitude is learned, or more correctly, indoctrinated, by the constant bombardment of an idea from the home, the school, the press, and other media of communication. The idea, sinister and evil, is that unless an individual secures a college degree he is a nothing, he has no place in this world, he is a millstone around the neck of a society struggling in the sea of competence, achievement, and success. Stated another way, without a college degree an individual is relegated to the unacceptable role of a second-class citizen condemned forever to such repulsive and revolting tasks as store clerk, taxi driver, plumber, bank teller, carpenter, postal employee, or enlisted man in some branch of the service. The individual is indoctrinated with an attitude which leads him to see a person without a degree as something to be scorned. . . . All of the above seems to add up to an attitude in many students that without a college degree one is not needed and gains neither approval nor attention in this world. It leaves the individual with little self-respect or self-esteem. The integrity of the individual is reduced to a bare minimum; his resources for survival are just about nil except for his worship of the false god, College Degree. Threatened with failure in his struggle for possession of this false god, the individual develops symptoms of anxiety and depression.

And now a college degree is no longer adequate for self-respect. One must go to graduate school.

We believe that a university education, as we know it today, is not appropriate for everybody. Learning in universities today is a highly symbolic, highly abstract task. The student who is not verbally or mathematically facile, or who doesn't get a kick out of that kind of task, should have other admired alternatives available to him. There are many bright people who get great satisfaction out of working with the concrete world, shaping it into something useful, or meaningful, or beautiful—something that works—and who don't care much for intensive involvement in abstractions.

Those of us in universities must resist the temptation to transform into people like us—i.e., people who value, enjoy, and are productive in the world of abstractions—individuals who would prefer a different kind of life but who are ashamed to seek it. Ours is not the only model of a good life, and the good life is surely not measured solely, or perhaps even primarily, in economic terms. Our society should seek to provide young people with a variety of admired and socially valued models from which they can choose, and a variety of ways of educating themselves to create their own model of the good life. We believe universities, with their great prestige in this area, must provide the leadership in this effort.

Second, we are suggesting that the phenomenon of college dropouts implies a basic flaw in our entire educational structure, and a fundamental distortion of our values in regard to different forms of human activity. We need to invent forms of education that are appropriate for those who are not highly effective as symbolic learners, or who—though effective at it—don't care to learn that way. A young person should have the opportunity to choose among several avenues for continuing his or her education, and should be free to make that choice with the confidence that all avenues are socially approved and valued. Our federal and state programs should give emphasis not only to "more" higher education but also to "new forms" of higher education.

We believe universities must lead the way in inventing new social strategies for education to fit that world we are rapidly creating, in which fantastic increases in control over our environment and our bodies must be matched with new views of ourselves, and additional ways of making our lives meaningful.

# PART II

# THE PERSONAL DIMENSION

DEAR PARENTS:

I think that the best way to describe my study problem to you is to say that I feel guilty about achieving in my studies. Unbelievable? But I'm telling you exactly how it feels. There may be something of the same element in football and in other areas of difficult achievement.

. . . if I thought you would not approve of what I was doing—doing *intellectually*, in this case—I would experience guilt for having transgressed against you, the original source of right and wrong for me. Understand that I am speaking largely of the workings of my mind at a subconscious level.

Let me be specific in order to clarify my point. Realizing that you are both fairly fundamental and conservative in your religious thinking, subconsciously I am reluctant to let my mind absorb new knowledge which compels me to form conclusions about religion different from those which you hold. This could have broad effect, because I think it is safe to say that the large majority of the scholars whose writings we study here did not (or do not, if they are living) have religious convictions which resemble yours. Another area is sex. My mind will be reluctant to absorb knowledge and to reason along lines which will lead me to formulate sexual morals which differ from yours. I could go on to cite politics, economics, general life philosophy as regards materialism, etc.

Virtually everything I learn, both from books and from day-to-day experience, impels me to formulate conclusions which differ from your own. Nevertheless, you must allow that my beliefs are just as right and true *for me* as yours are *for you*. Truth is relative and not absolute;

the sheer diversity of world thought forces this conclusion upon us.

The overall point is that my experiences are molding me and are causing me to mold myself into an individual who is distinctly separate from you. As I see it, this is inevitable and desirable. . . . I want to emphasize here, however, that when I say that I must inevitably become "an individual distinctively separate from you," I don't mean separate from you in love and respect, the essential ties which bind a family together. I can hold ideas very different from yours and still respect your ideas. I can live in a way different from yours and still respect your ideas.

Out of all this I have been left with a feeling of guilt *at being myself*. I cannot go on feeling this way, for not only is the feeling preventing me from getting a formal education, but it is making my life generally very unhappy. I don't know whether you consider me basically boy or man, but I implore you to recognize my manhood at least to the extent of allowing me to develop freely.

With love,

Jim

—Letter written by a student in academic trouble who was considering dropping out. He never mailed it and remained in college.

# CHAPTER 5

## PERSONAL DETERMINANTS AND THEIR INTERACTION WITH ENVIRONMENT

THE EDITORS

THE STUDY OF dropout phenomena and the development of potential talent in college students becomes mechanical and piecemeal to the extent that it concentrates only on arriving at generalizations based on the statistical analysis of surface data. The reasons for leaving college that appear on any institution's books are subject to the practical need for simplifying the complexities of human experience. But a need that meets the convenience of the institution may also offer the withdrawing student and college as well an opportunity for escaping from any constructive confrontation with limitations and problems. By the way of illustration, the vague category of students withdrawing for personal reasons does little to define or illuminate the fundamental sources of difficulty, whether in the college or the student.

There are obvious exceptions to the thesis that all dropouts, of whatever sort, must have at least some personality factor operative in the dropout event. The exceptions are particularly obvious if one's view of dropping out is that it is an untoward event, or at least evidence of dysfunction in the individual's life. A student may start at a small college and through maturation come to need a large college. He may start with an ambition to major in history and develop an interest in anthropology, which is poorly represented in his college's faculty. And although there is vastly increased opportunity to find inexpensive education, or financial support in education which is not inexpensive, occasional students have to make their education discontinuous for financial reasons.

Nevertheless, the exceptions seem far fewer than those that follow the rule. Usually students with well-integrated personalities and high motivation to the goal they originally sought can overcome difficulties, whether put there by institutional oddities, family difficulties, or merely by the unkind shafts of fate. The admiration due the student who overcomes a difficulty to continue in college should not interfere with our desire and obligation to understand and, if appropriate, modify the factors which lead a student to drop out of college.

This section of the book deals with the psychological factors which allow or prevent the student's success in obtaining his degree on time. Obviously, the interaction between institution and individual is important, but even this is halfway a function of the student's personality, ability, and motivation.

### *A Period of Transition and Potential Growth*

Study of an individual or process involves particular points in time or stage of development. Comprehension of the dropout must wait on comprehension of the conflicts and issues facing the college student. Conversely, comprehension of the individual dropout necessarily leads to increased comprehension of growth and development in late adolescence and early adulthood.

Early personality theorists tended to neglect the significance of this period of time in the formation of personality. Recent investigators have directed greater attention to it as interest in ego functions has increased. The ideas of three recent theorists are of particular interest to understanding the dropout.

Erik Erikson's concept of identity formation has had a profound influence upon the thinking of clinicians working with college students. Erikson describes the issues of this period as identity versus identity diffusion, of intimacy versus distantiation and isolation. The individual may grow toward an increased awareness of and confidence in who he is and where he is going; he can develop the capacity for interpersonal intimacy in the form of friendship, combat, leadership, love, and inspiration. On the other hand, he may remain unable to define himself adequately or to take hold of life; he retains or develops distantiation, which means that he is ready to "repudiate, to isolate, and if necessary, to destroy those forces and people whose essence seems dangerous to his own."[1]

Sullivan was also influential in emphasizing the significance of the adolescent and late adolescent stages of development.[2] For him the issues during this period of change centered around the need for intimacy, for heterosexual activity, and for stabilization of the self-system. Growth toward maturity means a sympathetic understanding of the limitations, interests, possibilities, and anxieties of oneself and others. It means an ability to deal with these anxieties and a freedom to express one's talents and satisfy one's needs while respecting the rights and feelings of others.

White's concepts of natural growth are particularly helpful in appreciating the developmental tasks of late adolescence. He describes four directions of change:

*Stabilizing of Ego Identity.* This involves growth toward a sharper and clearer identity, relatively consistent and free from transient influences. The self-concept becomes progressively autonomous from the daily impact of social judgments and from experiences of success and failure.

*Freeing of Personal Relationships.* This involves an increase in ability to respond to people according to their actual traits, as new individuals. Stereotypic responses tied to past relationships tend to be dropped. Personal responses tend to become more flexible; the true adult has an ability to interact fully with people and has a capacity for empathy.

*Deepening of Interests.* This involves an increased absorption in objects of interest, an increased sense of regard in doing something for its own sake, independent of outside support or praise.

*Humanizing of Values.* The growing individual increasingly discovers the human meaning of values and their relationship to the achievement of social purposes. The individual is able to see the relativity of values and brings his own experiences to bear upon a value system. Conflict and challenge

1 E. Erikson, "Identity and the life cycle," *Psychological Issues,* 1959, Monograph 1, p. 95.

2 H. S. Sullivan, *The interpersonal theory of psychiatry,* New York: Norton, 1953.

lead to a set of values that is clearly one's own and which represent a unifying philosophy of life.[3]

Although these tasks described by White are lifelong processes of growth, their urgency is extreme in late adolescence and early adulthood. Clearly they are not easy tasks. Few if any can proceed with them entirely smoothly and uneventfully. Some college students will have major difficulties with them. Such difficulty does not necessarily mean disruption in other areas of life, especially the cognitive, but it often does. In many ways these four tasks are prerequisites to setting mature, realistic goals, either short or long term. Certainly, when the individual is failing in these developmental tasks he seldom has such goals. Such an individual is the one who is lacking in motivation; he seems to have run out of gas. Either voluntarily or involuntarily he may drop out of college.

### *The Cost of Academic Success*

Adolescence imposes unique tasks and conflicts; college imposes additional unique demands. The college environment presents special intellectual and social challenges to its students. It has a particular impact which provides the opportunity for growth and change but which may stimulate regression and rigidity.

Growth and development during transition from high school to college has come under careful study by the National Institute of Mental Health. Its staff has studied both students who had severe emotional decompensation in their first prolonged separation from their families while living and working in a university,[4] and also students who were extremely successful in coping with the college as a new learning environment.[5] These studies describe the tasks of transition from high school to college thus: learning new academic skills and intel-

[3] R. W. White, *Lives in progress*, New York: Dryden, 1952.

[4] R. L. Shapiro, "Adolescence and the psychology of the ego," *Psychiatry*, 1963, 26, pp. 77-87.

[5] E. Silber, D. A. Hamburg, G. V. Coelho, Elizabeth B. Murphey, M. Rosenberg, and L. I. Pearlin, "Adaptive behavior in competent adolescents," *Archives of General Psychiatry*, 1961, 5, pp. 354-365; G. V. Coelho, D. A. Hamburg, and Elizabeth B. Murphey, "Coping strategies in a new learning environment," *ibid.*, 1963, 9, pp. 433-443.

lectual competencies; dealing with the physical separation from family; regulating the need for relatedness to parents; development of meaningful friendships and productive work-relations with peers; and extension of heterosexual interests and feelings in preparation for courtship and marriage.

These tasks, like those of adolescence themselves, are numerous and complex. Almost by definition the college transition causes stress in most, if not all, students. In recent years, additional stimuli add to the stress: increased competition for entrance, increased competition for good grades and for graduate schools, the growing emphasis on excellent marks as a definition of fulfillment, and the increasing complications of modern life.

The effects of stress on the students are often hard to measure. The increasing use of psychiatric and counseling facilities by college students probably testifies both to their relative sophistication concerning psychological difficulties and to increased level of stress. Undeniable is the fact that the suicide rate among college students is significantly higher than the suicide rate among non-college young people.

The stresses of this age and the college experience fall differently on different subgroups. Often it is our "best students" who pay the highest price for academic success. The compulsive worker is keenly aware of the unspoken assumption that time not spent on academic pursuits is "wasted." A student taking an evening off to go to the movies wonders if he should not be back studying in the library. One such student who soon became a patient left a Princeton-Dartmouth football game with the score tied in the third quarter because he was not able to enjoy it, thinking that he should be back in his room working on a long paper on which he had blocked psychologically.

The compulsive student learns early that he must do his homework himself, on his own. He tends to sense high standards of academic accomplishment without being told explicitly; he adopts the highest of these standards for his own. He is responsible to a fault. In college he is aware that many (up to 80 percent in some colleges) will be attending graduate school or professional school and that in this race to the victor belong the spoils. Often he has been conscious of such pressureful knowledge since kindergarten.

These characteristics often produce the most admired and most valuable members of both student and general society. Paradoxically, traits which so often lead to success sometimes lead to psychological symptoms. The answer to the paradox is that the characteristics may represent a psychological defense against anxiety. When functioning well, these defenses aid success but even in doing so may rob success of joy. When functioning poorly, they cause or permit symptoms. The compulsiveness becomes inefficient repetitiveness or overattention to minor details, or it no longer wards off the basic anxiety so that the individual becomes paralyzed psychologically.

These types of decompensation may lead to dropping out by themselves. Other students drop out when they realize that their lives have been devoted to academic success to the exclusion of growth in other areas. How many of the reports of loss of interest in studies and lack of motivation express recognition of earlier non-academic tasks which have gone unmet? How many express the feeling that the cost of academic success is too great?

### *The Psychology of Learning and Individual Psychology*

Study of the college dropout and of the dropout process informs not only about personality development during a crucial life period but also about the learning process itself. The process and content of learning are rarely free of the dynamics of the individual's personality. For better or worse, the meanings of education, subjects and courses, teachers and exams become colored by the individual's past life experiences in general and by his past experiences in learning in particular. The public judgment of education is that it is "good." But for many students the meaning is far more complex. The intrusion of logically irrational but emotionally real meanings is frequent. The descriptions that follow, illustrating some of the influences interfering with learning and intellectual development, have particular relevance to students considering dropping out.

Not infrequently, students view education largely in terms

of *financial investment*. The goal of increased future income which a college degree is widely believed to guarantee is substituted for the more subtle and intangible rewards of learning; and failure to be interested in the curriculum or to decide on a vocation evokes anxiety and guilt in proportion to how much a student fears he is wasting money or is making a poor investment.

For some students learning appears to be part of a masculine or feminine role. For example, one study suggests that achieving women consider achieving relevant to their own roles, but that underachieving women view it as more appropriate to masculine roles.[6]

For other students, learning is blocked because it arouses underlying fears of venturing into *forbidden competition with the father*. One such student reported feeling guilty over being at a rich university, contrasted his own status with that of African natives, and revealed that his father had been too poor to go to college. He further recalled problems in competing in high school when he literally wore his father's boots to school. Another student, majoring in biology, told of how highly esteemed his father was as a biologist, and of his own doubts of success in this field. Still another, after counting up the exact number of years of education his father had, chose a field involving more education and a higher degree, only to drop out before he had surpassed his father.

To another group, learning, with its seemingly arbitrary assignments and deadlines, represents the kind of *unwilling submission to those in authority* that must be endured in childhood and passively, if not actively, resisted in young adulthood. One student described a contact he had with his father while in high school: his father paid him a dollar for every "A," fifty cents for every "B," and he had to pay his father a dollar for every "C." Another student in academic difficulty, who later dropped out, recalled being alternately struck and wept over by his mother when as a child he made errors in his homework. On one occasion his father beat him when he had

[6] G. S. Lesser, R. N. Kravitz, and R. Packard, "Experimental arousal of achievement motivation in adolescent girls," *Journal of Abnormal and Social Psychology*, 1963, 66, pp. 59-66.

brought home a poor report card. Outside play was forbidden during the early school years, and often as a high-school student he would spend time in his room daydreaming while presumably studying. At college, the urge to daydream and to distract himself from his work seriously interfered with his studies. Another student, also in academic difficulty, reported: "I work and fear that I'll get clobbered by my parents if I fail. I've been taught that only studying matters and everything else is a reward for that." Probably, experienced teachers can all call to mind numerous examples of how the defiant rebellion of "I won't" can become the passive rebellion of "I can't."[7]

Frequently, the learning process is disturbed by distortions in the reaction of students to professors, determined more by past experiences with parents and parent-surrogates than by the professors themselves. Katz has described this phenomenon as *transference in the classroom.* He refers to the following passage by Freud on the parentlike significance of teachers for students:

> I do not know what aroused our attention more: the scientific subject matters we were presented with or the personalities of our teachers. . . . With many of us the road to learning led only via the personalities of our teachers. Some of us remained stuck on this road and for a few of us—why should we not confess it?—the road was for this reason permanently blocked. We wooed our teachers or we turned away from them, imagined sympathies and antipathies on their part which probably did not exist. We studied their character and fashioned and misfashioned our own in reference to theirs. . . . At bottom we loved them very much if they gave us any reason for that at all; I do not know whether all of our teachers observed this.[8]

Those educators who look find many examples of Freud's thesis. There are students whose arguments with professors

[7] H. Halpern, "Psychodynamic and cultural determinants of work inhibition in children and adolescents," *Psychoanalytic Review,* 1964, 51, pp. 5-21.

[8] J. Katz, "Personality and interpersonal relations in the classroom," in N. Sanford (ed.), *The American college,* New York: Wiley, 1962, pp. 365-395.

recapitulate their arguments with parents. Others fear controversy with them as they feared it with a parent. Some seek to depend on them. Still others are so fearful of rejection that they cannot make the slightest request. Just as one student tends often to see a teacher as a source of inspiration and a model, so another has grown up inclined to view him as a target for rebellion, to the detriment of the learning process.

A final highly personal variable affecting this process is the *degree of anxiety aroused by examinations and written assignments.* It may exist only to the mild, healthy degree that serves to stimulate students to put forth their best efforts, or it may reach an extreme state of panic that paralyzes thought and prevents occasional students from having access even to material they know perfectly well under non-stressful conditions. Menninger in an early article noted that "the sudden panic some students experience in facing examinations is really related to unconscious fears that they are about to be questioned in regard to hidden guiltiness."[9] One student may fear he will fail to live up to the imagined or real expectations of teachers. Another may regard the examination, in a manner verging on the paranoid, as an attempt on the part of the teacher to attack him, cut him down, or reveal hidden weakness. Or a student may be so highly sensitive to shame and humiliation that feelings of this kind dominate the examination situation.

The inexperienced teacher, unfamiliar with the severe crippling of thought processes that examinations and papers can produce in some students, is apt to suspect willful negligence, abysmal ignorance, or flagrant disrespect when a blank examination paper is turned in or a deadline goes by without the completion of a written assignment. Even after listening to the student's explanation, he may be skeptical or perplexed unless he takes the trouble to inquire more than superficially or casually into the student's reasons for the difficulty. If he does so, he may discover that the student is dealing with a clearly recurring pattern of personal handicap, extending back

[9] K. Menninger, "Psychoanalytic observations on the mental hygiene problems of college students," *Journal of Nervous and Mental Disease,* 1929, 69, pp. 642-650.

into the past. Or he may be confronted with the need to evaluate the more complicated story of a student for whom the work-block is a new experience, apparently related to how the task of the moment touches upon some personal Achilles' heel. For example, a student complaining of inability to write a paper on Kafka's "Metamorphosis" described how the feelings of Gregor toward his parents coincided with conflicting feelings in his own life, about which he was in stalemate. Many similar examples could be cited by those who have opportunity to witness the personal dimension of student problems—a dimension that has considerable practical importance for teachers in expediting the learning process and in making fair judgments about the performance of students.

Examination anxiety, writing-block, and the other interferences with learning discussed above are, of course, not the exclusive property of dropouts and would-be dropouts, for the handicap they impose are found in non-dropouts as well. But particularly when students appear to be in difficulty or are non-conforming, attention to the personal dimension, with its fascinating variety of influences, can teach lessons having a much broader application than to a single individual about opening up the way for progress toward maturity, as well as toward educational growth. It has often been pointed out that the non-conformist is in a sense the conformist's loyal opposition, in that he constantly forces the latter to reexamine and improve traditional habits of thought, which easily harden into dogma when they remain unchallenged.

### *To Drop out or Not to Drop out*

Dropping out of college voluntarily is but the final step in a continuing decision-making process of varying intensity and duration. Many go through preliminary phases without ever dropping out. Some call a halt only after it has gone forward to the very verge of withdrawal. A more numerous group entertains the idea, even if only briefly, during times of crisis and stress.

The meaning of the final decision to withdraw also varies considerably from student to student. At its worst, it is a sign of decompensation in the functioning of the individual. At its best, it represents a healthy and realistic coping device.

Among the influences that determine the decision to drop out, such as dissatisfaction with the college or with the self and a host of special reasons which the examples in the introduction to this book serve to illustrate, the role of identification is often critical. Identification, involving the conscious or unconscious patterning of the self after an ideal model, is essentially an imitative process. It is, however, distinguished from the more transient and superficial qualities of simple imitation, as in playful or experimental mimicking, in being rooted in the deeper recesses of the personality. The latter are reserved for such persons as parents, admired teachers, and personal heroes who have a special and enduring emotional significance.

Because an individual makes multiple identifications in the course of his development, and because by the time he reaches his college years he is or should be also actively engaged in fashioning an identity of his own, it is not surprising that students are often harassed by identity conflicts, which they sometimes try to solve by dropping out of college.

It is noteworthy that Eckland found that students whose fathers were college dropouts were more likely to become dropouts themselves than students in other categories, including the sons of fathers with only an eighth-grade education. (These dropout sons of dropout fathers, however, were also among the most likely to return to college.)[10]

Princeton each year witnesses students dropping out to transfer to the colleges attended by their fathers. One outstanding student who said he was leaving college to get to know his father better spoke of returning to major in his father's vocational field. Another, after the death of his father, a career officer, withdrew to go into military service with a military career in mind. A third, in poor academic standing, related that his father had flunked out of graduate school and that his girl friend was about to fail in college.

[10] B. K. Eckland, "A study of college dropouts and graduates ten years after matriculation, with special reference to social origins and intergenerational mobility," unpublished doctoral dissertation, University of Illinois, 1964.

In the case of a surprising number of dropouts, a parent, sibling, close friend, or favorite relative had previously dropped out of college. A comment by an alumnus is relevant here: "One of my classmates who left school has an interesting history. He comes from a long line of Princetonians, and the family has always been a supporter of the school. The interesting point is that to date not one member of his family has ever graduated. Perhaps he just didn't want to mar the record."

In the examples just cited, the attempt to solve the identity problem was in the direction of increased identification with an important figure. But in other cases withdrawal is related to movement away from the important figure, a process which has been called counter-identification. Here the student strives to avoid becoming like him. Instead, his behavior becomes rebellious, as in the case of the student who, after having compulsively tried to fulfill parental expectations of excellence, revolts to become a laborer or beatnik. The important feature of counter-identification, however, is that the rebellion is not only against those with whom the individual originally identified but also against some norm or model that has already become a part of himself, since identifications, especially those of early life, are tenaciously held.

For example, a student dropped out because he was uncomfortable about becoming more and more like his father. He found himself having similar difficulties with women, similar "superficial" values, and similar desires for success in business. Having tried unsuccessfully to dissociate himself from these tendencies, which he disliked, he planned to withdraw, work on a ranch, and then travel as cheaply as possible.

Those who attempt to solve identity problems by way of counter-identification, according to Greenson, often have a common clinical pattern, a constellation of feelings and characteristics that frequently recurs from individual to individual.[11] He presented a number of cases seeking to deny any resemblance to a hated person, most often a parent, by adopting traits and acting in ways directly opposite to what was

[11] R. R. Greenson, "The struggle against identification," *Journal of the American Psychoanalytic Association*, 1954, 2, pp. 200-217.

characteristic of the hated individual. Withdrawing students frequently exhibit this pattern. They are eager to find new models, but in a transitory, superficial, and experimental way. They complain of feelings of estrangement and emptiness, moodiness, boredom, and disturbances of eating and sleeping. Greenson noted that while they resemble depressed patients, they are not primarily depressed. Rather, being chiefly afraid of losing their own identity, they must combat the identifications made with parents and others in earlier years.

In addition to the influence, often deep-seated and powerful, of identification and counter-identification with important figures in early life, two other influences seem significant in reaching the decision to drop out. They are concerned with contemporary events in the student's life and therefore are more likely to make themselves consciously felt. One is the influence of a student's peers, with whom he may identify to some extent, and the other has to do with the alternatives that confront him should he leave college.

During the college years, most students discuss withdrawal, in a general way or as a serious possibility, with their fellow students. The impressions they obtain register more or less deeply, depending on their sensitivity to campus sentiment and the number and strength of their friendships. Although dropouts frequently like to view their decision as their own, they usually talk it over with friends, frequently reporting that the latter tell them they, too, have considered dropping out but do not have the courage to do so. As a result of such discussions, the student may come to view dropping out as good or bad, strong or weak, brave or cowardly. Such attitudes toward dropping out will often play a vital role in the final decision about withdrawal.

On rare occasions, these discussions lead to a group decision to withdraw, as when seven students left Princeton together. One member of the group wondered whether the members had been initially attracted to one another because they shared similar characteristics, or whether they had influenced each other toward a common decision.

The student culture may, on the other hand, discourage dropping out. At Kyoto University, once a student becomes a member of the campus family he is not expected to leave. Withdrawal would reflect unfavorably on the college's sense of responsibility to him.[12]

Obviously, the alternatives ahead once the student drops out often play a crucial role in reaching a decision, although some drop out without giving them serious consideration. Practical matters, like arranging to transfer to another college, obtaining financial aid, what to do, where to live, how to test ability to live independently, the chance of being drafted into military service, may expedite or deter the decision to withdraw.

In sum, those in the colleges whose work brings them into close touch with students who voluntarily drop out or are considering doing so find that *students seldom make the decision lightly.* Not only does it involve complicated intra-psychic forces, social pressures from the adult world and the peer group which in themselves may be formidable, if not conflicting, and a realistic appraisal of alternatives to remaining in college, but for the very reason that such a variety of forces and pressures must be considered the decision is, more often than not, the focus of considerable doubt and anxiety for the potential dropout, as well as for his elders.

### *The College Impact: Student-Environment Interaction*

> A student went to Amherst when he should have gone to Bates; to Bowdoin when he should have gone to Yale; to Williams when he should have gone to Rensselaer. Mistakes of this kind are so easy and so costly that one wonders why practically no safeguards against them have been developed.[13]

The preceding discussion has emphasized the importance of taking into account the multiplicity of personal variables that enter into interaction with the environment. The variations among colleges are also myriad: coeducational, men's, wom-

[12] E. Levenson and M. Kohn, "A demonstration clinic for college drop-outs," *Journal of the American College Health Association*, 1964, 12, pp. 382-391.

[13] F. L. Wells, "College survivals and non-survivals at marginal test levels," *Journal of Genetic Psychology*, 1950, 77, pp. 153-185.

en's; sectarian or non-sectarian; local, state, or private; vocationally oriented or liberal arts; college or university; and so forth. Many other variations, not so obvious, may be the product of official policy and attitudes, or they may be the product of student mores. To choose but one example: is there an honor system at the college and, if so, how do students view it? Do they respect and desire it, or do they regard it as an imposition to be evaded? Do they restrict its influence narrowly, or does it set a tone for many phases of student life?

Many colleges desire to communicate values as well as facts. A strong spokesman for this point of view, Dean J. Douglas Brown of Princeton, has written:

> It may be argued that the inculcation of a sense of values is the job of the church or of the family, and that university faculties should not tamper with such personal concerns. Students and faculties alike, it is said, appear self-conscious when personal values are discussed.
>
> But this is a narrow, unreal and peculiarly recent notion about higher education. The communication of values goes on, whether overt or not, in an institution in which young men and women spend years in intense intellectual and emotional activity. The university cannot take responsibility for providing the environment for four years or seven years of the most impressionable period of a man's life and claim that it is neutral in influencing the value system of that man for life.[14]

The values that enter into a student's choice of a particular college may represent those which he feels match his own, or those to which he aspires, or he may not be able to identify them clearly, simply believing he will feel at home there among fellow-students whom he already knows.

As for intellectual values, the college hopes that their representation among the faculty and students will lead to favorable changes in the newly admitted. The desirable changes, according to prevailing criteria of American college life, are an improvement in critical thinking ability, a lessening of stereotypic

[14] J. D. Brown, "The squeeze on the liberal university," *Atlantic Monthly*, May 1964, pp. 84-87.

beliefs, a more receptive attitude toward new ideas, and a decrease in dogmatism.[15] These values become a part of the life of the college student, affecting even the dropout. Consonance and dissonance with them influence the student's tendency to remain or depart from the college.

Many other characteristics of colleges, however, vary extensively, according to the work of Pace and Stern.[16] The majority of students seem to make a successful choice of a college fitting their needs and providing a match or fit between them and their environment. But an appreciable number have a distorted image of the college they prefer, or an unrealistic recognition of themselves and their needs. The resulting misfit then may lead to non-fulfillment of potential or to dropping out. Stern found that at the University of Chicago a minority group of authoritarian-minded students contributed most heavily to the withdrawal rate. They complained of looseness in the pedagogical approach that tolerated smoking in classrooms, did not require attendance, and expected students to answer their own questions.[17]

Similarly, Funkenstein reported results which "suggest that the hypothesis that when the 'basic attributes' of individuals are markedly incongruous with the 'basic attributes' of a college, a strain is produced. . . . Some of these failures in one school are doing well in other schools where the incongruities between students and institutions are not so great."[18]

Consonance or dissonance between student and college can be very specific. Sometimes, the topic is primarily cognitive and intellectual. Malleson described the findings of Furneaux that certain types of students have difficulty in one area, while

[15] I. J. Lehmann, "Changes in critical thinking, attitudes and values from freshman to senior years," *Journal of Educational Psychology*, 1963, 54, pp. 305-315.

[16] C. R. Pace and G. C. Stern, "An approach to the measurement of psychological characteristics of college environments," *ibid.*, 1958, 49, pp. 269-277.

[17] G. G. Stern, "Environments for learning," in Sanford (ed.), *op.cit.*, pp. 690-730.

[18] D. H. Funkenstein, "The implications of the diversity of students, colleges and medical schools," in C. E. Bidwell (ed.), *The American college and student personality*, New York: Social Science Research Council, 1959.

others have difficulty in another area, suggesting a relationship between type of work and type of student.[19] Katz and Sanford pointed out: "Within the same institution, at the same time, there are undoubtedly students who would benefit most from one type of curriculum and other students who would benefit most from a different type, and yet that institution offers and defends as universally good a single curriculum."[20]

Similar problems pertain to the ways in which the curriculum is presented. Patton has found that students who reject traditional sources of authority and are highly motivated toward personal achievement are most favorably disposed toward experimental classes run by students themselves and most able to handle the responsibilities involved in such classes.[21] More generally, McConnell and Heist pointed out that students in private and public institutions tend to express different interests. They reported, "Facilities in public institutions that want to interest students in ideas will have a difficult challenge and a considerably different problem."[22]

Bay noted that students with an intellectual bent will tend to feel in accord with professors who reward independent intellectual efforts, but will regard the professor who rewards efficiency in memorization as an obstacle to be overcome. In contrast, more narrowly grade-oriented students will be confused and antagonized by the former and will see the latter as reasonable and competent.[23]

It is tempting to believe that students have a fund of knowledge which can be tapped by any means of assessment. There is evidence, however, that students perform differently on different tasks. Claunch divided college students into concrete and abstract types. He found that abstract students were significantly superior to concrete subjects in performance on an

19 N. Malleson, "Operational research in the university," *British Medical Journal,* 1959, 1, pp. 1031-1035.

20 J. Katz and N. Sanford, "The curriculum in the perspective of the theory of personality development," in Sanford (ed.), *op.cit.,* pp. 418-444.

21 J. A. Patton, "A study of the effects of student acceptance of responsibility and motivation on course behavior," unpublished doctoral dissertation, University of Michigan, 1955.

22 T. R. McConnell and P. Heist, "The diverse college student population," in Sanford (ed.), *op.cit.,* pp. 225-252.

23 C. Bay, "A social theory of higher education," in *ibid.,* pp. 972-1005.

examination involving a complex criterion (essay), but not in a multiple-choice task. On essay examinations abstract students were better able than the others to integrate comparisons of different theoretical points of view.[24] Thus, examination performance and grades reflect personality style or mode of cognitive functioning. More generally, grades reflect the interaction between the individual's mode of operation and the tasks set for him by his environment.

These findings suggest that a fit between student personality and college characteristics encourages the fulfillment of talent, but that mismatches may encourage dropping out. But were it possible to create a perfectly homogeneous student-body in complete harmony with the college, the resulting community would probably not be particularly desirable. The stimulus to students of having to meet the challenges of varying personalities and requirements would be minimal, and the community would discourage some of the desirable values described above of improved critical thinking, lessening of stereotypes, a more receptive attitude toward new ideas, and a decrease in authoritarianism.

The task of the colleges is, of course, not to create this kind of impossible homogeneity, but rather to avoid ignoring the personal variables in students, the inevitable crises of late adolescence, and the possibility that there will be harmful effects from stress and challenge instead of stimulus and growth. Douvan and Kaye described the practical aspects thus: "The dropout and exchange rates in American colleges suggest that something goes seriously awry in the choice process . . . transfer rates seem to reveal a widespread choice based on inappropriate or transitory needs. The shopping around that occurs *after* the adolescent is already in college must cause him a great deal of loss and unhappiness. One suspects, at least, that some of the grief might be prevented by more careful counseling of students at the time of initial decision."[25] Ford and his asso-

[24] N. C. Claunch, "Cognitive and motivational characteristics associated with concrete and abstract levels of conceptional complexity," unpublished doctoral dissertation, Princeton University, 1964.

[25] Elizabeth Douvan and Carol Kaye, "Motivational factors in college entrance," in Sanford (ed.), *op.cit.*, pp. 199-224.

ciates at Pennsylvania State University have, indeed, inaugurated a program with just such aims.

### *Summary and Implications*

The problems concerning college dropouts and the development of talent sketched in this chapter are manifestly as complex as human nature itself, which is certainly far from being at its simplest and most predictable during the college years. They often transcend attempts at classifying them into narrow categories. Academic problems turn out to be rooted in personal difficulties, and vice versa. A seemingly maladjusted student subsequently progresses well after weathering a temporary crisis. And the "nice guy" whom everybody likes and whom Peter Vierck might suspect of being "overadjusted" ("public smile; private blank") is assumed to have no problems at all. Or the essential trouble is that a student has come to the wrong college.

Many of these problems, perhaps the majority, never come to the attention of college counselors and psychiatrists, being distributed instead among all those who work with students—professors, instructors, coaches, chaplains, deans, and so forth. The latter, particularly when they talk with their clinically trained colleagues on the campus, tend to deny having any psychological insight or knowledge, yet manage to be highly sensitive to subtle signs of the failure or success of the educational process in individual students. Some seem to have an unerring instinct when it comes to ferreting out students in difficulty or identifying those with emotional disturbances.

But whether students come to professional counselors or to faculty and others on the college staff seems of secondary importance compared with the recognition that their problems have a twofold dimension, involving both the personal and the social sphere. College students are apt to be in conflict not only with those who stand for the socialization of the individual, but also with themselves, chiefly because of the close connection between morality and the passions; for as Philip Rieff observed, "Morality derives its energies secondhand, from a process of reaction against desiring."[26] It is precisely at the time when people are increasingly being handled in masses that the colleges need to learn all they can from the experience of individual students, the successful as well as the unsuccessful, about how to improve the interaction on the campus.

[26] P. Rieff, *Freud: The mind of the moralist,* New York: Viking, 1959.

# *CHAPTER 6*

# READMISSION TO COLLEGE AFTER PSYCHIATRIC MEDICAL LEAVE

MICHAEL A. PESZKE, M.D. &
ROBERT L. ARNSTEIN, M.D.

THE LAST TWO decades have seen a tremendous expansion in demand for college admissions but no corresponding increase in enrollment for many of the private colleges. This has led on the part of prospective students to an intense competition for admission to these colleges and on the part of the admissions committee to a feeling that each class place should be occupied by a student capable of (1) meeting the academic requirements and (2) utilizing as fully as possible the opportunities offered by the college. Thus, a goal of the admissions committee might be to select a class which would graduate all of its entering members in the normal curricular period.[1]

This goal is rarely, if ever, attained; the average experience indicates that a significant number of students will fail to graduate in four years. A recent study of two graduating classes at Yale revealed that approximately 25 percent did not graduate on time. Of these, some will graduate at a later date, some will graduate from another college, and others will never receive the B.A. degree. The reasons for the interruption vary, but usually involve academic failure, disciplinary suspension, resignation for personal reasons, or medical leave of absence, either physical or psychiatric.

In general, it can be said that a student who drops out of college is in difficulty of one sort or another; he may have

1 This goal, of course, implies that graduation is the measure of success, and it could be argued that such an "achievement morality" is arbitrary, and that for any given individual there may be more important tasks at this particular stage in his life. This is a possible viewpoint but could only be incorporated into a research study by using a later point in the individual's life to evaluate the total impact of the college experience. While beyond the scope of this study, such a project would be a worthwhile, if difficult, endeavor.

several possible ways of coping with the difficulty, but one of these is to leave college. Obviously, on occasion withdrawal may be involuntary as a result of administrative action. When it is elective, however, the decision to leave will result from a complex interaction of factors, including the attitudes and wishes of the student himself, the college attitude toward students taking leave, parental attitudes, perhaps peer attitudes, and the possibilities of readmission.

This study, a sequel to an earlier study done at Yale on students who drop out for emotional reasons, focuses on the group of undergraduates who are readmitted after a "psychiatric medical leave."[2]

Before discussing the problem of readmission, some factors relative to the granting of leaves need to be described, for it has become quite clear that readmission is more difficult to evaluate if the terms of leaving are unclear. The term "psychiatric medical leave" is more difficult to define than it might appear. In a college where superior academic ability is a prerequisite for admission, every student who enters probably has the intellectual capacity to do the work. If he fails, does one therefore automatically ascribe this to emotional disturbance? The answer depends in large part on the definition of "emotional disturbance," and is relatively clear-cut if he is hallucinating and is in the midst of a psychotic reaction. If, however, he is simply rebellious and rowdy, or if he is beset by an unexplained apathy, it is more difficult.

Over the years at Yale a kind of operational system without rigid categories has evolved which seems to work reasonably well and to provide some guide lines for the Dean's Office as well as the Health Service. There are essentially three types of "dropouts," each type having subcategories. First, there is the student who is dropped for academic failure or disciplinary breach. In almost all such cases the action is taken by the Dean or his administrative committee. On very rare occasions the college psychiatrist may intervene and ask that the action be made a medical leave if there is evidence of gross psychiatric

[2] R. W. Harrison, "Leaving college because of emotional problems," in B. M. Wedge (ed.), *Psychosocial problems of college men*, New Haven: Yale University Press, 1958, pp. 95-112.

difficulty which has not been previously apparent. Secondly, there is the student who resigns voluntarily for a variety of reasons, including financial problems,[3] vocational indecision, general dissatisfaction, or family difficulties. Included in this group are a number of students who seem to be having problems of maturing and/or adjustment difficulties which are not sufficiently clear-cut or severe to warrant a medical leave. Thirdly, there is the "medical leave," which is given for physical illness or for emotional illness when the psychiatric condition is acute, incapacitating, and clearly diagnosable.

The decision to leave involves various considerations. These range from a more or less immediate medical evaluation of the student's ability to function successfully in his environment to the broader question of whether the student is deriving the maximum possible benefit from his college experience. It seems fairly clear that the latter concept has been affected by the post-World War II experience that many veterans, whose college careers had been interrupted, returned and performed in far more distinguished academic fashion than during their preservice period. On the other hand, a student's plan to leave may be a rather impulsive response to a period of acute discouragement or frustration that he needs only to face and weather in order to finish effectively and with adequate rewards. The task of any advisor—dean, counselor, psychiatrist, parent, or friend—is to help a student to evaluate the situation accurately and to determine the best course of action.

The stated reasons for considering a leave are many and varied. In some cases the student feels totally unable to complete his work as a result of anxiety, depression, or apathy, which probably includes elements of both anxiety and depression. The precursors of these symptoms again may be multiple, varying from conflict with parents to unexplained inability to sit down and work. In other cases the student may be doing objectively satisfactory work but for some reason feels inwardly that his performance is unsatisfactory or that he is not achieving the kind of results he knows he can achieve. He may feel

[3] At Yale, with its heavy financial aid program, the meaning of the term "financial reasons" usually is more complex than simply lack of money to pay tuition and boarding costs.

either that he is heading in the wrong vocational direction, or that he is essentially directionless. He may be subject to the pressure which grows out of his knowledge that he must achieve academically in order to be selected for the next phase, and yet he may question whether the final rewards are going to justify the struggle. He may be overcome with a kind of school fatigue which afflicts him and makes him yearn for a period in which he can experiment without feeling that a failure will significantly affect his ultimate academic progress. Or he may wish to do something irrelevant to the academic; the desire to "bum" or travel frequently crops up as a fantasy, and recently various humanitarian occupations, such as the Peace Corps, have become popular. In many cases that are being considered in this study, the withdrawal will have been precipitated by some symptomatic outbreak such as an acute anxiety attack, a suicide attempt, or a psychotic reaction which makes the leave medically imperative, but frequently some of the more chronic problems can be found to underlie the acute reaction, and perhaps are the real precipitating causes.

Once a student has decided to leave, latitude may exist in the type of leave, and, although this may seem trivial, there are some hidden implications. As has already been pointed out, the student who is dropped for administrative reasons has little choice. In selecting between medical leave and resignation, however, it generally has seemed preferable to the psychiatrist to restrict medical leaves to students with severe illness. Although there has been a tendency for psychiatry in general and the college mental hygiene division in particular to extend the territory covered by emotional problems, it seems preferable in administrative matters to be less expansive, because the stricter application of the term "medical" helps with the readmission process, as will be explained below. In addition there are other pertinent factors. In some cases it seems preferable therapeutically for the student to take a more "active" role in the decision to leave by resigning, in contrast to the more passive "being placed on medical leave." In other cases a medical leave is preferable in order to underline the fact that the student is ill and should be treated as such. This may be important in terms of the student himself, his family, or even the college administration. Occasionally a student will favor one or the other for essentially irrational reasons and this may be a difficult problem for the psychiatrist. Sometimes these reasons are not entirely irrational, but have some ulterior aim such as the relative advantage of having a "medical leave" on the record as opposed to a "resignation."

At present at Yale there is no very rigid policy regarding recommendations to a student who goes on leave nor are there specific requirements that must be met prior to his return. The current rather flexible policy has evolved gradually as a result of experience gained by various deans and staff psychiatrists. At one point there was a fairly strict rule that students who went on medical leave were required to be absent for a period of at least one calendar year. This is no longer required and occasionally students are readmitted before a full year has passed. However, there is a general feeling that, up to a point, the longer the student is out, the more likely he is to have solved his problems and to be able to cope with the Yale environment. Thus, it has been frequently found that a student who drops out in one semester and attempts to return the next may have simply resolved the immediate difficulty by flight and fooled himself into thinking that all will be well when he returns, which it usually is not. Most students who leave for emotional reasons will have psychiatric treatment recommended to them. Although treatment may be strongly advised, the student who returns without following the recommendation will not necessarily be barred from readmission. This apparently contradictory policy has grown out of the feeling that psychiatric treatment undertaken solely as a prerequisite for readmission will probably not be very effective.

When a student who is on psychiatric medical leave applies for readmission, some evaluation must occur. In general, Yale follows the policy that students who are admitted initially will be given a second chance. This will hold for almost all types of dropouts, but obviously in the case of medical leaves readmission is more or less automatic once medical clearance has been obtained. On the other hand, there are very few third chances given, and for the majority of the psychiatric medical leaves there will be no third chance because it is felt that if a breakdown occurs twice while at Yale, the Yale environment may be creating some sort of stress even though it is difficult to describe precisely what the stress is. Therefore, the timing of the readmission is rather important, for, if it is premature, it may well have far-reaching effects on the student's educational career.

For students on psychiatric medical leave, a regular readmission procedure has been established. This consists of an interview with a senior member of the Mental Hygiene Division staff; preferably, but not absolutely required, a report from the applicant's psychiatrist if he has been in treatment while away from college; and, in addition, the submission, to the Dean's Office, of letters from employers and/or a transcript from any interim educational institution he has attended. Administratively the final decision regarding readmission always is made by the Dean's Office, but in cases involving psychiatric medical leave no action will be taken by the Dean until clearance is received from the Mental Hygiene Division. Occasionally, in the course of psychiatric evaluation, psychological testing will be done. This usually consists of a test battery including Rorschach, WAIS, TAT, and is performed by a clinical psychologist on the staff. In addition to automatic interviews for the students who are on psychiatric medical leave, the Student Mental Hygiene Division may be asked to interview and give an opinion on an individual who has resigned if the Dean's Office feels that emotional factors were rather important in causing the resignation.

In the readmission interview the psychiatrist must consider three aspects. On behalf of the individual, the psychiatrist must take into account the student's current state of health and attempt to evaluate whether return to college will undermine gains or cause another breakdown; he will also be concerned about the effect of premature return on the student's academic progress. From the standpoint of the college, he will be concerned with the effect of the introduction onto the campus of a sick individual who might cause difficulties for the institution; in addition he will be concerned about the college's investment in the individual student and may attempt to prevent a student who is unable to function from occupying a place in an already crowded institution. From the standpoint of the family, he will be concerned with preserving the student's health and, secondarily, perhaps protecting the parents from paying tuition when the student is really not able to utilize the college experience.

The readmission interview is not an easy one. In addition to the necessary reliance on subjective impressions, there are other pressures on the evaluating psychiatrist. The applicant may be extremely eager to return to college either for his own reasons or because he is subject to parental pressure. He may be able to cover up the degree of his current illness and present a quite convincing argument for readmission. Furthermore, the report from the home psychiatrist may not be particularly helpful. He may tend to side with his patient's manifest wishes; he may be unclear about the college pressures acting on the student; he may feel that there is no medical "danger" to the patient, and, therefore, see no reason for barring him on medical grounds; or he may be subject to considerable pressure to write a favorable recommendation. Thus, the external pressures on the evaluating psychiatrist are all toward clearing the student, and this may be his own inclination also inasmuch as it would seem to require very good evidence to postpone further the student's natural progress in his educational career.

What then are the criteria which can be used in determining a student's readiness to return to college on a full-time basis? In a sense the current study originated because one of the investigators found the readmission interview a difficult experience, frequently ending with a subjective evaluation in which the interviewer felt he was rendering an opinion without a very clear set of criteria. Furthermore, it was noted that a certain number of students who were readmitted had recurrences of their difficulties during the year and were forced to drop out again. The current study was undertaken, therefore, in an effort to elucidate criteria for readmission and also, if possible, to gain information which could be used in making recommendations to the student who was leaving.

A general review of the psychiatric literature reveals only

three studies, two published and one unpublished, pertaining specifically to the problem of readmission after psychiatric medical leave.

Harrison in *Psychosocial problems of college men*, edited by Wedge, reports a study done at Yale, which was the forerunner of this one.[4] Harrison's study differed from the present work in that both graduate and undergraduate students were included. Of a group of 179 students who left Yale because of emotional reasons during the five academic years from 1947 to 1952, he found that 86 students, or 48 percent, had returned prior to August 1955; and of this total, 59 (69 percent) graduated. He then compared a group that returned and graduated with a group that returned and dropped out again. The following criteria were compared: (a) class at time of leaving; (b) academic status before leaving; (c) psychiatric diagnosis at the time of leaving (in some cases this was made by psychiatrists reviewing records *post hoc*); (d) psychiatric treatment before and after leaving; (e) length of time out of school; and (f) treatment after returning to school.

Harrison's conclusions were as follows: three of the above variables were significantly related to the student's chance of success: (1) graduate students did better than undergraduates; (2) students who were in academic trouble prior to leaving were more likely to have to leave again; (3) students with a diagnosis of a psychotic or neurotic disturbance were more likely to finish successfully than those with a diagnosis of character disorder. The three findings were all significantly related to each other; that is, the student with the diagnosis of character disorder was more likely to be in academic trouble prior to leaving and the incidence of this diagnosis decreased as the educational level went up. In his study, however, Harrison found the following to have no significant bearing on success or failure after admission: (1) whether a student had treatment before, during, or after a leave, and (2) the period of time that the student stayed out of school. In this study Harrison also confirmed a fragmentary study done by Darling at Cornell and reported in 1955, in which it was stated that

[4] Harrison, in Wedge (ed.), *op.cit.*

a psychotic diagnosis is not inimical to success on readmission.[5] Darling noted that of ten students who left because of psychotic reactions, five returned to college within a year, and of these three were performing well the following semester.

A second study was done at Harvard and described briefly in *Emotional problems of students,* edited by Blaine and McArthur.[6] The authors stated that of 160 students of the class of 1956 who had to take a leave of absence because of emotional problems, 76 returned by 1957 and 60 were still in good standing at a date which was not specified.

A further extensive study, so far unpublished, was done on Yale undergraduates by two Yale seniors, Iman and Altemeyer, who studied all sophomore, junior, and senior students who dropped out, returned, and were no longer at Yale during a ten-year period from 1952 to 1962.[7] The authors grouped the reasons for dropout into ten categories, of which two have a direct bearing on the present study: (1) those students who left for emotional reasons and (2) those students who left for a combination of academic and emotional reasons. The other categories used were: academic, medical, financial, disciplinary, and various combinations thereof. Of the 563 individuals in the study group, 78.8 percent went on to graduate; and of 22 students who left and were readmitted a second time, 18 graduated. They compared the students who graduated and the ones who dropped out a second time on a number of variables, such as length of time out of college, number of terms to go on return, academic load on return, type of secondary school attended, financial aid, reason for leaving, rooming situation on return, marital status, and activity while away from Yale.

They found that the student who was married on return had a much better record of success, except in the "emotional" category, where no difference from the average appeared. They also found that the fewer number of terms to go, the greater

5 Case reports of the Cornell University Infirmary and Clinic, *Student Medicine,* 1955, 3, pp. 102-109.

6 G. B. Blaine, Jr., and C. C. McArthur, "Problems connected with studying," in G. B. Blaine, Jr., and C. C. McArthur (eds.), *Emotional problems of the student,* New York: Appleton-Century-Crofts, 1961.

7 S. Iman and R. Altemeyer, "Readmission study: 1952-1962," mimeographed, Yale University.

was the chance for success. Another point made in a more tentative way was that a heavy academic load on return did not seem to be too difficult for the student who had left for strictly emotional reasons, in sharp contrast to the student who had left for academic *and* emotional reasons. The length of time away from school, if shorter than two terms, appeared not to favor success, but beyond this no positive relationship could be distinguished, although those with long absences had good success on return. According to the study's categorizations of reasons for leaving, the group with academic and emotional problems—which, incidentally, was the second largest category—had the highest rate of second dropout, with the "straight" emotional category next. In terms of activity while away, those who had been in military service had the highest percentage of success on return. Travel had a positive correlation with success on return, and "staying at home doing nothing" a negative one. There was also a hint that students who lived by themselves, whether on campus or off campus, did better than students with roommates, but there were several contaminating factors in this finding. Many of these findings, however, were not statistically significant and appeared only as trends.

Iman and Altemeyer say of the "emotional cases" that approximately three-quarters were successful on return. Marriage was not a positive factor, as in the total study group, and a heavy academic load not a negative factor. Single rooming situations boded well for success, and number of terms to go was a less significant indicator, although the number was small. Those who had been hospitalized while out of school (presumably indicating more severe illness) showed only a slightly higher degree of failure on return than the "emotional" group as a whole.

Of the "academic-emotional cases," only two-thirds were successful on return. The rate of failure in this group was significantly higher for the students from a prep school, whereas marriage meant almost certain academic success for the returnee. Academic load and success were directly proportional, but a single rooming situation did not improve chances of success. Length of time away showed the same general trend but long absences seemed less hazardous, and the optimum absence time was somewhat longer. Again the activity while away from college seemed difficult to interpret.

The current study is limited to a period of seven years from 1956-1963. The study group is comprised of all undergraduates who interrupted their college career during this period because of known emotional problems and then reentered during the same period, a number totaling 101. Data were gathered on a series of variables, and the statistical results are shown in Table 1. Although an attempt was made to define the group rather rigidly, some comments are necessary about the selection process. First, an individual was included in the group if he was seen by a member of the Mental Hygiene Division prior to readmission, whether or not he was technically on psychiatric medical leave. Secondly, over the course of the seven-year period there has been some shift in the concept of medical leave and, consequently, criteria for medical leave during the latter part of the period were probably stricter. Thirdly, although most of the readmission interviews were conducted by a single interviewer, he had begun this activity only in 1958 and experience may have affected his performance as interviewer in the later years.

As one might expect, the percentage of successful students returning after psychiatric medical leave is somewhat lower than the percentage of success of all students returning after a period away as determined by the Iman and Altemeyer study at Yale, which found that almost 80 percent of returnees graduated. Of our study group, only 70 percent have graduated or are still in good standing as of June 1964, and of the six still in school, some may fail to finish, so that the final figure for graduation could be slightly lower.

Thus, our study indicates that of those readmitted approximately two-thirds will complete their degree. The inspection of specific factors (Table 1) makes it clear that none of the criteria chosen as variables will predict success on readmission. In the total picture, the only significant finding is the number of terms remaining prior to graduation at the time of leaving. Seniors who leave have a significantly better chance of success than freshmen. Otherwise all diagnoses, all combinations of

TABLE 1.

This study comprises 101 Yale undergraduates who were placed on psychiatric medical leave during 1956 through 1963, and who were readmitted during these same years. Statistics are compiled as of June 1964.

| | GRADUATED: 64 | | DROPPED OUT: 31 | | IN COLLEGE: 6 | |
|---|---|---|---|---|---|---|
| | *Number* | *Percent* | *Number* | *Percent* | *Number* | *Percent* |
| *Diagnostic Category* | | | | | | |
| Adolescent adjustment | 12 | 18.7 | 4 | 12.9 | 3 | 50.0 |
| Schizophrenic reaction | 18 | 28.1 | 9 | 29.0 | 1 | 16.6 |
| Psychoneurotic disorder | 11 | 17.1 | 5 | 16.1 | 2 | 33.3 |
| Character disorder | 14 | 21.8 | 4 | 12.9 | 0 | 0 |
| No diagnosis | 9 | 14.0 | 9 | 29.0 | 0 | 0 |
| *Class When Medical Leave Taken*[a] | | | | | | |
| Freshman | 7 | 10.9 | 8 | 25.8 | 3 | 50.0 |
| Sophomore | 15 | 23.4 | 11 | 35.4 | 3 | 50.0 |
| Junior | 23 | 35.9 | 10 | 32.2 | 0 | 0 |
| Senior | 19 | 29.6 | 2 | 6.4 | 0 | 0 |
| *Secondary School* | | | | | | |
| Preparatory | 24 | 37.5 | 14 | 45.1 | 5 | 83.3 |
| Other | 40 | 62.5 | 17 | 54.8 | 1 | 16.6 |
| *Financial Aid at College* | 16 | 25.0 | 8 | 25.8 | 1 | 16.6 |
| *Activity During Medical Leave*[b] | | | | | | |
| Hospitalized | 23 | 35.9 | 14 | 45.1 | 2 | 33.3 |
| Outpatient therapy | 41 | 64.0 | 24 | 77.4 | 6 | 100.0 |
| Armed forces | 8 | 12.5 | 1 | 3.2 | 0 | |
| Study | 19 | 29.6 | 6 | 19.3 | 0 | |
| Job | 31 | 47.1 | 13 | 41.9 | 4 | 66.6 |
| *Length of Medical Leave in Months* | | | | | | |
| 0 — 6 | 11 | 17.1 | 6 | 19.3 | 1 | 16.6 |
| 7 — 12 | 28 | 43.6 | 16 | 51.6 | 2 | 33.3 |
| 13 — 18 | 11 | 17.1 | 5 | 16.1 | 3 | 50.0 |
| 18 + | 14 | 21.8 | 4 | 12.9 | 0 | |
| *Treatment in College* | | | | | | |
| At time of medical leave | 31 | 47.1 | 14 | 45.1 | 1 | 16.6 |
| Self-referral | 19 | 29.6 | 4 | 12.9 | 1 | 16.6 |
| After return | 23 | 35.9 | 15 | 48.3 | 4 | 66.6 |

[a] This refers to the first leave, if more than one was taken.

[b] This is a cumulative column and includes more than one category for most students. E.g., student X may have had Rx and held a job. He would be counted in both columns.

therapy, hospitalization, and absence of therapy, and all lengths of time away include cases that have both succeeded and failed on return, and none is statistically significant, using the Chi-Square Test. Inasmuch as the *N* in several of the subcategories is rather small, it is conceivable that a larger study group would lead to significant findings in these areas, but the current sample contains at best only suggestive trends.

A few cases will serve to illustrate the nature of the readmission histories. The cases are selected not to demonstrate a particular point, but to show that the evaluation process is characteristically imprecise. They are presented in skeletal form to indicate that there is a wide variation in individual patterns, and it is difficult to select even retrospectively the significant fact or facts in the history which determines success or failure on return.

(1) *A* was a student who had sporadic contacts with the Division of Student Mental Hygiene throughout his first three years of school. He was obviously quite disturbed emotionally, but very able and highly motivated academically. During his senior year, he suffered an acute psychotic episode which necessitated hospitalization. He remained in the hospital for three months and received several electroshock treatments. On discharge he continued with psychotherapy and returned to college after eight months. On readmission he was seen in intensive treatment and throughout the entire year was maintained on drugs. Despite some extremely shaky periods he managed to graduate with a fine academic record, although his average on return was not quite as high as before.

This is a clear-cut case of an interruption caused by a psychotic episode. The student was "successful" in completing his work on return, although considerable therapeutic support was necessary and the prognosis for the future must be guarded.

(2) *B* was originally referred by the medical department while in the Infirmary. It was commented that he was confused and tired, and after interview it was felt that there was probably an underlying schizophrenic process. He entered psychotherapy with a private psychiatrist, and in May dropped out of school. He was seen the following September but was not re-

admitted, in part because of the short time he had been away. He reapplied in January after working during the previous two or three months. He was readmitted and was seen in treatment the following fall by a Division of Student Mental Hygiene psychiatrist. He had a rather erratic year, and eventually was again placed on psychiatric leave.

This is obviously a student whose impairment in functioning was severe, and probably of psychotic magnitude. It is not clear whether further time away or a more consistent therapeutic situation during his leave of absence would have made a difference on return. Actually he is one of the few who received a third chance, and the final outcome is not yet determined. It is interesting that on his last return he commented that he should not have been readmitted at the time of his second application.

(3) As a junior, *C* ran into a number of difficulties of a personal nature at school which culminated in his leaving Yale in February and going home. He suffered from fatigue and anxiety and was hospitalized for evaluation at home. He received some psychotherapy, but family interference caused termination. He was interested in a professional theatrical career, which was very much opposed by a successful lawyer father. *C* applied for readmission the following fall and appeared very well integrated in the readmission interview, but he came back into treatment following readmission. He became acutely anxious again in October, had to be put in the Infirmary, and decided to leave Yale.

This student probably was beset by problems of growing up, although a rather poised and sophisticated exterior may have served to disguise more serious psychopathology. In retrospect, he probably should have been made to remain out longer before return.

(4) Originally *D* was referred by his faculty advisor because of tension and anxiety during exams and because of poor study habits. His school work deteriorated and he was placed on leave during his sophomore year. There was a background of family difficulty and pressure, and the student was encouraged to seek treatment. On readmission after twenty months, he presented himself as feeling better and knowing clearly his

goals. He had seen a psychologist for counseling and felt better able to handle his family difficulties, although the conflicts were not solved. In spite of treatment and his apparent improvement, his study difficulties recurred and he was dropped for academic deficiency at the end of the year.

This student appeared to have problems of maturing initially, but his subsequent course suggested an incorrect diagnosis. The readmission interview either failed to assess accurately the degree of upset potentially inherent in the family pressures or was too accepting of the evidences of improvement presented.

(5) *E* "disappeared" from Yale with the intention of entering military service in the spring of his freshman year after a rather disastrous academic record. He did not consult with anyone at the time because he was so ambivalent about his decision that he was afraid he might get talked into staying. He enlisted and spent three years in the army, most of it in Europe. After discharge from the service, he completed a summer school session. Although there was no medical reason for barring his readmission, the interviewer noted that the only overt reason for readmitting him was that he said he wanted to come back and he had been away a substantial time. The student was admitted and graduated successfully with a truly outstanding academic record.

This is a confusing case, but it probably represents an individual with adolescent problems whose motivation for studying crystallized as a result of time and the maturing process of his service experience.

(6) *F* was a senior who became quite upset and began to indulge in rather bizarre behavior and in addition failed to meet his academic obligations. This caused considerable concern on campus, although it was not sufficiently flagrant to demand emergency hospitalization. He was referred to the Mental Hygiene Division and came rather reluctantly. He was persuaded to go to the Infirmary to await the arrival of his family, who took him home. He was seen in therapy while at home and applied for readmission a year later. At that time in the interview there was evidence of inappropriate affect, loose associations, grandiosity, and poor planning. He was tested

psychologically and the test report indicated some mild thought disorder. Medical clearance was refused and he returned home.

This is a case of a borderline patient who showed sufficient disturbance in the evaluation to make it seem inadvisable to clear him. His therapist later reported that he had decompensated markedly on his trip to college, presumably as a result of leaving home and/or facing college. This case illustrates a difficulty confronting the evaluating interviewer, who is not necessarily seeing the same emotional state in an individual that his own therapist may have seen even as recently as a week before.

The six cases described schematically include individuals with a psychotic episode who returned and succeeded; a psychotic episode who returned and failed; a problem of immaturity that returned and succeeded; a similar problem that returned and failed; an apparent immaturity reaction who probably returned prematurely as a result of incorrect diagnosis and failed; and a borderline psychotic reaction who was not readmitted. Even this very small sample demonstrates that the complexity of the interacting elements makes it impossible to predict success accurately on the basis of diagnosis or experience while away from college.

What conclusions then can one draw about the process of dropping out and readmission? Is it worth having an interview with a psychiatrist? If so, are there any guides that come from the study? Are there recommendations that can be made to the student who is leaving?

First, the seven-year experience indicates that in purely statistical terms, the evaluation interview will in a high percentage of cases grant clearance eventually. During this period only five students were refused admission, although admission was deferred in several cases. Presumably in the cases where clearance was not granted there was sufficient psychopathology so that the bar to readmission was an important action both for individual and institution. It could be argued, however, that any interviewer with some experience in evaluating students would have been able to assess the situation sufficiently to reach a similar decision. When, however, the college has a psychiatrist available, there probably are real advantages in having the psychiatrist make the evaluation: (1) because it relieves the administrator of having to make a decision in an area in which he does not feel particularly well trained; and (2) because it makes clear to the student and family the source of the problem and may lead to therapeutic action. Furthermore, the fact that there is a readmission interview required may well cause the individual to consider more carefully the decision to return.

The readmission interview is usually a semi-structured one which is carefully defined at the outset as designed to provide information on the individual's readiness to return. It is also made clear that an opinion will be forwarded to the Dean. The applicant is usually asked to describe the circumstances at the time of his leaving, his activities in the interim, and his evaluation of his current psychological state. If he has been in psychotherapy, he is usually asked to describe his feelings about this experience. Then any special areas of difficulty are explored. These may range from questions about specific anxieties known to have existed previously to investigations of current parental pressure for return. He is usually asked about his reactions to Yale and about alternative plans in the event that he is not readmitted. Finally, he is asked whether he feels that he currently has emotional problems and also about his reaction to the readmission interview.

In terms of the readmission procedure the guides are not very clear. In general, it is probably better to demand a longer time away than a shorter, although there are no absolutes. If the student has been in academic difficulty prior to leaving, it is usually advisable to demand some evidence of academic performance prior to return, and the Dean's Office has come to require this. If, on the other hand, he has maintained a good average prior to leaving but has had acute emotional problems, evidence of therapy or a considerable period of time away seems desirable. If the interviewer feels some real uncertainty, it is frequently valuable to have psychological testing done, because cues which may be minimal in the interview situation are often highlighted on the tests. On the one hand, the testing may reveal intellectual impairment, psychotic intrusions, and disorganization that are not readily visible in the clinical interview. On the other, it may show a reasonably integrated psychological state with no intellectual impairment and relatively little confusion or interference with mental functioning, which also may not be apparent during the clinical interview because of anxiety connected with the evaluation process itself.

In an attempt to determine whether there was any improvement in the predictive success of the readmission process, the readmissions in the last three years were studied. Of those admitted in 1960-1961, nine graduated and five dropped out; in 1961-1962 and 1962-1963 combined, 22 graduated, four dropped out, and six remained in college. While one would assume that of the six remaining some may eventually fail to finish, as of June 1964 the percentage of success for the three years cumulatively was 80, and for the last two years, 87. It would be gratifying to believe that this result was not chance, and that it could be maintained. If one assumes it is a significant finding, the explanations probably are threefold: (1) additional interviewing experience on the part of the chief interviewer; (2) more careful clarification of the medical leave status and the requirements of readmission; (3) additional use of psychological testing in doubtful cases. A further factor which is hard to evaluate but which probably has been important has been the development of a more open, collaborative relationship with the deans most responsible for readmission decisions.

If "experience" is helpful, can this be analyzed and described? It is not easy and such "hunches" as have developed are not really substantiated statistically. Nevertheless, some discussion is in order. Unquestionably, experience makes for a greater ability to withstand the pressures tending toward clearance and a greater "toughness." Although it has not been possible to measure the effect of this numerically, it should in theory improve the percentage of successful returnees. In addition the insistence on *some* accomplishment, either of an academic nature, employment, or military service, seems important in most cases, particularly when the time away has been short or the individual was having academic difficulties prior to leaving college.

In all cases, attention to minimal cues is important, because in the inevitably brief evaluation interview the individual is usually able to present a reasonably good façade. The intuition of the interviewer plays an unfortunately large but significant part in the final decision. In cases of doubt, delaying a final decision may be useful, for the passage of time and the gathering of additional impressions and information may clarify the situation considerably. Although no questions are absolute indicators, it is frequently useful to ask what alternatives have been considered and what the individual's feeling about the readmission interview has been. If no alternatives have been considered, this is usually worth further investigation to discover (1) the amount of parental pressure or (2) a lack of flexibility which may cause difficulty later. The question about the interview will often reveal resentment or considerable anxiety which may illuminate some of the other material. The applicant will frequently regard the interviewer purely as an obstacle to be hurdled, which is in a certain sense realistic. If, however, he can be convinced that the interviewer is primarily interested in his welfare, which is equally correct, it is usually possible to make a more accurate assessment of his real feelings about returning. Other than this, the interviewer will find all combinations of reticence, openness, enthusiasm, resentment, clear motivations for return as well as the opposite, and none seemed necessarily to predict success or failure.

In listening to students in the readmission interview describe their experiences during the time away from college, one is impressed with the diversity of benefits. In general, most fall under two headings—either a gain in general confidence, or a settling of vocational direction. The steps leading thereto, however, vary widely. Some individuals are affected by as mundane an experience as attempting to get an "interesting" job without a B.A. degree and realize thereby the importance of completing college. Others, having found a job in a particular field, are inspired to continue in that field and see clearly that additional training is essential. For many, success in job performance leads to increased confidence and an inner conviction that they can cope with problems. Those who go into military service sometimes are affected by the "boredom" and become convinced that education is important through their own experience, not just because parents or teachers say it is. Others in this situation gain considerable confidence from finding that they can survive and compete successfully in the "real" world. Some will have married, which has a "settling" effect and underlines mature responsibilities. Marriage also may have resolved some of the doubts and conflicts in the area of heterosexual relationships, making for less inner turmoil. Another important feeling often noted is an increased sense of independence and emancipation from family control which results from the individual's living on his own and supporting himself during the time away from college. Many in this particular study group had, in addition to these more conventional experiences, undergone psychiatric treatment, which seemed frequently to be very important in the elimination of symptoms of anxiety and depression through the resolution of identity problems and by enabling changes in relationships with family and peers.

What then can be said in more theoretical terms about the leaving and return of a student? After considering the cases involved in the study, it was tempting to divide the group into those who had rather clear-cut psychopathology and those whose problems might be more accurately described as "developmental" or proceeding from immaturity.

Clinically, there are methods of distinguishing the two, although the sharpness of such distinctions may be less clear than one might anticipate. The first group will be more likely to have diagnoses in the psychotic, psychoneurotic, or severe personality disorder categories; the second, either "adjustment reaction of adolescence," or milder forms of the psychoneurotic diagnoses, such as anxiety or depressive reaction. Obviously individuals in either group may show traits from the other, and descriptively the distinction may be quite confusing because of the wide range of symptomatology that may occur in either group. In the first group, the range may include symptomatology from mild anxiety to acute psychosis, and in the second group the process may be variously described as anxiety, rebelliousness, apathy, identity diffusion, lack of commitment, vocational indecision, immaturity, lack of motivation, and plain laziness.

If, however, one could accurately distinguish these two groups, the recommendations on leaving and criteria for readmission would probably be clearer. For the first group one would recommend strongly the undertaking of psychotherapy and discourage any of the pursuits, such as military service or travel, which would interfere with this recommendation. In the readmission interview one would look for specific signs of improvement in adjustment to situations similar to college and be more inclined to utilize psychological testing as a means of plumbing the below-surface stability and the intactness of intellectual functioning, The length of time away from college would probably be of less importance than an evaluation of the state of ego functioning. With the second group, therapy would be less important and recommending a variety of "maturing" experiences while away would seem appropriate, whether or not they were directly related to the problem of academic progress. The time away from school should be longer rather than shorter, and a minimum of a year might be enforced. On the theory that poor academic performance is on occasion a means of protest against family "values," every effort should be made to evaluate family pressure to return and the degree of rebellion remaining, if this seemed to have been prominent initially. Clarity of goals, immediate or distant, would probably be important also.

In summary, a study of readmission after psychiatric medical leave was attempted in order to clarify the role of the psychiatrist in evaluating the returning student. In the process it became apparent that no study could be done without considering some factors affecting the initial decision to leave. The relevant theoretical considerations touch on problems of diagnosis, the concept of motivation, and the process of development during late adolescence. The study revealed that developing distinct criteria for readmission after psychiatric medical leave is difficult, for none of the variables studied distinguished between success and failure on return, with the exception of the number of terms to go—the fewer, the greater the chance of graduation. It also revealed, however, that the percentage of those graduating after return from psychiatric leave was over 65 percent, and only slightly lower than the percentage of those graduating after dropping out for all reasons.

The psychiatric evaluation interview turned out to be a "clearance" interview in most cases. The only applicants refused clearance were those who were on or over the borderline of psychosis. In a few instances, however, return was deferred because the student seemed unready or because he was beneficially involved in psychotherapy and an interruption was judged to be undesirable. The psychiatric evaluation interview has probably three major uses: (1) the fact that a readmission interview is required may cause more careful application for readmission and perhaps acts as an unseen selection process; (2) the psychiatrist with the help of psychological testing may be in a particularly advantageous position to assess borderline psychotic applicants who might well break down again rapidly under the stress of college; and (3) it serves as an opportunity for the applicant to discuss with a presumably neutral person his real feelings about return. In fact, if there is one particular lesson suggested, it is that ideally the psychiatric evaluation interview should be a discussion aimed at deciding whether it makes sense for the individual to return at the given time rather than a strictly judgmental procedure. Although it is necessary at times to invoke the authoritarian aspect of the situation, skillful interviewing can frequently minimize such occasions, and even a "refusal to clear" can be in a certain sense a joint and constructive decision.

Inasmuch as the study was initially undertaken to clarify the role of the psychiatrist in evaluating returning students, the focus has been on aspects of this problem. In closing, however, it seems important to note a rather different fact that emerged from the study: namely, that over two-thirds of those students who returned after dropping out because of emotional problems were able to graduate. This certainly is impressive evidence that a diagnosed emotional problem—even a relatively severe one—is no automatic bar to recovery and eventual success in college. It remains, of course, to construct a study in which information is gathered about the students who drop out for emotional reasons and do not apply for readmission. Although no figures are currently available at Yale, it is felt that the number is relatively small. Another and perhaps more difficult study would attempt to ascertain how many of those who drop out for apparently non-emotional reasons actually have hidden emotional problems precipitating the withdrawal. If feasible, this would provide an additional dimension of information about the role of emotional difficulties in preventing clearly talented and able individuals from completing their basic education.

# CHAPTER 7

## ADAPTATION, EDUCATION, AND EMOTIONAL GROWTH

BENSON R. SNYDER, M.D.

A PLANT, IN order to survive, undergoes specific modification which fits it more perfectly for existence under the particular conditions of its environment. Exposed to a northern climate, the sap system of the leaf moves back into the stem and the leaf becomes a needle. In this way the plant adjusts. This is Webster's definition of adaptation. The plant that is unable to shift its chemistry when confronted with drastic environmental change is lost. From an ecological perspective, however, the plant's presence also alters its environment, diminishing its harshness, or at least the $CO_2$ content of its atmosphere.

In the context of a recent conversation about scientific education, a physicist spoke of the altered circumstances of optical engineers. A lens of any complexity was until recently the product of months of trial-and-error calculations. The computer now makes such a computation in minutes. The optical engineer, having achieved accuracy through extended periods of tedium and hard work, finds this experience suddenly irrelevant to the task at hand. His education and his life have prepared him well for what has now become obsolete. As with plants, the educational environment may for some students extend the range of adaptive patterns, while for others it may freeze the student in one stance. This is the dilemma and the danger that we face.

In the process of achieving mastery of a human task, the cognitive and adaptive styles of an individual may become so fixed that his ability to cope with altered circumstances becomes limited. Obsolescence may then be one price that is paid for a parochial success in the mastery of adolescent tasks. The student may maintain a high grade-point average by closing off all activity and feeling which he considers extraneous to the task at hand. Such a student, by putting blinders on and judging commitment and interest by their instrumental use in achieving high grades, runs significant risk of growing up unable to cope with more than a narrow and probably stressful range of stimuli.

Does the educational institution ask this of the student for him to be successful? Does what the institution asks run counter to the developmental task of adolescence? While doing well in school, is the student still able to develop, for example, the achievement of intimacy, successful sublimation of instinctual drives, a range of adaptive mechanisms appropriate to a variety of stimuli? What are the long-term consequences of immediate mastery in adolescence?

This chapter will examine various aspects of the relationship among adaptation, education, and emotional growth. Much that I will discuss bears directly on education's influence on adaptation. It is drawn from a current study of the adaptive mechanisms of late adolescents in a particular institution. We have gone far enough to have reasonably informed hunches about education's effect on emotional growth.

Educational institutions can be viewed as special environments in which one group deliberately intends to alter another group, in part by setting explicit and implicit tasks, pressures, and satisfactions to which the second group must adapt. The members of this second group will use various strategies in coping with the environmental demands—some may schedule their time to the minute; others may work hard only when the pressure is on and thus move from academic crisis to academic crisis; still others may play the academic game by ear. Judgments on whether a particular strategy is good or bad, sick or healthy, depend on one's position and perspective with respect to the hoped-for outcome for the student.

Should our yardstick for measuring the strategies of immediate mastery be emotional growth, we will come up with quite different judgments than if our yardstick be adjustment—"niceness of fit" to specific social demands.

The aims of an educational enterprise do not necessarily include emotional growth. For instance, a vocational school is almost exclusively concerned with developing technical skills. The educational environment may have a significant effect or almost no effect on the student's emotional growth. This may occur irrespective of or in spite of institutional intent. The institution may limit emotional growth or foster it by virtue of the adaptive mechanisms its structure favors. The consequences, in terms of emotional growth, of the student's adaptation to his educational environment is the central theme of this chapter.

Before discussing our research and the questions which it raises for both psychoanalysts and educators, I will contrast two very different academic cultures. Consider the possibilities for self-definition, for cognitive style, for adaptive modes implicitly sanctioned in these separate schools. Consider the student strategies employed for academic and social survival. Pay special attention to the different images of man in these two academic cultures. Consider what it would mean to be suddenly transplanted from a school preparing students for an introspective understanding of their world, to the technical institution preparing its students for an instrumental mastery of their environment.

One is a woman's college with gently rolling lawns and well-pruned trees. The buildings are American Gothic, the faculty and administration tend to use the biological image of the plant to describe their students, members of the college community informally describe their tasks as the cultivation of their students by supplying them with the proper nutrients to promote firm, straight intellectual and emotional growth, as though their function were similar to the gardener's. Introspection, as a means to a fuller self-realization, is shared by both students and faculty. The liberal arts curriculum, with its emphasis on "Know thyself," is an institutionalized expression of this concern. For example, individual motivation and individual ethics are carefully examined in courses in literature, history, and philosophy. Another trend runs parallel to this. Students and faculty are polite, anger is contained, aggression is seldom directed outward, but rather in upon the self. The student confronted with an academic problem will almost always look at herself, asking what is wrong within. The fact that she shares the college's image of the plant, with its implied ethic of the bad seed, subtly reinforces this response.

Most students in this academic environment are preparing themselves for a future role as mother, and accept the current social definition of woman's role. There is some irony in the fact that some faculty at this particular institution depreciate women and defensively exaggerate the intellect's importance. This was exemplified by the gifted student who felt obliged to hide her delight in intellectual competence. She was afraid that it would interfere with her forming a close, lasting relationship with a man and was strongly supported in this notion by two women faculty members.

Many students in such an institution feel that their personal worth, their self-esteem, in part derives from knowing the culture and serving as its carrier, providing both a biological and social continuity. The student's time sense also bears some similarity to the concept of time in an agricultural society. It is extended and associated with the continuity of tradition and with the expected recurrence of patterns over time. A relatively small number of students, often with some estrangement from their peers, move across the boundary into science. By and large, these science majors are impatient with the above notions, being far more preoccupied with today than tomorrow or yesterday, and intent on manipulating and understanding immediate and palpable reality. All this is obviously a gross oversimplification, but there is enough truth in it to make the caricature intelligible.

In contrast to this, the university specializing in science and technology is laid out in geometric patterns with large, utilitarian, Roman-like temples alternating with small, square patches of lawn, which are rapidly being encroached on by the ever-expanding parking lots. The imagery of the machine rather than the plant is used when the faculty and the administration talk about their students. Students refer themselves to the Dean or to the psychiatrist for a tune-up, a retool, to add gas, to get the carburetor adjusted—these are phrases that are heard as students describe their need for help when faced with difficulty.

While there are obvious differences between the theoretical physicist and the civil engineer, they do share common notions of cause and effect, and a predilection for operational definitions, which they find congenial. This is in contrast to the more Platonic tradition-oriented definition of reality characteristic of the liberal arts college, with its emphasis on an inner ordering of one's perception of the world. Both faculty and student at the technological university ask, "How well does something work?"—many adding, "Why does it work?" The philosophy of the gardener has been replaced by the perspective of the scientist. The aims, aspirations, and the means for achieving them are different in these two cultures. This results in a different socially sanctioned basis for self-esteem in each environment. The necessary and sufficient conditions for feeling pleased with oneself vary, creating a shift in the areas of primary concern for the developing adolescent.

The imagery of the machine may allow at times for a frank and honest self-appraisal without contamination by a crushing sense of personal failure, by a turning of aggression in upon the self. It may, however, also lead to an unproductive search for an external cause of a difficulty that arises from some internal source. If difficulties arise for the student at the university, he characteristically first looks outside of himself to find what is wrong. Problems are more often externalized or projected; thus the professor is making unreasonable demands or the courses are too hard, or the exam is too tricky, or the unknown in the chemistry lab is contaminated. Anger is expressed. There is of course politeness and regard for social decency, but when one compares the pranks of the students in this university with those in the woman's liberal arts college, there is a degree of sophistication and imaginativeness, and certainly aggression, expressed by the university students which far exceeds that found in the latter. It is possible that this may be a sexual difference, though not all the variance is related to gender. The point is that there are different sanctions for the modes of expression of aggression, different strategies for mastering the several tasks of each environment. The range of successful adaptive patterns in each of these schools may significantly influence the change in level of libidinal development, the shift in ego ideal—in sum, the opportunities for emotional growth.

For the past two years, a small group of us have been involved in a study of the adaptation of students to MIT. Professor John Rule of MIT, and other MIT consultants: Professor John Seeley of Brandeis University, Professor Martin Trow of Berkeley, Dr. Merton Kahne of McLean Hospital and Dr. Dorothy Huntington of Beth Israel Hospital, are the senior colleagues in this work. It has been supported by the Grant Foundation for roughly a four-year period. We have been concerned with describing the nature of the interaction between the institution and its students, and making explicit some of the social and psychological consequences of the interaction for both the student and the Institute. Among the specific questions with which the research has been concerned are (1) What are the cognitive styles, the perspectives, and the values that are characteristic of a given scientific discipline, and what, if any, impact do these have on the students in those disciplines? (2) Are there modal adaptive patterns for students in achieving commitment to and/or mastery of a given field? Do the patterns of adaptation vary by field? (3) Does the institutional structure in effect limit the range of adaptive life-styles which can be successful in it? Are those limits necessary or unnecessary? Productive or unproductive, for some or all?

In the study, a random stratified sample of 67 sophomores was requested to come in for two interviews—54 responded, and 45 returned for a third interview during the spring of their junior year. The final round of interviews is planned during this, their senior year. These partially structured interviews were designed to provide data for at least preliminary answers to the preceding questions. The findings from these interviews are being correlated with a related study of the movement through MIT of the entire class from which the sample was drawn.

One of the fundamental tasks for the research has been to attempt a description of the average expectable environment at a given institution for different groups of students. This has been attempted in several ways. The students have been grouped by their major field of concentration as well as by various personality characteristics—for example, clustering of defenses, and quality and nature of object relationship. Their successes, survival, and failure, as measured by institutional criteria, have then been noted over time. We have been concerned with the extent to which (1) the structure of the Institute, (2) the division of courses, and (3) the social and psychological laws which govern the individuals within this Institution determine, define, or limit the possibilities for adaptation. As a psychoanalyst I have been concerned with how the structure of this particular society influences both the elaboration of instinctual drives and, even more, the development of the ego in late adolescence. The primary query here concerns the extent to which the structure of a particular society determines the forms of action or of behavior having the greatest adaptive chance of survival. Essentially we are asking how the individual can express his uniqueness and still survive in this specific environment. What does he have to give up or alter in drive expression, in restriction of pleasure, or flight from pain in order to achieve even a temporary equilibrium with his surroundings?

Taking our lead from Hartmann, we have been inquiring into the extent to which a given line of development is determined by a particular average stimulation from this environment. Can ego development be deflected or altered by environmental influence? This is not simply a question of magnitude of change, but of direction of change. We are looking for those factors in the external situation that are most salient for ego development.

A number of students are able to describe their reactions to their common environment, while they react consistently to a different and private environment to which their reality sense is attached. In the study of adaptation, one must avoid taking as evidence of adaptation the adjustment to this public common environment alone. One must have a clear picture of the private world that the student senses as real. For example, "All teachers are dangerous," "All women are evil," would be examples of the felt formulations that might well be acknowledged by the student to be unrealistic, but which nevertheless serve as the basis for his actions. Educators commonly have access to the public environment, psychoanalysts to the private. In order to understand adaptation—and, beyond that, to assess emotional growth—they must compare their notes on the same phenomena.

In the evaluation of adaptation, we have attempted to determine the amount of stress experienced by a student, the degree of support which he felt he received from specific elements within his environment, the degree of support he received from internal adaptive maneuvers, from the use of certain specific defenses, and the degree to which situational factors affected crucial conflict areas. We have focused on the opportunity for growth, for expansion of relevant choices, for autonomy and success in a given environment. At the very least we are gathering descriptive detail about the variety of situations in which the ego's reaction to environmental pressures may affect its functioning and its development.

Observing the movement of students through an institution over time will help us to understand the interaction between the student and the institution and the factors that influence their adaptation. The choice points and patterns of movement that characterize the students as they move through MIT have been worked out. We have plotted the course-to-course movement, as well as shifts in major areas of concentration and grade level and living groups of an entire class, through four years at the Institute. ("Courses" at MIT correspond to departments or major fields of concentration at other universities and colleges.) Demographic, sociological, and psychological variables have been examined, using analysis of variance and correlation matrices, as well as transitional probabilities, to determine which of these variables characterize students taking specific paths through the institution. The data come from our pilot study of the class of 1963, and the major study of the class of 1965.

The class of 1963 had been given the Minnesota Multiphasic Personality Inventory and the Myers-Briggs Type Indicator during the first week of their freshman year as part of another study which kindly supplied us with the scores. The classes of 1965 and 1966, the population for our research, were given the Omnibus Personality Inventory (developed at the Center for the Study of Higher Education at Berkeley) in the first week of their freshman year.

We noted, first, three patterns of growth among the courses (or fields) at MIT. The first group, with a heavy concentration from the Engineering School, retained most of the students who started in it. The small loss from transfer, disqualification, and withdrawal was matched by transfers from other courses. The total population of students in these courses remained relatively constant over the period of study. The second group, with largest representation from the School of Science, lost a large proportion of its original population (roughly one-third to one-half) during the sophomore and junior years, by transfer to other courses or by withdrawal or disqualification from MIT. The third group began with a small population, of whom roughly a third left, but these courses underwent rapid and very considerable growth as large numbers of students transferred into them.

We note that the probability of survival is not uniform in all courses, and that it is in part a function of the grading system, the demands of the curriculum, and the adaptive characteristics of the students. Let me illustrate this with several examples. The ability to delay gratification, as measured by the Omnibus Personality Inventory, was positively correlated with high grades. Students who were low on Impulse Expression did much better in their grades than students who scored high on this scale. Further, students with high scores on scales that attempted to measure originality and creativity left some courses in much greater numbers than left certain other courses.

We are dealing with data about the students, but we are on the verge of drawing inferences about the nature of the academic climate by considering who survived, who prospered, and who failed. These are rough measures of adaptation to a particular environment.

Let us take one scale on one test administered to the class as freshmen, which showed significant differences between students who stayed in a particular course for four years and those who were disqualified or withdrew from that course. I will summarize the items which the person scoring low on the Sensing-Intuition scale of this test, the Myers-Briggs Type Indicator, responds to. This will put you in a better position to judge for yourselves what aspects of personality may be at issue in the successful adaptation to these separate courses.

The sensing person would admire the conventional, the inconspicuous man of common sense, rather than the original, conspicuous man of vision. He would prefer teaching facts to theory and adjusts to facts as they are. He prefers to be seen as a practical and conservative man rather than the man who is ingenious and always coming up with new ideas. The intuitive person is described as the converse of this: original, unconventional, with an interest in theory.

Course A in engineering demands much theoretical knowledge which then must be applied to concrete problems in the design of "hardware." This course falls in the first group—a stable pattern with the few transfers in balancing those leaving. (Of the students who left MIT from this course, 70 percent withdrew, 30 percent were disqualified.) The students who stayed in this course to graduation had a *significantly* lower mean score on the Intuition scale than those who left by withdrawal or disqualification from MIT. (SN mean score for stayers, 55.7; for withdrawals, 68.4; significant at the .001 level.)

Course B, though in science, was also concerned with applications of theoretical knowledge of structural relations. This course has the same general movement characteristics as the preceding one, though the proportion of students moving in and moving out was greater than in Course A. (Of the students who left MIT from this course, 30 percent withdrew, 70 percent were disqualified.) Obviously the probability of academic dismissal is greater than in Course A. The students staying in Course B for their entire MIT career also had significantly lower mean scores on the Intuition scale than those leaving by disqualification (the majority of those leaving) and withdrawal. (SN mean score for stayers, 57.0; for withdrawals, 69.8; significant at the .01 level.)

Science Course C is highly theoretical, without necessary application to the material world. This course is characteristic of the second group—high input, higher outgo—with some drop in over-all number of students in the course from sophomore to senior years. Half of those leaving MIT from this course were disqualified, half withdrew. Students staying in the course had a significantly *higher* mean score on the Intuition scale than those disqualified or withdrawing. (SN mean score for stayers, 62.2; for withdrawals, 56.2; significance level, .05.)

These differences in means represent signal, not noise. Specifically, two courses lose students that score higher on intuitive ability than those that stay, while a third course loses students who score lower on this capacity than the stayers. All three courses put a high premium on this characteristic.

It is possible that the intuitive, original, unconventional student has less chance for success in Course A or B unless he can effect some temporary strategic shift in his cognitive horizon and adaptive patterns.

One of our important findings from the work to date is that data on psychopathology appear to have considerably less power to predict future patterns of adjustment than do variables relating to ego strength. Our efforts are directed toward explaining how the student manages to master, or by what means he integrates his experience, rather than pursuing the fate of a neurotic conflict *per se*.

While we have been looking for those mechanisms associated with the development of disturbance, this has not been our primary focus. In some respects this differs from the characteristic psychoanalytic approach to the study of adaptation, with its emphasis on describing those conflicts which the ego must solve—i.e., conflicts with the id, with the superego or with the external world. Significant differences may emerge when ego operations are evaluated in terms of their impact on the individual's orientation to reality, rather than in terms of his role in the management of conflict. Specifically we have been concerned with how differences in specific defenses influence the individual's ability to cope with both his adaptation to his environment and his conflicts. We are also considering how intellectual development, the level of energy available to the individual, also affects the ability to cope. There is an extensive psychoanalytic literature which deals with the problem of adaptation and the processes involved in adaptation in relation to internal conflict. Following the lead of Anna Freud, Hartmann, Erikson, and others, we are attempting to describe these ego processes in relation to their role in allowing the individual some mastery of specific aspects of his reality. The programmatic and research consequences of these different perspectives are not the same. An emphasis on conflict as the basis for adaptation directs our attention toward therapeutic intervention. The emphasis on adaptive mastery relatively independent of conflict directs our attention toward the nature of the interaction between the student and the college. The research has been addressed toward clarifying our concept of both conflict and achievement in normal growth and adaptation in the average expectable environment, and ultimately its effect on development.

In our research we have dealt with the relationship between education and adaptation by defining the tasks which the Institute sets for its students. We have gone on to consider how the setting of such tasks imposes conditions to which the late adolescent ego must adapt. The study of which students follow which paths through MIT will be correlated with our knowledge of the task or hurdle system for each path. We are in the process of describing the variety of ego defenses and adaptive and coping mechanisms used by the students for successful mastery of given tasks. We hope in time to be in a position to explore the impact on ego development in late adolescence of a given task system as a function of an educational system. First let us consider tasks that are common to all college students, later taking up several tasks that may be specific for MIT.

A high-school student's pattern for achieving and maintaining self-esteem is subject to dramatic challenge following his move to college. An institution of higher learning calls upon discrete and different psychological functions of its students, by virtue of the overt and latent tasks it sets before them. A student must complete assignments, write papers, pass examinations. He must organize his time and decide between work and the pursuit of pleasure. Should work give pleasure, the student has quite an edge on his classmates at most elite universities. Beyond this he must cope with a number of implicit, unspecified tasks imposed by the social and academic structure of the university. There are many unstated personal tasks that derive from the student's altered circumstances away from home, from his position in late adolescence. He must master new concepts in mathematics, reevaluate his Newtonian view of matter, reassess in varying degrees his philosophy, politics, and religion. He must learn to read cues from dress and manners that tell him where he stands with his fellow students. The personal tempo of his life is subject, at least at MIT, to major revisions. There are deadlines to be met and little opportunity for reflection or repose. The implicit task is the development of inner control over impulse, the extended delay of gratification. Students must learn to neglect selectively at least some of the work assigned. This is especially difficult for undergraduates who, in their high-school experience, could easily do far more than had been assigned. Their image of themselves is frequently shaken by finding limits to their competence. Without deliberate intent to do so, the institution requires an intense dedication to purposefulness, to making the right decision, to maintaining at least the appearance of totally excluding all tribally unsanctioned, non-goal-oriented activities.

The tasks confronting the ego of the student in late adolescence may also involve profound shifts in the conscious and unconscious conditions which he sets for maintaining his self-esteem. This becomes particularly relevant when one considers the actual conditions of the environment and the consequences of these conditions for ego change in late adolescence. The student is taken up with making short-term and long-term choices about his courses and his career. He is shifting his allegiance from a prior to a present ego ideal. He is developing competences which will in time permit the aspired-for reality to become a present one.

In an effort to make these issues more explicit, let me conjecture a central social task for the freshman at MIT which is latent, unstated, non-obvious, and taken by the student to be inherent in this system. The task, in simple words, is to know the world in rational and conscious terms. That which can be manipulated in man's environment is to be reduced to concepts and/or formulae which permit at minimum the illusion and at maximum the fact of mastery of the environment. Let me conjecture that the major thrust of the MIT freshman curriculum is toward making the world comprehensible in some operational sense.

Let us take several students and briefly consider how they perceived these tasks and how they went about attempting to integrate them into their late adolescent egos. And, in addition, let us speculate on how the process may have affected their pattern for maintaining their self-esteem. The narratives which follow represent a condensed summary of the data on these students. These are not patients' histories, but those of students selected from the random, stratified sample of our study.

Smith did well in high school without the expenditure of effort. At MIT he had his first experience at failing quizzes, of not understanding immediately and easily all that went on in his classes. From his account of his childhood it appears that in his early years he had a conviction that he could not influence his parents' relationship to him. His image of father bordered on that of a super-father who could only be influenced by magic. His father's, indeed the entire family's ethos, did not allow for acknowledgment of failure or personal distress. In Smith's adolescence his family had been faced with an economic crisis which the family first denied and then "explained" by referring to magical and fateful forces.

Football and other strenuous high-school pursuits were replaced in this young man's scheme of things during mid-adolescence by his increasing concern with developing a potent, unbeatable intellect. There is much suggestive information in the interview that supports the inference that he identified with the aggressor, saw himself defensively as a super-boy. His anxiety about his weakness, his terror of defeat and thus of his impotence, break through a counter-phobic defense at several points. For example, he recalls going into an exam in his freshman year at MIT and observing the fright among his classmates. He was surprised when, after half an hour, he froze, his memory failed, and he flunked this particular exam.

Science and engineering seemed to serve as this student's special bridge to his super-brand of masculinity. His encounter with MIT had taken on for him the qualities of a magical initiation rite. He explained his almost total failure in the second year as memory failure and reacted by putting his books under his pillow. In many ways he was trying to use his scientific education as a form of magic to strengthen his mind. All the while he was defending against the anti-magic bias in the content of his courses. He obviously did not find confirmation for his belief that such propitiation could produce good grades.

This young man apparently had considerable latent ability, but his cognitive processes were caught up in a pervasive neurotic bind. Thinking, learning, and grade-getting all assumed a special defensive significance which crippled his ability to see the tasks. He had to manipulate his environment and in his desperate effort to maintain his self-esteem relied on propitiation. The first-year task, reducing the environment to knowable parameters, dealt a central blow to his defensive stance.

The second student, Jones, having done very well, decided while still a sophomore in an elite high school that MIT was his first choice for college. He considered high grades a result of hard work, but added that they should be achieved without becoming a grind. His A's in high school have continued through three years at MIT. By making sure that all his work is done beforehand, "so nothing can creep up on me," he is able to protect himself from failure. It is evident that he can concentrate and apply his energy with singular effectiveness. First impressions are important to him, and it is important for him to make a good impression on others. The reassurance from the feedback of the good impression he has made helps him to carry himself farther in the face of anxiety. "It is dangerous if you start off a course too low," not because of intellectual difficulty, but because one may get discouraged. He related his only academic difficulties, which were minor and restricted to the humanities, to their being more personal than the science courses. In terms of the task of selective negligence, it is noteworthy that he actually read every word in his humanities assignments—Thucydides, Plato, Aristophanes—in the first four weeks.

Jones did not like being proved wrong or being outdistanced in the classroom or in sports. He gave up a sport because he could not gain sufficient weight to achieve the position he desired, and moved to another activity where everyone "has the same equipment."

His interest in engineering dates back to early adolescence. On one level it appears to be associated with his need to know, to master, to get ahead. He associates engineering with powerful equipment that is "streamlined; it is a wide-open field, pioneering, offering opportunity for originality." He is most interested in the applied areas of his field. In this regard he notes that accidents arise from the fuels in current use. He wants to work in this line and develop better fuels. He is aware that it will be three years before he can get his first assignment directly related to his interest.

Jones does feel some threat from the indulgent life of the delinquents, from those students who "play around" at MIT at the expense of their studies. He appears to defend against his fear of letting up and falling into this group by his adherence to a rigid schedule. It is interesting that a reason he gave for not dating was to avoid being tied down to any fixed responsibility.

Jones is fascinated with practical engineering, with space and distance. There was little evidence of introspection throughout the interview protocol. At minimum, introspective thinking does not appear to be usual for Jones. He pushes problems and concerns away from himself and is constantly trying to understand how the institution will react, how his friends will react, how a professor will react, not how he finds himself feeling or reacting. From data in the interview, it appears that distance, space between people is perceived as safety. Whether or not closeness is necessarily associated with friction and fighting, it is impossible to say. His personal life style prepared him well for learning "the facts" of environmental mastery.

What evidence of maturation or of growth do we see in Jones? In his sixth term he was still problem-oriented, concerned with mastery, with what was necessary to "get ahead." His self-esteem continued to be based on mastery and control of aggressive impulses. The institution challenged him in his third year by putting him more on his own. Working out a schedule and living by it was no longer, by itself, sufficient conscious motivation. In his junior year, he spoke of being shaken temporarily by the fear that he had lost his inner system of order and control. His major adaptive mechanism involved real or fantasied action, muscular or cognitive mastery. The childhood ideals, the parents or their substitutes, are typically seen during this period in a new and harsher light. The ideals are redefined and the integration of the new ego ideals painfully and as a rule slowly worked through.

Jones may be a modern Icarus. He appears to be rationalizing his aspirations, not working through any lasting alterations in his aims. As a junior he spoke of giving up the notion of going on immediately after graduation for a Ph.D. in favor of a job. Though he described this as a temporary postponement, there was much evidence that he didn't really believe this himself. He continued to push as hard as he could to get as far as he could, but strikingly took the minimum number of chances. He assumed only known risks where he could carefully calculate his odds. He picked little puddles to be the big frog in, did (for example) much organizational work which led to limited acclaim which he then inflated. To paraphrase, he appeared determined to get as high as he could, and his means to this end were calculation of the odds and control of the impulses and, if possible, of the environment. He chose the alternatives which he calculated would offer him the most favorable odds.

This young man was not shaken by his experience in school until the third year and then only briefly in the face of a less structured, more open-ended series of assignments in his classes. He associated to this experience with annoyance, and at this point in the interview went on to describe his change in plans, the job in favor of the Ph.D.

Finally, a brief reference to Thomas. He was a straight A science major, with a structure bearing some similarity to that of Jones. In contrast to Jones, Thomas expressed an increasing gratification from the use of his intellect as a means for mastery of problems in science. At the same time, he expressed a concern that his intellect should not set him apart from close relationships with his classmates or from women. He handled the de-idealization by coming closer to his father—skiing with him, for example—even while he felt some gulf between their relevant worlds. As a freshman Thomas had been involved in a seminar which was a "most exciting experience." He developed "a feeling and attitude about research." This came from seeing both the tedium of getting equipment to work and putting little bits of information together to begin to understand "what was happening physically in a crystal." He got a great deal from his "relationship with the professor." "He was not just putting on a demonstration and occasionally made mistakes." This contact altered his view of science and his image of himself. In his junior year Thomas used laughter and thoughtful introspection to handle "what may be a temporary disaffection with science" He was seriously debating a move into medical research after graduation. As he moved through school there was less denial, less externalization, and an increased gratification from interpersonal relationships, less reliance on grades for maintaining his self-esteem. This experience in the freshman year was crucial in the constructive working through of his de-idealization. The educational environment played an important role in challenging his earlier view of himself and was a positive experience.

These three examples suggest that this—and, I suspect, all—educational institutions intervene haphazardly.

Several hypotheses are suggested by these and other data. First, the mechanisms which students employ will have crucial consequences for the extent to which and the way in which they interact with their environment. Let me be specific. Externalization is an ego mechanism by which an inner state is managed so that a constant dialogue develops between the student and his environment. He continues to be relatively open to alterations in his aspirations and in his basis for self-esteem. Projection or denial, as seen in Smith and to some extent in Jones, may lead to an angry covert or overt withdrawal from interaction with the environment.

The energy demands on the adolescent ego are maximum. There are many situations, and colleges are high among these, where energy is expended in the face of gross demands from the environment for cognitive developments or for developing new relationships to replace old ones. With these case vignettes in mind, and reminding you of the comparison of two academic environments which began this chapter, let us look at the possible effect the college environment can have on the student's self-esteem.

The college environment changes the basis for its students' self-esteem by challenging the equilibrium between the student's self-image and his ego ideal, by attacks on his self-esteem. A common resolution occurs with the student's integration of new ego ideals and alteration of his image of himself. The environmental demands on the self-esteem system may be diminished by the student's excitement in mastery, in stretching himself, as Thomas reports. The crucial issue is whether the environment provides means for achieving a new and altered equilibrium in the self-esteem system. An educational environment, by its task organization, can significantly affect the opportunities for the student to reevaluate his self-esteem. It is in this area that education can influence the major changes occurring in late adolescence. Consider a situation where learning occurs without stress to be the basis for self-esteem, as appeared to be the situation with Jones. He learned much with high competence in the face of an inferred, devalued self-image, without apparent change in ego structure or in self-esteem. His immediate reality confirmed his judgment about his competences—i.e., he got A's from his instructors. The institution may never intend to challenge its students' self-esteem or self-image, and to this extent limits their opportunities for change and growth. The institution, without intent or knowledge, may play into an infantile, archaic set of aspirations without providing challenge and alternatives to the student's basis for his self-esteem.

Smith, Jones, and Thomas perceived the world in different terms and coped with what they saw in very different ways. It is necessary for us to be clear about the portion of the college environment available to each student and, having determined this, to understand how he then copes with what he has perceived and experienced. The student reaction to a major threat to his self-esteem may be a drop in his available energy for active coping with the threat. Subjectively he will feel powerless to achieve his aspirations. Feelings of helplessness will be triggered in each instance by a set of circumstances which are related to the perceived inability to obtain either his aspirations or gratify his predominant emotional and physical appetites. Frustration or blocking in the means allowed by the environment for achieving crucial individual ends produces in the ego either a state of helplessness, a defensive stance, or a significant realignment of means and ends.

The first two students described here were not involved in an educational experience, but in a kind of vocational training at best. Smith was unable to change because of prior difficulties and a particular adaptive mechanism that effectively cut him off from interaction with the environment. Jones, primarily because of his structure and his adaptive mechanism, sought and found confirmation of what he thought of himself. This reduced his chances for change. Thomas underwent significant changes in his basis for self-esteem, his cognitive horizons, his life goals. The formulation which is suggested by the statistical data in the early part of this chapter and the cases which have been reviewed is that education, by virtue of the adaptive demands which it places on its students, will affect their emotional growth. In this context, education is concerned with providing means and altering aspirations and appetites by intervention in the self-esteem system. We must focus on the relationship of that system to the actual conditions of the environment in order to evaluate the consequences for emotional growth in late adolescence.

A further crucial, though controversial, issue remains. Our model of the self-esteem system may not take sufficient account of the student's developing sense of competence of effectiveness. The college experience may expand, for instance, the opportunities for mastery, for adaptive choice, and in some measure free the student from his reliance on a previously rigidly held defensive position, regardless of his sources of self-esteem.

The social and psychological environment defines and limits the possibilities for adaptation. Certain forms of behavior will have the greatest adaptive chance. Whether they consist of compliance or creativity is at minimum a separate issue. Our project and the work reviewed is an inquiry into the extent to which a given line of development may be determined by a particular average, expectable, stimulation from a given environment. Two central questions concern us—one primarily addressed to behavioral scientists, the other to educators. What data does the behavioral scientist have or need to have in order to infer the action or behavioral consequences of change in ego function? What data does an educator have or need to have from which to draw inferences about an educational institution's impact on its students' development and emotional growth?

# CHAPTER 8

# THE COLLEGE DROPOUT IN CLINICAL PERSPECTIVE

LOUIS E. REIK, M.D.

SINCE 1954, THE MENTAL health service at Princeton University has had the opportunity of gathering a great many impressions about the attitudes and issues involved in dropping out of college. In that year, the administration favorably received a proposal that undergraduates withdrawing for any reason be routinely offered a withdrawal health check by the psychiatrist, or by some other member of the health services staff in the event that an occasional student objected to seeing a psychiatrist. The check was not to be put on a compulsory basis, nor was it to imply that the various members of the administrative and health staffs assume the dropout is necessarily mentally ill, though inevitably there have been those who misinterpret the procedure in this fashion. Rather, it aims primarily at providing an opportunity for those dropouts aware of psychological or health difficulties to review their progress, with the idea of discussing what steps they might take during the interval away from college to solve their problems. In other words, it was not designed as an investigative statistical study, which would require that the procedure be made compulsory for all dropouts. More especially, it looks for those who seem to need to undertake the therapeutic encounter rather than toward generalizations about dropouts as a group.

Nevertheless, even such a loosely structured project, with no more than about a third of the dropouts participating, has provided considerable clinical data about the attitudes toward withdrawal from college and the issues involved. Indeed, the fact that it attempts to keep the focus primarily on the clinical approach and consequently on the general welfare of the individual instead of solely on academic or research considerations has advantages, not the least of which is to facilitate spontaneous and frank interchange about non-academic as well as academic aspects of the dropout's life.

What such a project accomplishes cannot be adequately summarized in terms of precise details and statistics. Its chief value is the opportunity it provides dropouts to discuss what for most of them is a momentous event. Knowing that "dropout" has come to be "a bad word in the popular press and the American home town," as Ford and Urban remark, the students themselves are in general far from taking a casual attitude about it. There are, of course, rare exceptions, like the boy who in matter-of-fact fashion summed up his reason for withdrawing: "My father dropped out to go into the family business, and now I've decided to do the same thing." On the contrary, even though they may expect relief by escaping academic pressures that they regard as boring or intolerable, students are not prone to see dropping out as an unmixed blessing. Some express regrets over giving up extracurricular pursuits they enjoyed and leaving their friends. Many voice misgivings about the whole new set of problems and anxieties that withdrawal brings in its wake: what to do next, what are the present and future implications of withdrawing, how can it be viewed in a constructive spirit when it is felt as a defeat.

Perhaps, the most poignant are the problems of that sizable group of dropouts who, having demonstrated ability to obtain grades that are not only satisfactory but in some cases excellent, find themselves alienated from their work because for the first time in their lives they are faced with a discrepancy between what they begin to realize they can hope to achieve and the dazzling expectations they held in the past. Having been able with the help of parents and teachers to maintain the illusion of superiority in earlier years, they are peculiarly vulnerable as they are confronted increasingly by the necessity for independent accomplishment and by the impersonality of the great world, which is less interested in them as individuals than in what they can contribute to the common good.

The dilemma of many dropouts can be best expressed in terms of the age-old conflict between what the world expects from the individual and what the individual expects from life and the world. It is only natural that, coming recently from the comparative shelter of home and school, the college student, barely out of adolescence, often remains unable to reconcile the expectations of society with the desire to assert the primacy of the self. Unable to come to grips with the paradox that he who would save his life must first lose it in something that transcends the self, the dropout's focus is apt to be on questions that have perplexed mankind since the world began, such as what *he* is, what *his* happiness demands, and what goals *he* should have—in short, questions concerning the purpose of his existence and his unique identity. He is apt, therefore, to be powerfully drawn to writings on identity problems, like the senior dropout who wanted more than anything else to talk over his problems with Erik Erikson, whose book *Young man Luther* he was carrying with him. This elusive quest for selfhood, which normally proceeds in a somewhat disturbing but orderly fashion during adolescence as a prelude to adulthood, finds open expression in gifted dropouts. It is as though the very gifts themselves, by placing heavy demands on the self for maximal utilization, invite the frustrations and dangers that Roy Schafer discusses in his important and illuminating chapter in this volume on "Talent as Danger."

In addition to the intricacies of self-realization, the college dropout also is faced with the dawning discovery that the impersonal world, apart from family, friends, and a few vaguely sympathetic teachers, attaches no real importance to perpetuating childish tendencies toward egocentricity and self-aggrandizement, which, in fact, it regards as obnoxious in adult life. Where these tendencies nevertheless remain strong, frustration evokes correspondingly strong reactions and attitudes. They include loss of self-esteem and other symptoms of a depressive kind, feelings of confusion or panic, passive rebellion as typically shown by beatniks and the bored, a bitter attitude toward a world that is felt to ignore the individual and to bless only conforming faceless men in gray flannel suits, or else an attitude of lofty disdain for the demands of those who refuse to pay homage to His Majesty's Ego. But fortunately experience teaches that, thanks to the resiliency of youth, reactions and attitudes of this kind are neither alarming in degree nor of prolonged duration in the majority of dropouts. Yet they are commonly seen among students in this category.

The clinical encounter with dropouts also inevitably provides a wealth of data from parents, professors, deans, and others about their own attitudes toward withdrawal. One of the most important lessons to learn from these attitudes of the older generation, colored as they often are more by emotional bias than by a desire to understand the dropout's point of view, concerns what Edgar Levenson describes as their *transactional* nature. The more the older generation tries blindly to impose its own arbitrary demands on the younger, the greater the likelihood that each will be isolated from the other. A cold war of this kind obviously not only runs counter to the educational process but also delays the maturing process as well. The only value of such a war is to protect the contenders from the disheartening realization that both sides may be in the wrong.

A more common attitude toward the would-be dropout than the hostile one which brands him as an aberrant individual is a display of oversolicitude regarding withdrawal based on considerations other than the student's educational welfare. There are many variations on this familiar theme. The student is exhorted to think of his ailing mother or his doting father. He is reminded that a diploma in modern society has become a symbol of status and success. He is offered a vacation in Europe or a new car if he will only remain in college. These maneuvers, which might be called education by seduction or bribery, undoubtedly sometimes prevent dropping out in the physical sense but seem of dubious value as substitutes for a genuine desire to be actively engaged in the educational process.

The emotional attitudes of the older generation arise so naturally and spontaneously and are felt by their holders to be so entirely justifiable that they are rarely examined from the standpoint of whether they will merely make matters worse for the dropout. Nor does the latter, particularly if he happens to have shown signs of talent in the past, realize the effects of his withdrawal on his elders—on dedicated college personnel, for example, who in pursuit of excellence have private misgivings about how well they are actually carrying out their mission, and who thus experience in a different context the same kind of anxieties that parents often have. It is, therefore, not surprising that in both the dropout and his elders the act of withdrawal is apt to evoke subtle and deeply rooted emotional reactions that prevent a calm, dispassionate view.

The clinical attitude, on the other hand, with its emphasis on neutrality and objectivity, seeks to minimize the distortions and non-rational consequences of emotionalism by making the emotional attitudes themselves the central objects of study. Seeing the disadvantages as well as the advantages of a narrow, dedicated partisanship, whether on the part of the professor for his subject, or of parents for the student, or of a student for personal matters apart from a social context, the clinician has the difficult and sometimes superhuman task of studying in a spirit of detachment the emotional excesses that often accompany dropping out. Needless to say, the scientific attitude which he tries to approximate, and which demands constant awareness of the sources of error in the observer as well as in the observed, is relatively simple in the world of impersonal objects as compared with the sphere of human emotion. The latter, as Freud has shown, is governed by laws far different from those of everyday logic, allowing contradictory feelings to coexist simultaneously, without reference to intellectual considerations, reverting automatically under stress to habits developed in childhood in spite of subsequent knowledge and experience, and demanding expression of desire and impulse regardless of consequences. Ordinarily, the intellect likes to imagine, nevertheless, that these laws have been superseded by a higher and more civilized code, and this is, indeed, the case for the most part in ordinary life. But in times of crisis, such as many dropouts experience, the primitive power of the emotions is apt to reassert itself.

It follows, then, that the clinician's strategy of focusing on the emotions and the degree to which they do or do not make sense in terms of the dropout's welfare is better accomplished when he remains relatively impersonal. But just as many students complain vigorously about what they call the paternalistic attitude of college authorities, many others complain about those authorities' aloofness and impersonality—advocating, for example, better student-faculty relationships. Wanting recognition and encouragement from their elders, needing guidance and advice because they are excessively fearful of making mistakes and wrong decisions, they are prone to interpret the impersonal attitude as unfriendly or even hostile. It is of little avail to point out that the feats of science and much of the world's most helpful business are carried out in a spirit of impersonality, which, though it can exclude a great deal of intercourse at the personal level, is yet neither cruel nor necessarily opposed to individualism. In dealing with the individual dropout, who, after all, like late adolescents in general, is often an incredible mixture of sophistication and childishness, self-sufficiency and dependency, altruism and egocentricity, the clinician must be alert to the emotional basis for misinterpretations of this kind. Where they occur, there is apt to be the more important misinterpretation that the impersonality or neutrality of the world in general toward the individual is also hostile and therefore to be feared. Above all, it is necessary to recognize that the problems of the dropout in late adolescence are special problems, coming as they do at an important time of transition between childhood and maturity, between the protected past and the dangerous future, between submission to benevolent despotism in early years and the opportunities for self-assertion in the later ones. Being special problems, they require a special approach that sees them against the background of this period of life, as William Harvey brings out in his chapter on the treatment of depression in late adolescence.

Parents and society in general deplore dropping out as a sign of failure or waste of talent. One father wrote, after learning that his freshman son was planning to drop out: "We are in a state of mental shock. However, we did avoid hitting the panic button *and* the ceiling . . . for the boy did make a significant statement: 'Don't you think that I, too, am concerned about the mess I am in?' "

In addition to the emotional reactions and attitudes, dropping out raises many complex issues. Is it realistic to expect all students to commit themselves for four years to a given college before they have come to terms with other aspects of life? Must they all be expected to develop smoothly and uniformly in these other spheres, including the social and sexual, which, though seemingly far removed from intellectual development, yet often present problems that interfere with concentrating on education? Does the prejudice against dropping out tend to stifle rather than promote the unfolding of original talent by arbitrarily limiting opportunities for free experiment?

When questions like these are raised, we soon come to another issue that is also heavily freighted with emotion. It has to do with the eternal dilemma of the older generation in its dealings with the younger: whether to be more or less permissive. In the minds of the older generation, especially in the United States, permissiveness is becoming increasingly synonymous with softness and overpermissiveness, which, in turn, evokes the specter of unrestrained license. The younger generation, on the other hand, confuses authority with tyranny. The student who described his father as "blindly authoritarian" offers a typical example of how the younger generation tends to view the older. What appears to be really at issue here is the desire of the young to emancipate themselves from the domination of their elders—a desire that even the latter concedes need not always be unhealthy or in the service of evil.

Yet along with this desire for freedom, there is the equally important desire for help and support from the powers that be, a desire that youth characteristically neither readily acknowledges nor consciously accepts. Nevertheless, the need for support and approval serves constantly to check open rebellion against the older generation, once the latter has drawn clear lines between what it will tolerate and what it forbids. Exaggerated demands for more liberty, or behavior that superficially seems defiant, often turn out to be trial balloons designed not particularly to defy those in authority but rather to test where they stand. Naturally enough, tests of this kind become more frequent and troublesome when the rulers themselves are unwise, vacillating, or inconsistent. But sending up these trial balloons is probably inherent in the maturing process, since it provides the young with concrete information about the attitudes of their seniors that sometimes they could not obtain in any other way. A junior, for example, expressed a fervent desire to drop out. He feared, however, that his father, a devoted alumnus and a man for whom he had much respect, would oppose it, and so was reluctant to discuss it with him. Once he had been persuaded to do so, he became convinced that his father tolerated the idea in good spirit, and after returning reported he no longer wanted to withdraw, going on to graduate.

The issue remains whether the student who proposes to withdraw is capable of making a wise choice, particularly when his reasons seem unclear or colored by emotion. William James once remarked on the difficulty one mind has in comprehending the inner "scenery" of another. The difficulty is compounded by Freud's discovery of an unconscious side that prevents a man from always knowing clearly even what is in his own mind. For example, an underclassman on his own initiative comes to the clinician complaining of inability to force himself to do the work in one particular course he dislikes, but which is a prerequisite for later work that he wants to undertake. In his other courses, he is doing well and no other problems emerge except for a long-standing problem with what he calls self-discipline—probably in reaction, he thinks, against parents whom he characterized as strict. The questions such a case raises are many, particularly when it soon appears likely that he has no gift for introspection, fundamentally accepts himself as he is, and looks for solutions by expecting the environment to modify its demands, which, indeed, seems to have been his experience with his "strict" parents.

Cases of this kind suggest a further problem, especially prominent in our time, concerning the degree to which universities should be arbitrary in their demands on students in order to accomplish their mission to educate. At issue is the tough-minded tradition, with its emphasis on submission to the discipline imposed by recognized masters, on the one hand, and, on the other, the discovery Freud made in his early attempts to reeducate patients by arbitrary suggestions, on the assumption that they would carry all the weight of his prestige as a physician in authority-oriented old Vienna. He found that his suggestions not only were sometimes completely ignored or merely temporarily effective, but were also, in retrospect, premature or faulty in the light of subsequent data that put matters in an entirely different light and so led to some previously unexpected dénouement.

At issue, too, in view of the incredible variability and complexity of an individual's assets and liabilities, is the question of whether the college shall consider its duty done when, with the aid of statistical investigation, it can satisfy itself that its curriculum and policies accomplish the greatest good for the greatest number. The facts of life, even for an institution, are such that there must be some degree of individual treatment for the non-conforming minority, not only as a matter of principle when important decisions such as withdrawal have to be made, but also for the familiar if somewhat disconcerting practical reasons that colleges must deal with sons of distinguished alumni, or that an occasional dropout manages to achieve eminence without benefit of a degree from his ex-alma mater.

Important and clear-cut as they seem at first glance, the more such issues are examined, the more elusive they become. Obviously, the individual approach of the clinician, like the statistical one, has its own limitations as well as its strength. The dropout phenomenon seems to cut across the neat categories of the clinician, whose experience is that it transcends the narrower question of mental illness or mental health. Likewise, it refuses to observe the sociologist's dichotomy of society and the individual, since both are in constant interaction, thanks to man's inability to remain static and to his irresistible desire to change his environment just as the latter seeks to change him.

The case of a gifted freshman who was valedictorian in his high school illustrates some of the complex issues involved and the futility of oversimplification. Midway in his first semester, finding he did more poorly than he had expected on some tests, he proposed dropping out of an all-male college in order to transfer to a coeducational one. He came on his own initiative to the clinician and revealed doubts about his sexual orientation, having for several years felt physically attracted to both sexes. But he also expressed doubt whether, after all, he might by dropping out be exaggerating his fears or be seeking an easy escape from difficulties that all young men encounter in growing up. Initially, he seemed to want to place the clinician in the flattering category of an omniscient being whose opinion he said he was prepared to accept without question, since he felt he had no way of estimating the extent or importance of his problem. He was encouraged, however, to arrive at a decision by the more difficult route of exploring the problem further and judging on the basis of what he experienced. During the remainder of his freshman year, seemingly by accident, he gravitated toward those with a similar problem, found himself more repelled than attracted by them, and finally reached a firm decision to transfer to a small coeducational college that in the meantime he had visited on several occasions.

Where problems can be so highly complex as to strain the limits of knowledge and wisdom, the clinical approach has, of course, great value. Its success, however, depends on time-consuming attempts to understand individual students by inquiring into the context and background from which their problems emerge. Most of all, it depends on the principle that students themselves must actively participate in the unpleasant task of searching for the inner weaknesses, often obscure and always defended, that gave birth to their difficulties. Once these are clearly identified and experienced, effective and rational ways of dealing with them can replace the formerly unavailing struggle against the more formidable fears generated by the unknown.

Particularly since World War II, the nation's colleges have encouraged more than ever before the clinical approach to student problems. Counseling and psychiatric services have become increasingly widespread and heavily patronized, and the end is not yet in sight. College teachers and administrators are relying more and more on special services of this kind. Frequently, in referring students to the clinician, they comment in self-disparaging fashion about being "just a layman when it comes to this sort of thing."

There are undoubted advantages in this development, which relegates the problems of individual students to the so-called "experts," for it allows teachers and administrators more freedom to concentrate on their own special fields. But the highly important question remains whether there are also significant disadvantages in regarding the intimate workings of the educational process in students as belonging more or less exclusively to the clinical field. One disadvantage is that students in need of academic assistance are apt to continue isolating themselves from those on whom they depend most for educational development, difficulties go unrecognized until they culminate in failure or dropping out, and students and faculty alike forfeit the mutual benefits that can come from freer interchange at the personal level.

It has often been noted that education and psychotherapy have much in common. Both meet with rather stubborn and unreasoning resistance in the individuals they are designed to help, though the resistance may be concealed or denied. And both inevitably encounter the problem of dropping out. On the other hand, they differ chiefly in the degree of importance attached to meeting the individual on his own grounds and to the recognition of the crucial role played in human development by gifts and limitations unique to the individual. The relentless pressures of mass education and a conforming society tend to obliterate consideration of these individual differences until they manifest themselves in the highly individualistic but abortive and unacceptable models of psychopathology.

It has long been axiomatic that early recognition of the sources of difficulty and stress can prevent an undesirable outcome. If educators aim to reduce the dropout rate and to improve college education in general, they will inevitably face the issue of gaining knowledge of student progress and difficulties not only from the official academic record but also from personal and firsthand contact with individual students themselves, before troubles have reached the crisis stage. The dropout problem is, of course, important and complex enough to call for a many-sided attack.

# CHAPTER 9

## SOME SOCIO-CULTURAL ISSUES IN THE ETIOLOGY AND TREATMENT OF COLLEGE DROPOUTS

EDGAR A. LEVENSON, M.D.

THE INCREASING efforts being expended to salvage the dropout attest that he is in a fair way of becoming the prodigal son of American education, whose return to the fold bringeth more joy than the predictable performance of ten Merit Scholars. In the parable of the prodigal son according to St. Luke, the good son (who is significantly the elder son) berates his father for showing more gratification at the return of the prodigal than at all his own years of dutiful service. The father responds, "Son, thou art ever with me, and all that I have is thine: but this thy brother was dead, and is alive again; and was lost, and is found." In the sense of the parable, that may be extended to mean "part of *me* was dead and is alive again." For the prodigal son, the dropout from filial responsibility, is recognized as having, in spite of his malfeasance, a more authentic and vital relationship to his father than the compliant, imitative son. He is, in an existential sense, the link to his father's unlived life.

Harry Stack Sullivan[1] called adolescence the period in which we are, perhaps for the last time, most truly human, for adulthood often presages a life of increasing restriction of spontaneity. Moreover, this attrition of potential is expected to occur painlessly; i.e., our popular concept of mental health requires a consistent and harmonious functioning. To quote Goodman, "Our scientists have become so accustomed to the highly organized and by-and-large smoothly running society that they have begun to think that 'social animal' means 'harmoniously belonging.' "[2] On the contrary, it may be said that the *sine*

[1] H. S. Sullivan, *Concepts of modern psychiatry*, Washington, D.C.: White Psychiatric Foundation, 1940.

[2] P. Goodman, *Growing up absurd*, New York: Random House, 1956, p. 10.

*qua non* of creativity is the ability to tolerate disorder. One can hear the Greek chorus of disgruntled parents, "Then from the evidence of my son's room, he should be a genius!" But, perhaps some variety of identity crisis with its concurrent disorganization and regression is necessary to the subsequent development of a productive life. Erik Erikson, from a somewhat different perspective, described this most clearly in his labeling of identity diffusion and conflict as the normal growth crisis of adolescence. Indeed, his book *Young man Luther* may well be read as a study of an ecclesiastic dropout whose explosive, regressive, even epileptic behavior portended an identity resolution that revolutionized European religious thought.[3]

I am suggesting that dropping out of college may be a psychosocial manifestation of just such an identity crisis, and may be viewed as an attempt by the student, however abortive or regressive, to find a way of life more meaningful and perhaps more honest than the milieu allows. Moreover, this rebellion constitutes a very considerable threat to his parents, peers, teachers and, last but not least, his psychotherapists, since his actions touch on their unresolved identity crises, their unlived lives. Everyone then hastens to label, isolate, and—most perfidious of all undercuttings—to "understand" the dropout; to do anything but acknowledge that he is a mirror held up to their own dissatisfactions and compromises. The psychotherapist, particularly, is much assisted in this undertaking by his "scientific" perspective, which endorses and dignifies this very pattern of isolation, description, and classification. So that whether we are for the dropout or against him, whether we talk of him as a "severe aggressive character disorder" or a "poorly motivated student" or even "the student with enough courage to buck the system," we are all playing the same game. He is *there* and we (thank God) are *here*! Only by investigating the dropout's past life experience, by perceiving his behavior as, to quote Erikson, "an adaptive if immature reaching out for the mutual verification by which the ego lives," and by recognizing how his experience impinges on our lives, can we arrive at a workable confrontation.[4]

[3] E. Erikson, *Young man Luther,* New York: Norton, 1958.

[4] E. Erikson, *Insight and responsibility,* New York: Norton, 1964, p. 120.

No doubt, this position may seem overly romantic, a somewhat literary glorification of the dropout as a "hero *manqué*." There is no doubt that these students are immature, infantile, lazy, arrogant, uninformed, opinionated, often in retreat from severe obsessive-compulsive or even schizophrenic trends. But that is not all they are. They are frequently very bright, challenging, and totally contemptuous of sham and flaccid solutions. It will be remembered that they have passed often quite rigorous selection procedures on applying to college. In our population, which we have described in greater detail elsewhere, their median I.Q. was 125, in spite of the presence of considerable gaps between performance and verbal scores.[5] Potential was considerably higher. Of our total group, less than 10 percent had college boards of under 500, and over one-third had boards of over 600. Twenty percent were still doing superior work when they quit school and another 20 percent maintained average grades in spite of very spotty effort. We have also noted that after separation from college they may show impressive efficiency and application in jobs unrelated to scholastic achievement and to which they do not have to make a lifetime commitment. For example, one student, a listless young man, showed great energy and application in a summer job working with underprivileged youngsters. Several others have worked for newspapers with enthusiasm and sufficient aggressiveness to assure their advancement. A number of students, initially bland and somewhat vacuous, have discovered a variety of talents and rediscovered the pleasures of commitment to work. I am certainly not implying that the psychopathology of the dropout is unimportant or can be ignored in psychotherapy, but there is certainly some modicum of truth in the Orwellian dictum that "Sickness is health." It is crucial to acknowledge that the behavior of the dropout is not *only* illness, but rebellion, or at the very least a passive dissent, against the goals and expectations of his parents and his society; and, as such, he is at the same time an immense threat to the equanimity and a spur to the discontents of the

[5] E. Levenson and M. Kohn, "A demonstration clinic for college dropouts," *Journal of the American College Health Association*, 1964, 12, pp. 382-391.

world around him. As Norman Mailer put it in another context, "Exceptional leverage upon the unconscious life in other people is the strength of the artist and the torment of the madman."[6]

It is evident that I am using the rubric "dropout" in a rather special sense; i.e., I am restricting it to those students whose intelligence, talents, and interests should lead one to expect adequate, if not exemplary, college performance. There are undoubtedly many students who leave college because of situational maladjustments, lack of funds, disinterest, or ineptitude. There are also some students whose emotional disturbance is in no way related to being in college; i.e., their difficulties would have overwhelmed them regardless of the environmental setting. But I would agree with Farnsworth that over half of the total dropout population have a significant emotional component in their difficulties.[7]

These observations are based on a clinical project undertaken at the William Alanson White Institute of Psychiatry, Psychoanalysis, and Psychology.[8] My comments on the dropouts and their families is a compendium of the experiences of the many people contributing to this project: therapists, psychologists, social workers, and ethnologists. Over a two-year period we received 133 applicants. Of these, 89 received a complete screening, and an additional 31 were partly screened. Thirty-eight patients were carried in psychotherapy for periods ranging up to two years. We also interviewed the parents and maintained a parent psychotherapy group and two student psychotherapy groups as ancillary sources of data. These students were referred to us by the colleges and, of course, there was a natural selection process, since not all dropouts at any one college were referred to us, and not all who were referred came

[6] N. Mailer, *The presidential papers*, New York: Putnam, 1960, p. 88.

[7] D. Farnsworth, "We're wasting brain power," *Journal of the National Educational Association*, 1959, 48, pp. 42-44.

[8] The work was supported by National Institute of Mental Health Grant No. MH-867 and was intended to demonstrate the feasibility of a community clinic for the investigation and treatment of college dropouts after their separation from the campus. We have described this group in clinical detail elsewhere: E. Levenson and M. Kohn, "A treatment facility for college dropouts," *Mental Hygiene*, 1965, 49, pp. 413-424.

or stayed through the screening procedure. Each student referred to us, unless grossly inappropriate or in need of immediate hospitalization, was offered a complete screening which consisted of (a) filling in an application, (b) an initial interview with the chief investigator, (c) an interview with our social worker, (d) a psychological battery of tests consisting of the WAIS, TAT, Selected Creativity Test (Getzel & Jackson), Rorschach, Human Figure Drawings, and Graphology. This material was then reviewed in a screening conference that included the screening participants and any of the therapists or other members of the staff who were interested in attending.

Acceptance for therapy depended upon two main criteria: (1) the extent to which we could estimate that the dropping out of school was causally connected with the college experience as an emotional crisis (i.e., not caused by a long-standing disinterest or difficulty which would have occurred at this time, in any other setting); (2) an assessment of the student's intelligence, originality, and genuine interest in learning. Diagnostic category and severity of pathology were, if possible, not weighed heavily and we rejected only a few students primarily because they were evidently too disturbed for treatment in an outpatient program. These are the vaguest possible selection criteria. Nevertheless, our two-year experience has demonstrated some very sharp differences between the groups selected and rejected for therapy. We have presented these findings in detail elsewhere, but, in general, it can be said here that the accepted group appears to be a much more rebellious and dissatisfied population, with other distinct differences in background and activity. Whether we intuitively selected the group most likely to respond to therapy or whether we simply selected the group we liked the most remains to be established.

From the onset, we planned to assess through systematic research procedures as many facets of the project as feasible. New research procedures were to be introduced as clinical insights arose and as time and personnel limitations permitted. Forms have been designed to record data systematically from the screening interviews and therapy and to collect additional information from colleges, patients, family, and therapists, particularly in areas where clinical hypotheses are evolving. To elaborate, at the conclusion of intake, the social worker fills in a form in which major aspects of the circumstances concerning the dropout, the patient's life situation after the dropout, clinical diagnosis, personal history, and family background are recorded. Each applicant for treatment fills in (a) a questionnaire on his previous school history and the nature of his parents' involvement with his school work; (b) a sentence completion test with items about the patient's attitude toward the past and the future, and his attitude toward work and the overcoming of obstacles; (c) an adaptation of Strodtbeck's V-scale to measure achievement striving; and (d) a self-attitude inventory designed by Goldberg, assessing the student's actual and ideal image of himself in various areas of his personality functioning. The parents of each of the patients in treatment have been asked to fill in a schedule which inquires in detail about their educational and occupational experiences and those of their parents, and another schedule which covers selected facets of the patients' developmental history. At the completion of treatment and/or at the end of one year of treatment, the patient's individual and group therapists fill in a specially devised assessment of change schedule. As in all other administrative details of the clinic (keeping appointments and being on time), both parents and students were remarkably cooperative in filling out this veritable mountain of forms.

These forms are, of course, subject to revision as our experience accumulates. The schedules were designed for later IBM processing which has much facilitated our exploring cross-correlations. In addition to the data forms, tape recordings have been kept of therapy sessions, group therapy projects, and all parent interviews. The parent interviews and parent group have been audited by an ethnologist. Our hope was to discover consistencies for the group of patients as a whole and to elucidate intra-group patterns. The absence of comparison groups (i.e., disturbed students who do not drop out, the less gifted dropouts who do not come to the attention of the clinic facility, normally achieving students, etc.) makes it difficult to assess the relative significance of our findings. We hope to rectify these gaps with comparison studies. There are a number of intra-group differences observable in the developmental histories of our male and female patients, time and nature of dropout, and family experience which we hope to present, in more detail, at some later date. Our data do strongly suggest that there are a number of typical patterns of family constellation which may be specifically related to college performance.

A total of 71 colleges were contacted and informed of our service. Sixty-two colleges responded favorably. A few of the smaller colleges were interested in us as an information exchange service, but were reluctant to send us students because of the "clinic" connotation and because they found it preferable to make arrangements with private psychotherapists of their own choosing. As one might expect, some of the more enthusiastic responses came from those colleges with a large number of relatively low-income students for whom private psychotherapy would not be ordinarily available, and from those where the income of the student was not the issue but where the college maintained a large, well-organized psychiatric service which was interested in collaborating with us. In order to place our population in the total group of dropouts from the participating colleges, we submitted questionnaires inquiring about various aspects of the student attrition rate. Our experience was in line with that reported by Summerskill, in that on-campus psychiatric services in many colleges are quite minimal and there is very little systematic attempt to collect data on dropouts.

Two-thirds of the students were from New York City schools and the balance from outside the greater New York area. Most of them (86 percent) were in coeducational colleges. Slightly over half the patients were living with their parents during their stay in college, but since their dropout two-thirds of the patients have been living with their parents. This high incidence of stay-at-home students certainly constitutes a major bias in our population. It would suggest a relatively immature or dependent population; or, at best, one relatively bound to their families. At the same time, homesickness or separation anxiety can be eliminated as a likely causal factor in motivating these dropouts. However, contrary to the implications of this residence data, at the time they came to the attention of the clinic, almost 70 percent of the patients were working either full-time or part-time. Also, approximately one-fourth of the patients were completely self-supporting financially. It is of interest, too, that, on the average, a period of only three months elapsed between separation from college and application to the clinic—half of the students applying within a month. These latter findings would imply a relatively high level of purposefulness.

The educational and socio-cultural background of the parents covers a wide range and is a remarkably representative cross-section. Of the total group, 39 percent of the fathers had only a high school education or less, 38 percent had some college education or graduated from college, and 23 percent had done some graduate work or completed graduate school. Mothers of the group are somewhat less well educated than the fathers. The occupational range in the sample is also quite wide. A quarter of the fathers were skilled, semi-skilled, or unskilled workers (the unskilled constituted only 2 percent). Eight percent were in clerical occupations, 14 percent owned small businesses, and 50 percent were professional workers or lesser professionals. Of the total group, approximately 28 percent of the fathers were self-employed. Most of the patients came from relatively small families. Patients coming from families in which they were the only child or in which there were one or two siblings comprised 82 percent of the sample. A relatively high percentage of the patients were the oldest child. These differences were approximately the same for male and female patients.

It is evident that because of our selection procedures and lack of adequate control groups, we cannot, strictly speaking, extrapolate from our group to the dropout population at large, or even the emotionally distressed dropout. Some of our most strikingly consistent findings may well be peculiar to our group, or even artifacts of our selection procedure. Nevertheless, although scientific discretion requires this apologia, we strongly suspect that many of our findings and hypotheses have considerably wider relevance.

To understand the dropout's behavior as a meaningful act

within his life context necessitates an examination of his family milieu. The following somewhat impressionistic profile of the dropout family was found to be present with very high consistency.

First, these parents demonstrate, even for this age of alienation, a rather remarkable degree of *unauthenticity* in their perception of themselves and of their relationship to their families. I use that graceless term "unauthenticity" advisedly, since I would emphasize that they are not simply dull or banal, but potentially able people disappointed in their use of their lives who are not quite honest enough to admit it. If they were really limited people with no yearnings beyond their immediate lives, or even terribly smug and self-satisfied, I believe they might make less trouble or, at least, another kind of trouble. But there is a faint air of despair about these parents, detectable in interviews with them and corroborated by details of their personal histories. In spite of their surface mien of absolute surety and self-confidence, they somehow marginally communicate this distress to their children. Their conscious devotion to order, duty, and hard work is staggering. We have never seen parents who on the whole worked so hard to be *good* parents, and yet they telegraph to their children an underlying note of discontent and rebellion. In this sense, the children might be said to be acting out, in their dropout behavior, the unconscious fantasies of the parents. We have indeed noted and described at length elsewhere how, when these students go off to college, a great deal of overt anxiety and depression may break out in the parents, particularly the fathers. The parents often make unconscious efforts to sabotage the student's school performance, offering veiled bribes if he drops out (a job in Daddy's firm, a new car) and, even before he leaves for school, furnishing excessive reassurance (e.g., he can "come home anytime"). If the dropout does return to school, after therapy, the parents often seem remarkably unelated and while his crisis mobilized their enthusiastic, if panicky, interest, his new-found scholastic competence may be met with apathy.

This terrible ambivalence on the part of the parents makes it vitally important that the child constantly reinforce the parents' self-esteem and reassure them that they are "good" parents. And, what is more reassuring in this day of scientific child-rearing than to have a "good" successful child? Consequently, the student is caught in a double bind: to wit, if he is really successful, really augurs a promising future, he is likely to stir up competitive anxiety in the parents who are busy deluding themselves about their lives of compromised respectable despair. Yet, if he fails, then perhaps they were not the good parents they must believe themselves to be. The inappropriate panic these parents often feel at any suggestion of failure in their children bears witness both to their marked ambivalence toward their child's scholastic success and to their marginal recognition that they are tacitly supporting the rebellion. It is of interest that the dropout caught in this network of mutually contradictory demands often sinks into an apathetic funk, almost a social catatonia; no action is acceptable, so he just doesn't move. He waits for the college to throw him out.

Historical data obtained from the parents and students support this description. In addition to the strong undercurrent of marital and vocational dissatisfaction in the parents' lives, it is of note that college often had a special significance for them. They were of college age at the time of the great depression, and a considerable number of them had to give up their schooling because of financial limitations. Some of them were older children (the Good Son of the parable) who interrupted their schooling to work to support the family while a preferred younger sibling was permitted to continue in school. Of course, this might be said to be true of many families, and if one looks hard enough, dissatisfactions can be found in anyone's life. For, as Scott Fitzgerald once said, "In America, sometimes nothing fails like success." But, the third ingredient —which is, I think, most specific—is that in *their* young adulthood, many of them—particularly the fathers—had shown a brief burst of open rebelliousness or lack of persistence in the work area. Sixty-eight percent of the fathers and 61 percent of the mothers had interrupted their education (not necessarily on the college level). Some had completed training in a particular area and then abruptly switched careers; e.g., received a degree in law and then never practiced. Many of them had briefly lived "bohemian" lives in the 1930's before settling into domesticity. Some had been active in early union agitation or left-wing political movements, again as a short-lived flare of protest. One-third of our group have histories of broken marriages, with a relatively high incidence of prolonged stalemated separations, sometimes lasting many years. When we grouped the following experiences—fathers' and mothers' severe disappointment in their careers, interruptions of schooling, openly expressed mental disorder, discontinuities of family experience (divorce, separation, or death of a parent), one or more of these factors was operative in over 80 percent of our population. In other words, in spite of their present conventionality and self-justification, they had, in their youth, rebelled or, if you prefer, acted out briefly.

In summary, these families consist of well-intentioned, hard-working people, conscientiously hewing to their prescribed social roles as "good parents." The mother tends to be the dominating parent, with the father playing a weak sibling role, fluctuating between seductive identification with his child and sporadic irascible, noisy, but not very effectual attempts to be the *pater familias*. The parents play their roles with great outer conviction, but a very prevalent sense, close to the surface, of despair and disenchantment. The student has a very complex homeostatic role in this family milieu, in maintaining the fiction of the "good life" and, at the same time, in affording the parents an outlet for their unconscious frustration.

The family profile is strikingly similar to Paul Goodman's description of the family of the "Beat Generation":

> Now it used to be said that middle-class parents frustrate the children more, to meet higher standards, but the frustration is acceptable because it leads to an improved status, esteemed by the children; the lower classes, on the contrary, are more permissive; nor would the discipline be accepted, because the father is disesteemed. What then is the effect, in the ranch houses, if the discipline is maintained, because the standard is high, but the status is disesteemed, first by the father himself, who talks cynically about it; then by the

mother, who does not respect it; then by growing children? *Is it possible to maintain and pass on a middle-class standard without belief in its productive and cultural mission?*

I wonder if we are not here describing the specific genesis of a Beat Generation: young men who (1) cannot break away from the father who has been good to them, but who (2) simply cannot affirm father's values; and (3) there are no other dominant social values to compensate.[9]

Although our project has collected no direct data in this area, we very strongly suspect that the college, *in loco parentis*,[10] often tends to recapitulate, in its transactions with the student, the same double-bind of intense surface righteousness and barely dissociated self-doubt and tacit support of the rebelliousness. There is a very considerable literature which deals with the inconsistencies, self-deceptions, and shortcomings of the educational system. But, on a more individual level, is it not possible that the college instructor, worried about tenure, told to "publish or perish," basking in the *ambiance* of ivy-covered halls and natural-shoulder suits and yet worried about his own standing within this establishment, might resent and, still, grudgingly admire the maverick dropout? Conversely, I suspect that students who play the role game and do not threaten their teachers are more likely to be sustained in college by their advisors and professors. To quote Katz and Sanford, "Nobody knows how many potential learners go out along with the unable and indifferent; nor do we know to what extent remaining in college is a matter of gamesmanship or capacity to adapt to conventional pressure."[11] Style of dress, haircomb, acne, or a well-turned knee may well be critical issues in the fate of the tottering student.

Psychiatric clinics operating on the campus are also, in essence, part of the establishment, and the self-image of the therapist or counselor is affected accordingly. What is the

[9] Goodman, *op.cit.*, pp. 122-123.

[10] *In loco parentis* has been aptly defined as "crazy like a parent." M. Freedman, *Chaos in our colleges*, New York: McVay, 1963, p. 203, quoting Elliot Cohen.

[11] J. Katz and N. Sanford, "Curriculum and theory of personality," in N. Sanford (ed.), *The American college*, New York: Wiley, 1962, p. 423.

status of the psychiatric unit? Is it in the basement of the gym building or in a magnificent new student health center? In some colleges, student mental health is an integral and respected service, but in others it may be barely tolerated by the college administration as a public relations nuisance. Moreover, what is the internal structure of the mental health service? Is the therapist a full-time university employee? Does he maintain an off-campus practice? Does he have affiliations with a group of more secular colleagues? I might add that similar questions could be asked of the therapist seeing the dropout off-campus. However, for all concerned with his college performance, his failure to *work* within the conventional, mutually validated structure of the culture is a highly loaded challenge. Virtually every authority encountered by the dropout on his way through the groves of academe is there by virtue of *his* ability to work very hard indeed, even though the motivation and intrinsic value of the work might not always bear too close scrutiny.

My thesis, then, has been (1) that the dropout can be treated as a special case of adolescent identity crisis; (2) that this crisis manifests such regressive and ineffectual behavior as to obscure the more positive searching aspects of the rebellion; (3) that the family experience and larger social milieu of the dropout predispose him to this particular course of action, or, if you will, "un-action"; and (4) that his failure to work touches on vestiges of all our own unresolved disenchantments, both neurotic and actual, and encourages us to isolate and stereotype him. What relevance does all this have for the psychotherapy of the dropout?

First, for the student, it facilitates his seeing himself in a fluid transaction with his environment, rather than simply as a difficult, cantankerous, or very lazy isolate causing his good, preeminently successful family and helpful advisors distress. The most devastating aspect of the adolescent identity crisis is a sense of terrible isolation and loss of connection, since the dropout is usually as puzzled by a failure to comprehend his behavior as are his parents. Let me give you a clinical example to illustrate the interplay between the parent's ambivalence and the child's behavior: this material was obtained, not from a dropout, but from a woman who was, quite incidentally, the mother of a dropout. Her son had been telling her, in response to her rather nagging inquiry, about an incident with his closest friend. The son apparently goes to a great deal of effort for his friend, doing errands for him and acting generally quite solicitously. The friend, whom the mother despises as an arrogant and exploitative person, puts himself out not at all, at least in the mother's frame of reference. Now, it is evident that these two young men have a considerable degree of intimacy. They are able to confide in each other, prefer each other's company and spend a great deal of time together. The son does not seem to mind that his friend is selfish and unreliable; the mother, who is generally a rather tolerant person, is amazed and disconcerted by what she recognizes to be an inappropriate degree of rage and contempt for her son's willingness to be a "sucker and a patsy." In response to her contempt, her son can only become morose and sullen. I suppose one could debate the relative merits of each position. Investigation of the mother's own relationships reveal that she is a woman with many extremely devoted friends. They profess, and often go to considerable lengths to demonstrate, great affection for her. She is, in turn, a most considerate person, tactful, kind, and willing to discomfort herself for her friends. It would certainly sound as though she had a rather solid platform for her disapproval of her son's way of relating. However, further detailed inquiry reveals that she has never, in her adult life, confided in another person. All her friends see is a wonderfully successful social persona, a mask. Moreover, she distrusts her friends. Although she is touched by their devotion, she cannot really believe it. Somehow it all seems slightly unreal. And, although she is very perceptive about her friends, she has never really confronted any of them with her reactions to them. There has never been a moment of truth. What she has developed is a Confucian network of carefully delineated social relationships, immensely supportive in a ritualistic social sense, but without real intimacy. One's friends, in this system, are accounted by the number of people who will come to one's funeral.

What is more, she is not far from knowing it and from

contacting her feelings of loneliness and isolation. Her son's ability to have a close relationship which transcends her *quid pro quo* style threatens to bring her into touch with her own dissociated longings. Although he may be struggling toward something more genuine than she has experienced, she must defend herself and her world by rage toward his "softness." There are, of course, alternate explanations for their exchange, but I think this illustrates the triad of characteristics I described before; that is, the self-righteous, sure parent, the rage toward the child for not performing according to Hoyle, and yet the barely masked recognition of personal failure.

For the psychotherapist, this perspective connotes a different mode of participation. As Erikson put it: "Young people in trouble are not fit for the couch: they want to face you, and they want you to face them, not as a facsimile of a parent, or wearing the mask of the professional helper, but as the kind of over-all individual a young person can live by, or will despair of. When suddenly confronted with such a conflicted young person the psychoanalyst may learn for the first time what facing a face, rather than facing a problem, really means."[12] If the therapist needs his patient's reassurance that he has found *The Way*, if he has not confronted his own doubts and longings, he will be frightened by the dropout and what he will defensively label as "acting out." If, on the other hand, the therapist can acknowledge that the patient is a real person having real impact on his life, then he can use his own anxiety to cue himself on a great deal transpiring in the therapy. Let me give a brief clinical example. In a group therapy project, one of the boys said to the therapist, "You may have more experience than I have, but I am much more talented than you." This was said with utter seriousness and conviction and resulted in the therapist's commenting to him and the therapy group on this boy's grandiosity, self-centeredness, and insensitivity to other people's rights. Later, in discussion with his colleagues, the therapist again focused on the boy's "narcissism," although it was evident to everyone that the therapist was irritated and rather shocked by the blatancy

12 Erikson, *Young man Luther*, p. 17.

and tactlessness of the patient's assertiveness. Now, in a characterological sense, he is no doubt an arrogant, self-centered, narcissistic person. But, he may well be more talented than the therapist. After all, that is one of the risks of working with patients.

It is also quite clear that the patient expected this reaction of anger, even though he professed not to understand why everyone reacts to him this way. If the therapist were not threatened by his patient's assertion of his superiority, perhaps he could have seriously considered the possibility that the patient really did have considerable talents, was in some way perhaps superior to the therapist, and then gone on to consider why the patient had not been able to utilize his potentialities. He might have considered the patient's boorishness as a defensive operation; i.e., by his offensiveness he guarantees the hostility of the authority, which then enables him to attribute his own lack of performance to a justified rebellion against the authority's aggressive disapproval. This variety of self-fulfilling prophecy is central psychodynamically to the dropout performance. It does not work if the therapist cannot be piqued. One might then argue that this is classic counter-transference —the inability of the therapist, because of his own neurosis, to tolerate the patient's aggression. But I would add that the patient's aggression is particularly effective because it is directed toward an area of psychosocial reality. The patient attacks the therapist's authenticity, his sense of value in his job, his own sense of creativity. Paradoxically, were the therapist really immune to this attack, he could not help the patient; his own complacency and lack of self-criticism would make any *entente* with the patient impossible. Therapy would degenerate into a coercion to normalcy. The good therapist can tolerate disorder, unclarity, ambivalence toward his own style of life and goals. It is his ability to live with anxiety, self-doubts, and uncertainties, *not* his sureness, which provides the dropout with a paradigm for successful living without self-deception. This approach would, at the very least, be novel for the patient and would afford him a corrective experience with an adult who is not frightened by the patient's drive or in flight from his own limitations. Why be so threatened by his arrogance? To know that existentially every choice, every decision, requires the relinquishing of alternate possibilities, and that the exigencies of life limit one's experience and potential, is no justification for our inflicting this middle-aged insight on the young. Expansiveness and even grandiosity may not be so terrible at twenty-one.

Although a brief psychotherapy, oriented toward giving the dropout some perspective on himself, the role he plays in his family and his college milieu, can be helpful for many students, more intensive insight-oriented psychotherapy may be necessary. In this case, the dropout must "work through" his problems in his relationship with the therapist; i.e., he recapitulates his neurotic dilemma in the therapy and through his corrective experience with the therapist develops new perspectives and new solutions. For example, it has often been noted that students, particularly in the first year of college, drop out because they experience aggressive competitiveness with other students as dangerous, even as a repetition of murderous oedipal impulses. It is possible, in a brief psychotherapy, to show the patient the psychodynamic correlates between aggressiveness and danger, even its historical development in his family experience. In a more psychoanalytically oriented therapy, he will "work through" in the transference his infantile fantasies about his destructiveness. Nevertheless, this remains benignly authoritative, the patient improving under the aegis of the therapist's assurance (tacit or open) that his difficulties stem from historically distorted perception of the present situation.

Although this perspective is, in a sense, both accurate and efficacious, I would consider it limited and in some cases actively deleterious. It is, after all, not inconceivable that the patient backs away from his competitive performance partly because it is not autonomous; it is not in the service of his own goals. He finds himself pursuing a scholastic course that has to do with gratifying his parents, not himself, and which promises in the long run a conventional success in which, as Goodman pointed out, no one really wholeheartedly believes. Failure may be the first autonomous act in the life of the student. If one asks dropouts, it is striking how clearly they experience that they were not committed to their work, or enjoying it. These same students will demonstrate quite remarkable aggression and assertiveness in jobs unrelated to parental goals.

Unfortunately one must break eggs to make this omelet. Students will not always return in a docile way to school. They may act out, experiment, move in unpredictable directions. But it is important that the psychotherapy be in the service of the patient, not of cultural homogeneity.

The successful treatment of the dropout becomes most feasible, then, when we stop "treating the dropout" and transfer our attention instead to the larger psychosocial field in which we all participate. The blatancy of the dropout's symptomatology should not divert us from the recognition that he is living through a developmental crisis; that, for many of these students, it would require much less energy and anguish simply to slide by with minimal grades. The commitment to failure may be a commitment to life—however lacking in awareness and ineptly implemented, an unwillingness to be trapped in the stereotyped "Good Son" role. This perspective offers, I believe, much hope for real change.

# CHAPTER 10

## TALENT AS DANGER: PSYCHOANALYTIC OBSERVATIONS ON ACADEMIC DIFFICULTY

ROY SCHAFER

IN THERAPEUTIC WORK with students we are used to thinking of their personal problems as interfering with the free exercise of their talents. Conflicts concerning sexual behavior, emancipation from parents, and relations with authority figures, to mention only a few common ones, occasion anxiety, low mood, apathy, rebelliousness, restlessness, insistent daydreams, and possibly symptoms. These all impair the student's ability to concentrate when and where he needs to. They lower his level of interest and his frustration tolerance. His talents may then lie fallow and his academic difficulties increase, sometimes alarmingly.

Although we are not oblivious to the fact that the student may view his talents as dangers, we are, I think, less used to considering this aspect of the problem in detail. Perhaps this is because we admire, envy, and idealize talent, and therefore see it simply as a blessing, as a source of pleasure, strength, and achievement. No doubt it can be that to a high degree. My topic, however, is talent as danger. It is a topic that includes but transcends that of the college dropout. It also includes but transcends the topic of so-called "underachievement," for close examination of the functioning of many students who appear to be living up to their expected level of academic achievement, students who may even achieve Phi Beta Kappa, Dean's List, and Cum Laude status or better, shows that they are at least uneasy with their talents and not always free to use them fully. These students are the secret underachievers and possibly even the secret dropouts. They make this clear in their therapy and we must ask what this is all about. The question may be put this way: What are the compelling subjective reasons to avoid using one's talents?

For the purpose of this discussion I shall restrict my remarks to intellectual talents. By intellectual talent, I mean superior cognitive aptitude and imagination in one or more fields of learning and inquiry. I shall not attempt a systematic analysis of the ingredients that go into talent, such as natural endowment, experience, and emotion. Any student who, on the basis of his intellectual qualifications, has been admitted to a college with exacting academic requirements may be considered talented. This is not, in my opinion, too liberal a use of the term "talent." And I shall assume that the talents of such a student have achieved the status of significant aspects of, and influences in, his personality.

Yet, however significant and influential in its own right, talent does not appear to remain altogether or permanently outside the sphere of influence of any of the major divisions of the personality defined by psychoanalysis—the id, the ego, the ego ideal, and the superego. While we must think of talent as an aspect of the adaptive ego, this does not mean that we exempt it from having or taking on instinctual, defensive, ideal, and moral connections. In fact, these connections appear in certain respects to spur on the development and utilization of talents, as when intellectual application brings love, blocks disruptive instinctual indulgence, leads toward fulfilling ideal self-conceptions, and constitutes an aspect of being proudly moral. In any of these connections, intellectual application is not just a matter of gaining mastery over particular subject matter, nor is it merely a matter of meeting external academic requirements. On the other hand, in any of these connections talent may become involved in conflict and the student may have to curtail or eliminate its application in order to spare himself intolerable anxiety and guilt.

In what follows I shall examine the types of conflicts or dangers involving the id, ego, ego ideal, and superego that are meant to be avoided by the blocking of talent. I shall attend to interpersonal as well as intrapsychic aspects of these problems. I shall be concerned with both the danger situations that talents may lead into and the danger situations into which otherwise relatively autonomous talents may be drawn to their detriment. As an addendum, I shall consider some special problems attaching to exceptional giftedness and achievement. In this chapter I can mention only some of the common psychoanalytic findings in these respects and can discuss them only in an incomplete and schematic manner.

First, the id: the extension of the sphere of influence of the id to the realm of talent leads to sexualization or aggressivization of the talent in question. That is to say, the exercise of the talent takes on some or all of the qualities of a sexual or aggressive act. One intelligent patient, for example, who finally reached the point of approaching an examination with adequate preparation and subjective confidence, experienced unmistakable physical sexual excitement with a genital focus as he began the exam; soon he was stricken with anxiety, developed an hysterical partial paralysis of his writing hand as well as subjective confusion, and could not complete answering the questions. Analysis revealed the presence of sexual fantasies accompanying and defining his feeling of intellectual competence. Another student could not complete a paper in which he was critical of two established authorities in the field under discussion; analysis showed that he fantasied these criticisms as violent, rebellious, and drastically punishable physical assaults.

If we accept a distinction between function and content, as has been proposed in psychoanalytic theory, either the function or the content may be sexualized or aggressivized. For example, the function of thinking in any form may be experienced as a dangerous aggression, as when insightful thinking is felt to constitute a hostile challenge to one's father, or specific contents of thought may be so experienced, as when wars, wounds, or weapons are felt to be taboo subjects. Or both function and content may be instinctualized, as in the sexualized instance of a student's feeling it to be bad enough to be curious about anything and especially so with regard to matters biological. The psychoanalyst will at one time or another encounter almost every ego function, and every talent, in a highly aggressivized or sexualized state, and thus as a party to conflict. He will observe too that these invasions by drives vary as to degree, and that it is beyond a certain point of intensity that the instinctualization becomes an interference. Lesser degrees may not matter or may add pleasurable feelings of excitement and release to the exercise of the functions. The turning point varies from one person to the next, from one function to the next, and from one set of circumstances to the next. All sorts of conditions may bring about sexualization and aggressivization and I shall not try to review them here.

It should be noted, however, that talents are not always blocked once they have become sexualized or aggressivized. Sometimes we observe that talent in action on a relatively primitive level: under the sway of striving for instinctual pleasure, its expression is limited to certain activities and contents that promise immediate gratification. Then its employment is too selective, too lacking in organization, too hasty, and too subject to fluctuations of emphasis to be a reliable and enriching enterprise. The use of the talent becomes almost the equivalent of a masturbation fantasy or part of a masturbation fantasy itself. For example, sadistically colored debate or daydream-like reading of biography, romances, or poetry of certain sorts may suffer this fate.

The action, rather than inactivation, of highly instinctualized talent is also sometimes observable in the setting of unusual creativeness. While not all truly creative work can be said to be id-dominated, the psychoanalytic study of creative persons shows that their achievements as well as their work blocks often involve at least transient regressions to instinctual modes, and with that to danger situations of an internal sort at least. We have no generally accepted and detailed formulation that explains why one person blocks under these conditions while another creates. In other terms, it is still far from clear what the difference is between a genius and a college dropout, though we must also keep in mind that these are not mutually exclusive categories: too many great men have been college dropouts. In any case, instinctualization of talents does not invariably lead to their inactivation.

The second sphere of influence to be considered is that of defense. It is, of course, defense or defensive inhibition that curtails the exercise of talent that has been sexualized or aggressivized. When the talent is no longer sufficiently differentiated subjectively from direct instinctual expression, its use may have to be suspended along with the invading impulse. My present point is not this one, however. It is that a talent may become loaded with defensive significance rather than instinctual significance. For example, following Anna Freud's description of the adolescent, his talents may become loaded with his defensive use of intellectualization and asceticism. Intellectualization and asceticism serve as major protections against the pubertal increase of the strength of instinctual drives. The student in this defensive stance will experience his talents in one crucial respect as the enemies of pleasure or gratification. He will see them as instruments of self-deprivation. Objectively, of course, it is not the talents but their employment that is in question, but this difference is often lost sight of by the involved student. We know that deprivation carried too far leads to overt or covert rebellions—the instinctual drives won't take no for an answer—so that, as so often happens, adolescent defenses are temporarily or enduringly overthrown to make way for instinctual outbursts. The adolescent becomes estranged from his security forces and wishes to be rid of them.

This estrangement comes about not only to appease drives, however. Another reason for it is that the adolescent is more or less alienated from the parental imagoes for whose sake and in whose manner he, to a significant extent, adopted his defenses to begin with. The defenses become no longer "his" but "theirs," and must be repudiated. If intellectual talent has served as a defense—and to some degree it inevitably will have served thus—it may have to be rejected in part or totally. While we, as citizens and educators, may value the talent and accomplishments of extremely disciplined college students, as psychologists (and perhaps as parents) we do wonder uneasily where the youthfulness of these students has gone and what the cost is to their total existence. I am not necessarily speaking of psychotherapy here, although we do often find the price paid in neurotic symptoms. Viewing the matter more generally, I am thinking of arrests in development in the spheres of sex and aggression and of the accompanying subjective ambivalence in the student toward his costly—because too defensive—talent.

In this part of my discussion I have been referring to wholesale employment of intellectualizing and ascetic defenses. The matter of maintaining self-discipline in pursuing studies that are not to one's liking, while not unrelated, is something else. Generally speaking, it falls under the heading of ego controls rather than emergency defenses.

Moving on now to the realm of ideals and to that suborganization of the personality called the ego ideal or ideal self, we encounter a new type of danger, or rather a set of two. One is the danger of an ego ideal set so high that no exercise of talent can meet its standards. Nothing is ever good enough. A grade of 90 is not 100, and a grade of 100 merely means that the exam was not hard enough or that the professor has been taken in. There is no achievement—only failure or degrees of failure. Under these conditions the vigor of striving toward goals can only diminish, and, perhaps more important, the pleasure in using one's talents, whatever the goal, is soured. Bearing in mind the distinction between function and content mentioned before, we distinguish sheer functional pleasure from pride in achievement. And in this grade- and score-oriented world, we must take care to remember functional pleasure—the joy of discovery, fascination, and the thrill of mastery. To protect himself against ideals that he has set too high, the student may not try to achieve; that way he may nurse the illusion that he has met his grandiose ideal or that he is capable of meeting it and is merely choosing not to do so.

The second danger with regard to ideals is this: recognizing and expressing one's ideals, even when they are not grandiose, may occasion fear of being laughed at or cut down to size by others, and may point to actions, such as competition, that seem dangerous. There is a dismal, shrunken security in keeping one's place or keeping one's aspirations in place, so there may be a specific intent to be a nobody, however painful that may be consciously. In this setting, inhibition of interest in and enthusiasm for applying one's talents can block the appearance of ideal self-conceptions, for nothing stimulates the flowering of dormant aspirations more than a touch of success.

Psychoanalytic investigation has revealed that in either case the disturbing ideal is not just out of reach or too daring, but sexualized or aggressivized in specific ways: to be "the best" or to be ambitious proves to mean to be the phallic superior of father and the usurper of his place, or the spiteful replacement through identification of the richly endowed but ungiving mother, or the destructive competitor of a sibling, and so forth.

Passing on now to the superego, considered here as the largely unconscious organization of childhood morality, we often observe that the exercise of talent has become a relentless moral imperative. In this case the subjective feeling is that, if you are not doing your best, you are being wicked, slothful, worthless and, more particularly, incestuous, destructive, greedy, dirty, or onanistic. Obviously, in speaking of the superego in this regard, I am distinguishing it from its offshoots—the mature conscience, moral code, and sense of responsibility that are attuned to reality. Also, numerous other forces of a non-moral nature participate in compelling one to be trying to do one's best always.

The primitive moral developments that constitute the superego have some of their roots in the connection made by parents between being a good and acceptable child on the one hand and a controlled, conscientious, and able little person on the other hand. The impetus to this equation comes not just from the environment, however, but also from the workings of the child's mind: in the child's fantasies, controlled, conscientious, and able activity is often an alternative to direct and dangerous instinctual expression; more than that, such activity often represents an undoing of or reparation for the overexcited and destructive aspects of his real or fantasied instinctual expressions.

What then if, as so often happens, the adolescent student attempts to revolt against his superego? I touched on this question before in connection with adolescent repudiation of defenses. Psychoanalysis has demonstrated that there is a crucial tie between the superego and the objects of infantile sexual and aggressive tendencies, especially the parents. This tie has fateful consequences. One such is this: in the course of his attempting to resolve the fresh problems of adolescence, including his beginning or further emancipation from his parents, the student may become violently ambivalent toward his deepest moral tendencies. Being good, which may include the productive use of his talents, may then become a danger because it is too closely tied to longings for and fears of these persons. In this respect, being outwardly bad may be for him a greater good. That is to say, in unconscious fantasy, being rebellious may be the only alternative to being too incestuous or homosexual or parasitic. Not that some persisting superego pressure may not still exact its toll of suffering, but that for him it is a lesser evil to be a delinquent student and a wastrel of talent. And at the same time the student will be expressing those destructive tendencies toward himself as well as others that normally are intensified in the course of adolescent development. Blocking of talent must be seen not only as a matter of inhibiting function; it is also a prime form of self-directed and other-directed destructiveness.

The combination of rebellious emancipation and destructiveness can only intensify the student's resistance to well-meant academic encouragement, exhortation, and discipline. The same may be said of any of the dangers touched on here.

Returning now to the ego, we may consider conflicts that develop within or around its adaptive functions. I shall refer specifically to the synthetic function of the ego, that function concerned with reconciling contradictory aims and contents and with coordinating or fusing diverse tendencies into the limited number of pursuits allowed by time, energy, and opportunity. I shall bypass the problems of directly synthesizing the demands of the id, superego, ego ideal, and defensive ego; some of these may be inferred from the preceding discussion and some will be implied in what follows, for the problems are not really that separable.

The first, most obvious problem of synthesis concerns the student's reluctance to commit himself chiefly to one line of endeavor and thereby neglect or close off attractive alternatives. When his talents lie in more or less unrelated fields, such as science and literature, he may have to sacrifice one talent to another. But each talent is a fragment of a way of life: it implies its own prospects of pleasure, achievement, and definition of self and community. It therefore is painful to choose between talents and to be reconciled to reducing one to a side interest, a hobby, or a forsaken future.

A second problem of synthesis is this: for many students the free exercise of intellectual talent creates the danger of enlightenment and, with enlightenment, choice. These become dangers because they involve the ego in contradictions or discontinuities. To appreciate this point we have only to think of the student bred to go into the family business but possessed of, and maybe possessed by, artistic or scientific talents: for him it may be a threatening matter to recognize, accept, and follow his personal bent inasmuch as it may involve him in ugly interpersonal and intrapersonal conflict. We are all familiar with some of the interpersonal problems: paternal and maybe maternal disappointment and anger, mutual recriminations and coldness, broken-off communication, and the student's rebellious disregard of studies or demoralized apathy; or, if the protest is repressed, anxiety, somatic symptoms, concentration difficulties, and the like.

What is often lost sight of in this type of situation is the presence of intrapersonal problems—the contradictions within the ego—for the student brought up this way will have internalized many of the expectations and demands of his environment. He will have adopted aims and values, and possibly may have even cultivated skills, in keeping with the pertinent identifications he has made. He will have made these identifications out of some mixture of functional pleasure, love, admiration, fear, and guilt. And so, when he comes finally to emancipate himself from his parents, whether loudly or silently, he will be at the same time torn inside himself.

It may be very difficult to bring this struggle out into the open. Often the student does not want to know anything about his internal acquiescence to his upbringing. He will insist that he is of one mind and his family is of another and that's all there is to it. How can he acknowledge even a little of his love and respect and fear when to do so would, as one patient expressed it, lead him to throw himself in tears into his parents' arms; when, in other words, to do so would flood him with old wishes to surrender himself to them? Determined autonomy and desperate arrogance may be his only protections, and yet he will never be at ease in this stance because ultimately he is locked in struggle with himself.

All this may result if the enlightenment and the possibility of choice are allowed to develop. Some students never let things get to this point: using an array of conscious and unconscious techniques, they ignore their talents, derogate their intellectual opportunities, ward off the spirit of college life, and sometimes blandly and sometimes morosely, apathetically, or drunkenly follow what is for them fundamentally a dismal path to their baccalaureate degree. In so doing, they are often following their parents' examples rather than their preachings. This point can hardly be overemphasized: superficially the details of the student's disrupted functioning may little resemble the outward features of his parents' lives, but the analyst repeatedly encounters powerful unconscious identifications with deep-seated, past and present parental patterns of failure, self-abasement, and corruption. That parents consciously encourage or pressure their children to be better persons than they themselves are is not decisive in this respect: identifications speak louder than words. And so, while many a professor may scorn or pity these demoralized students, the analyst sees them as too bound by their identifications and too hemmed in by potential severe anxiety, guilt, and irresolution to be educable in the grand sense.

Incidentally, it is not only the businessman's son who may be trapped this way. The children of professionals and career intellectuals may have their own built-in traps, and so may the gifted, aspiring children of poor, uneducated parents. Children do not escape from their families without identifications of enormous power. These old identifications may conflict with the full and pleasurable utilization of personal talents and the setting of aims and ideals commensurate with these talents.

Before leaving the problems of synthesis raised by talent, I would like to mention an additional discontinuity that may result from enlightenment—namely, the collapse of infantile and juvenile idealizations. In this respect, a lot of knowledge may be a dangerous thing, while a little knowledge and little skill may be safe. The occupations, the history, the religious and secular values, and all the customs of the family and the community are likely to be confused anew in the course of a vigorous, open-minded education. Nothing is sacred to the inquiring mind, or at least it need not be.

Idealizations are illusions that people and the world they inhabit are better than they are. Like anyone else, the student needs the security of these illusions, many of which, by the way, have been fostered by his earlier education. In part, idealizations provide the security of maintaining hope, but in part they also provide security against recognizing deep disappointments in and derogations of oneself and others. Behind superficial worldliness and cynicism, many students cling to their idealizations and close their minds and stunt their talents to protect them.

These idealizations may be of a general, impersonal sort, pertaining, for example, to the workings of our educational, political, or religious institutions, or they may be specific and personal, pertaining, for example, to the manliness and integrity of one's own father. And it is often the case that the general idealizations are extensions of family idealizations. But whichever type is emphasized, the idealizing student is often unconsciously complying with conscious or unconscious demands by his parents not to see, not to think, not to ask. His parents may be trying to conceal their own disillusionment with their society or, closer to home, their marital discord, patent infidelities, mental or physical illnesses, and failures of every sort that can't be lived down. Cases of pseudostupidity in childhood have been reported in which this defect appeared to be intimately connected with parental pressures against free inquiry in the family setting. And yet it is the family setting in which learning begins and where normally the heart is put into learning: with the heart taken out early by demands for selective ignorance that will support flimsy idealizations, all later learning, all later pleasure and security in using one's talents, may suffer greatly.

Before, I spoke of talent as a repudiated instrument of defense and archaic morality; now, I am speaking of it as a repudiated instrument of emancipation. In making these two points I am not necessarily referring to two distinct groups of students. Psychoanalysis repeatedly encounters contradictory meanings and feelings attaching to one and the same personal quality or behavior. Thus, to be talented may simultaneously stand for being a free man and a slave, potent and impotent, richly fed and starved, and the like.

Continuing with the theme of talent as a threat to secure and satisfying interpersonal relations, I will mention two more factors: deprivation and invasion. First, deprivation: we often see the talented student equating competence and achievement with being abandoned and deprived by others and consequently unconsciously going on strike and behaviorally blocking in his work. This equation will have had a long history, beginning with the birth of the next younger sibling or the stepping up of demands for instinctual control in early childhood, or at least being sent off to school. The subjective idea is that if you are any good, no one will bother to look after you; you are out in the cold or, what is even more embittering, made to take care of things when you feel most strongly that you are the very thing that needs to be taken care of. This is a matter of degree, of course, and normally the child also shows impressive strivings toward autonomy and away from dependence.

But recognizing these growth strivings should not blind us to the residue of nostalgia, loneliness, and bitterness that so often attaches to being "a big boy now" or "a big girl now." Where important enough, this residue may be intensified at significant turning points in the years after childhood, such as the time of leaving home for prep school or college, or leaving college for a life on one's own. Normally, graduation is a time of celebration but, to a variable degree, it is also a time of disappointment, mourning, and anxiety. Anticipation of this occasion may cause the leftover disappointment, mourning, and anxiety of childhood to go off like a time bomb. Then the student is left with the despairing question, Where has all my talent and effort gotten me?

Even before the approach of graduation, the conflict may show itself: the talented student may need to be academically weak, helpless, deficient, or in trouble in order to get individualized care and attention from the college faculty and administration. The care and attention may be sought even if they are stern and punitive, and in some cases especially when they are so, the setting of limits and the inflicting of punishment being for many important signs of love. The able student may unconsciously subvert his talents and achieve enough failures and incompletes to bring him the care he is seeking, though other factors may interfere with his benefiting from this care.

The other interpersonal factor I referred to above was invasion. I have in mind the student with weak ego boundaries. The concept of weak ego boundaries does not necessarily pertain to every student who claims to be in search of his "identity" or who makes a point of asking, "Who am I?" The concept applies typically to the schizoid person for whom it has been a lifelong problem to maintain a sense of separateness and orientation in the course of his relations with others. In his subjective experience this type of person is readily invaded by the qualities of others; he takes over external stimuli of every sort and makes transient or lasting internal demands or criticisms out of them. As a result he becomes confused as to where he leaves off and his environment begins, and he may always have the sense that his self and his companions are unpredictable entities and his feelings somehow false or hollow. Typically, he develops a psychic shell, cocoon, or hole in the ground within which he leads his inner life, hoping thereby to preserve some sense of continuity and inviolability.

As students, those with weak ego boundaries live under the constant threat of being invaded—invaded by teachers, by fellow students, or by subject matter. Some make excellent academic adjustments—and in all sorts of fields, too—but some are fated to spend most of their energy restricting their involvements with the collegiate world. Inevitably that means restricting the free and full use of their talents. We may say carelessly or uncomprehendingly that they are too withdrawn to be interested in their studies and the academic community, but it is closer to the truth to say that they are protecting themselves against getting all too involved in a way they fear will have malignant consequences. Needless to say, there are many other reasons why the schizoid student may perform below par.

Finally, I turn to a set of observations concerning the problem of exceptional giftedness and achievement. These observations cut across the boundaries of the preceding sections of my discussion.

An unusual gift, whatever its joys and blessings, can be a very heavy burden; perhaps it always is. For one thing, it excites the envy of peers, parents, and teachers, and so may draw down on its possessor special criticism, derision, and other forms of rejection. The student may perceive correctly that he is hated for his gift, and, if his previous development has sensitized him to being attacked, he may come to hate his gift too. In fantasy, his gift also challenges the gods and, in keeping with infantile conceptions and their mythological elaborations, he may dread the punishment for his hubris.

For another thing, his gift and its expression lead others always to expect something special of him. Consequently he may feel burdened by unceasing demands to do his best. It is not that he may not want to do so spontaneously, but there is a vast difference between offering giftedness to the world and being tyrannized by the world because of giftedness. The adulation and lionization that frequently impinge on the exceptionally talented student involve sets of demands for unflagging effort and excellence. The student may have internalized such demands long before his college years, so that at college he may have to contend with the synergistic action of relentless internal and external pressures. And these invariably imply, if they do not openly state, that the talent is not his: it belongs to the world, and so he must play that concert, write that piece, do that experiment; his emotional state, his needs for sex and love and laziness are irrelevant. In the end, then, he is irrelevant; only his talent counts. In response to the presence of this army of occupation, he may seal his talent off from the rest of his personality so far as he can, and allow it to remain an area of unclear self-boundaries and of undefined personal impulse.

Then there is the element of exhibitionism: exceptional achievements throw one into the limelight, and where infantile conflicts over exhibiting oneself sexually have persisted with too great force, these conflicts may intrude too much on—sexualize—the use of one's gift. One will wish then to be inconspicuous, which means ungifted. Further, a great talent sets one off from one's peers and family, and possibly from many of one's teachers, too. The remarkable student sees too much and understands too much of the mediocrity and pretense that surround him even in the best academic community, and he is impatient with the pace and quality of others. In these ways, his gift may accentuate his feelings of loneliness or distance from the surrounding world. He will wish then to be ordinary, which, again, means ungifted.

Sometimes we see other connections, consequences, or uses of great talents, such as maintaining incestuous ties, aggressing against others, carrying out atonements, concealing oneself and manipulating others. These factors have sometimes been taken as essential components of great achievement, but this is not a well-worked-out matter at all and the evidence is that they often make for barrenness rather than fruitfulness.

In any event, the burdens of exceptional talent and achievement are there, and for reasons extrinsic to the gift and perhaps intrinsic to it, these burdens may become too great and may alienate the student from part of himself. He may go on using his gift without joy, or, what concerns us here, he may intermittently or enduringly bury the treasure.

In this discussion, I have surveyed only one species of reasons why so much talent goes down the drain. I have concentrated on individual psychological factors and have essentially bypassed social psychological ones, such as certain institutionalized practices that may restrict free exercise of talent. Here I have in mind such deterrents as fixed and burdensome course requirements and course sequences, scholarly and administrative pressures that limit faculty interest in and opportunity for teaching students in the extended sense of teaching, and traditions of being "cool," well-rounded in interests, or high in grades that may be mutually reinforced by students, parents, and college authorities.

There are other limitations. I have not taken up differences between the problems encountered by talented female college students and those by talented males. Further, I have concentrated on the college years even though I recognize that many of my remarks apply to the years before and after college; there are, however, different factors or different versions of the same factors also operating at each of the developmental levels. And finally, I have not spoken of the college dropout as such. Nevertheless, I believe my discussion provides part of a necessary baseline for considering the psychology of the dropout: recognizing the dangers commonly associated with talent helps prepare us to examine the student whose dropping out is unnecessary from the standpoint of potential ability and thus challenges the understanding and resources of the clinician, the educator, the community, and, it is hoped, the student himself.

## CHAPTER 11

# IDENTITY AND DEPRESSION IN STUDENTS WHO FAIL

WILLIAM A. HARVEY, M.D.

IN SHAKESPEARE'S TRAGEDY, after Hamlet has staged the play which accuses his mother and uncle of "damned incest" and "murder most foul," he answers his mother's summons to her closet.

(*Enter Hamlet.*)
*Hamlet*: Now, Mother, what's the matter?
*Queen*: Hamlet, thou hast thy father much offended.
*Hamlet*: Mother, you have my father much offended.
*Queen*: Come, come, you answer with an idle tongue.
*Hamlet*: Go, go, you question with a wicked tongue.
*Queen*: Why, how now, Hamlet!
*Hamlet*: What's the matter now?

*Act III, Scene IV*

Thereafter, "putting on this confusion, this crafty madness," Hamlet, implacable, moves on to his own destruction and that of his mother and usurper "father."

In modern dress on a recent day, it was Jason Hughes, my twenty-year-old sophomore, who was telling me of himself: "The way I treated my mother. Gave her a birthday gift and said something to make her cry. She'd cry: 'Not the way to give a gift.'

"Why not? What's wrong? I'm giving you a gift. Why are you crying? Why are you upset?"

"To my father," he continued, "I love to speak civil words in a hostile tone. It confuses him. He can't understand it. Goes back to his newspaper."

"I throw people out by confounding them; say: 'I'm sorry I won't be able to do that because I have nothing else to do.' Good answer to confuse people. Two ideas, mutually exclusive, put them together in a causal relationship. Terrific weapon, powerful because it confuses, causes anxiety."[1]

He was speaking with relative easiness now. The choking vehemence of emotion, the frantic raging and despair which filled his first visits was now subsident. "You can't realize," he went on, "how they did that to us all the time, reversing the polarity switches so you're constantly being clobbered and beaten over the head. Mother offered to help and hurt you. She would want to help and her hands would hurt. I'd be practicing that organ. She'd come storming in, hissing, push you off the seat: 'God damn you. You're going to do it right.' You'd watch her horrible hands. I think of her hands and freeze. Half-hour later, she'd smile: 'How are you, Jason; I'm concerned about you.'

"It was always endless orders; no matter what you did, you'd only get another order. When she corrected, her lip curled. Horrible. But you always thought it was your fault. You didn't love your parents. She blamed us for her migraine. Never satisfied. Never happy with us. No use. We fought among ourselves. She'd wish she were dead. From the seventh grade, contemplating suicide, I'd sit by the railroad trestle, sit there for hours, afraid I'd do it.

"She was my companion. Took me to novenas, museums, and concerts. Father says she put grandiose ideas in my head, taking me into Chicago to the Museum of Science at four. He

[1] The import of these transactions need not be missed. How destructively this weapon conveys the force of cold, rejecting hostility, vengeful and unloving, is dramatized in the pathetic plight of Ophelia, "driven to desperate terms" of madness by Hamlet's confusing. As the players are about to begin:

> *Hamlet*: Lady, shall I lie in your lap?
> (*Lying down at Ophelia's feet*)
> *Ophelia*: No, my lord.
> *Hamlet*: I mean, my head upon your lap?
> *Ophelia*: Aye, my lord.
> *Hamlet*: Do you think I meant country matters?
> *Ophelia*: I think nothing, my lord.
> *Hamlet*: That's a fair thought to lie between maid's legs.
> *Ophelia*: What is, my lord?
> *Hamlet*: Nothing.
> *Ophelia*: You are merry, my lord.
> *Hamlet*: Who, I?
>
> ACT III, SCENE II.

has a terrific percentage in keeping me down, but he pushes me to the right schools and camp. Since I was having a lousy time at camp, I thought I was terrible. He always told mother I didn't have what it takes. Screamed at me to concentrate and said I couldn't concentrate. I believed it. In elementary school, I couldn't get myself to study. Got the idea I couldn't study. I have a terrific sense of fear in trying anything. Always caught hell. Their criticism scares me. Puts me in a frenzy. Since second, third grade, I'm scared to do any work. Then I'd give the wrong catechism answers to the sisters in Sunday school. The French teacher in seventh grade tried to help. I played being dumber. Wouldn't learn the conjugations. Provides me with an excuse. Not doing well because I don't learn the stuff. I take over my neurosis and watch myself being destroyed. I torture myself when I really get going. Felt I deserve it, to be punished. It's what my parents said."

Despite high intelligence, an exceptionally strong drive toward intellectual attainment, and his facility for manipulating ideas, Jason had withdrawn from his mid-western university because he was unable to do the work of the premedical curriculum.

He had asked for some help while still on the campus. With pressure of speech, he poured tirades of raging criticism on himself as he described his predicament: "I can't get the work done. I can't get myself to read. It bothers me, making no progress. I've been this way as long as I can remember, from the third grade. I couldn't get myself to do the homework. I'd sit in front of the stuff. Five minutes before a test, memorize a key outline or a brilliant first paragraph. I never learned definitions. If I memorized, I never knew what it meant. I refuse to understand it. It's out of my control. It's not fair. I had this in me by the time I was rational. I'm sick and God-damned tired of it. I can't get the work done. I'm so dissatisfied with myself." Anxiously despairing, he feared at the same time that his dropping out of college would cause both parents to have breakdowns.

In a few weeks' time, his depression had lightened as he came to mix raging attacks on his parents with tearing himself apart. His life was replete with examples of his continuous struggle to retain an identity of his own, of his endless protests against being owned and dominated by his mother. She was controlling, strangling, degrading, and she was also ungiving and seductive. "The main thing we were taught: to wait on her. She destroys my father. No male in our family. Mother complained she filled the role of both. Any success I had would go to her. 'You followed my advice and did it right.' When I study, I end with debates with my father and mother. They'd take me over body and soul if I did what they want."

His accountant-turned-banker father, Jason perceived as subtly hostile, cynical, hypercritical, and devaluing him, yet also as solicitous, judicious, and reasonable, always right. "Father knows it all. I can't win. I'll fail and father will smile: 'Aha! I told you so.' To have people smile at me confuses me. He goes after me, questions, questions, questions, so critical. Try to tell father a joke, he's correcting your grammar. You talk to him and get the idea you're a fool. Questions, questions. I remember a time I used to call myself an idiot for hours on end."

Jason felt he must be a genius, know it all before he could try to learn. "Trying, you're naked and vulnerable. I'll never be good enough. Why bother to do anything if you're not a genius?"

It would never be acceptable to do better than his father. It is unthinkable. It would cause "a crisis, a real disaster." Yet he knows he cannot exist as a shadow of his parent. He stands alone, having no identity of his own while tied to his parent and unable to establish an identity apart from him. Intellectually, he opposes everything and emotionally he rejects all relationships, has no friends. He does not know what he wants and his only identity is to oppose or destroy. He doesn't trust himself and he doesn't trust others. He saw immediately this meaning of his dream: "You were called on to perform an operation—foot deformed. You hadn't bothered to get scrubbed. Next you had taken off the person's foot. The leg came off. You said how it had to go. Brutality of the operation! You were so big! You washed your hands of the operation. If you were to throw me out, you'd say it had to be. Rub your hands.

The way I followed you down the corridor, I followed my mother. I know I'd be cured if I could trust you. Don't know if I'll be ready for that. I've never given anyone anything to work with."

Prepared with increasing objectivity, Jason was able to use new experience of himself for insights which revealed more and more the automatic operations of identifications which had long held sway in his unconscious: "Yesterday, showing Bob how to hit a golf ball, I was in a rage: 'No, do it this way!' And—I didn't want him to learn. Nothing changes. She's omnipresent." Thus, his drive to autonomy was mobilized. "I've got to get my parents out of my mind. I'm like a tool, an appendage. They can be hundreds of miles away. It's like I'm a robot. Or like the girl in the story who keeps a place set for her long-dead father."

Jason's has been a struggle for identity, for existence apart from either parent, and it has not gone well. He cannot tolerate separation and the ambivalence of his relationships is equally intolerable. Dependent on parental direction, he bitterly resents and fears it. He must change things, but he has no direction, so he destroys. "Feel like I'm being suffocated. Like having foam rubber all around me. Just closing in. Nothing I do has any effect. Feel like I want to set the foam rubber on fire." Neither parent offered Jason anything to identify with that was not ambiguous, unstable, and destructively ambivalent. He can say, as did Biff in Arthur Miller's *Death of a salesman*: "I don't know what the future is. I don't know—what I'm supposed to want."

An oppressive conviction of impotence is shot through with obvious rage and circularly feeds it. Exclusively recognizing, emphasizing, and even reacting to his rage puts him in the wrong again with those significant others—parents and now therapist—for whom he is always in the wrong, his impulses at fault. Such confrontation can, from the outset, interfere with the therapeutic intention to provide, as Freud put it, an after-education correcting for the mistakes of our parents. The work is impeded if the therapist fits too really well into the imago of the parent. It is here, therefore, aside from questions of technique, that the personality of the therapist—what he really is, rather than what he attempts to be—is of crucial importance.

By deferring interpretation of the concomitant instinctual wishes, sexual, sadistic, regressive, the therapist avoids reinforcing the patient's identification with the hostile aggressor who often told the patient that his impulses alone were at fault. As the patient experiences the therapist's protection against the introjected—and actual—hostile aggressor, the transference deepens and the tendency toward regression comes into the scope of mutual therapeutic investigation and of resolution. The opportunity is provided to master conflict and undo identifications through the acquisition of insight.

In the natural progression of human events, we begin to grow away from emotional dependence on the family at an early age, to mature, to become complete emotional units and to maintain clear identities. The identity of each finds clear and further definition from interdependent functioning with other persons in social living and in a role that is for each his own and in which he is well recognized.

The task of identity formation we begin to face with the first cognition of the difference between self and non-self. It is a long human journey from infantile narcissism through perception and progressive mastery of environment and of one's own impulses and drives to mature self-esteem. As the path emerges out of adolescence, there is to be attained and ideally is attained a sure sense of the continuity of oneself in past and present, while fixing on a way of life in which there is sufficient gratification to sustain the man.

It is, of course, in the family that there begins the coordinating interaction between the developing individual and his human (social) environment. The coordination is mutual. In the previous chapter, Dr. Schafer has described the student's complying with conscious or unconscious demands by parents not to see, think, or hear. The experience of analysts treating children has brought increasing awareness that the behavior and mood of the child are to be understood fundamentally in the context of intrafamilial, interpersonal relationships. Pathological relationships between mother and father and the child play a great role in helping to maintain distorted and unintegrated tendencies in the child.

The neurotic needs and wishes of the parent, whether of an excessively dominating, dependent, or erotic character, are found to be vicariously gratified by the behavior of the child or in relation to the child. Delinquent children have been found attuned to a permissiveness quite unconscious in the parent, the parent obtaining a vicarious gratification in the child's behavior.

We may say that the child adapts to survive, and when the experience and the demand (as to conform to parental need) is too threatening for the immature ego of the child, he may—and should, if he can—fight to survive. In our patients who fail, it has been a poor fight, frustraneous, self-defeating, compromised by hostile overidentification with disturbed parents, by dependent attachment, unconscious submissiveness, and conformity.

The therapist who deals with the aspect of motivational failure in the dropout is able to offer a conceptual approach derived essentially from clinical experience without which this failure and the significance of the failure can hardly be appreciated. This may utilize, as have the presentations in this volume, different avenues of approach: from the study of the intra-psychic processes in the individual, from an orientation emphasizing the current psychosocial milieu of the dropout, and thirdly, from an interest in the family as a homeostatic system of personal interaction. We can find, however, an eventual common theoretical basis for such formulations in the psychoanalytic theory of ego function.

Certainly Dr. Schafer tells of ego when he describes the inhibiting consequences of its defensive operations as it avoids anxiety. Dr. Snyder (Chapter 7) emphasizes the time-specific importance of the college years for the late adolescent ego and the tendency of the institutional environment either to extend the range of the ego's adaptive capacity or to freeze it. His study seeks to clarify how the university environment may "run counter to the developmental task of adolescence." Dr. Levenson could, I believe, be said to be postulating a failure of the individual ego to achieve a complete differentiation of itself from a family ego mass—if we may be pardoned for using such a term and so stretching the concept of ego to apply it to the family group.

The term "ego" has been used ambiguously in psychoanalysis to refer, on the one hand, to the whole personality and, on the other, to a coherent organization of mental processes—the sense of our usage today. As such an organization, it is defined by its functions. Our knowledge of "ego" began with the study of its intra-psychic defensive operations against the feared destructive force of impulse and innate drive of which Dr. Schafer has furnished a surpassingly excellent description.

The ego accomplishes the self-regulation necessary for man's life in this world. Functioning well, it is taken for granted; in its failures, it can perhaps be best appreciated. In its major failures, for example, we are confronted with the disaster of the psychotic disorganization of the ego. Thus, a twenty-year-old college junior became frightened as he entered a classroom that he might suddenly attack the instructor; at other times, that he might exhibit himself.

The ego, in addition to the functions of defense, must also accomplish adaptation to the environment and has what are called "executive functions" whose role is effective performance. How the one activity, defense, may compromise the other, adaptation, has been illustrated in the discussion of talent as an aspect of the adaptive ego. This ego, this organization of psychic functions, has a natural history of growth and development which parallels the bodily growth.

We thus recognize in man a development from dependency as marked as the physiological parasitism of the fetus and infant, to a mature entity, relatively self-sustaining physiologically, but also psychologically. The body grows by adding tissue, by taking into the organism other tissues which are assimilated into one's own. The psychological interaction with the environment is less concrete and more subtle.

We see the ego as gradually formed from the undifferentiated phase of earliest infancy, identification being the major process contributing to this early formation of personality. It is presumably initiated by pleasure in imitation, as in the building of model airplanes with father (cf. Dr. Snyder's sophomore, Jones). It eventuates in the assimilation of attributes of the other person into stable and permanent elements of the personality. The child has to rely on the adults. He participates in their reactions and thus acquires their methods of solving problems and coping with emergencies. This is the beginning of education, of what we study later as a capacity to achieve mastery of given tasks, mastery of the environment. The little child's ego, undeveloped as it is, has to rely on the auxiliary ego borrowed from the parents. The adolescent's ego lacks the support of the parents' auxiliary ego because the adolescent turns away from the parents. This loosening of ties with the parents is a difficult and protracted process, often accompanied by genuine mourning.

In effect, finally, to be able to do without the parents and to do well, the essential identifications must be integrated into a homogeneous and harmoniously functioning ego. When this is accomplished with reasonable success, the adolescent acquires an assured sense of adequacy, of inner continuity and social sameness, and what I would describe also as a separate wholeness. This well-being derives from the ego activity, from manipulation of the environment, from successful function, from pleasure in function. Then, "work gives pleasure." It is important for us to note that this means the overcoming of the infantile state of helplessness and any fixation thereto. For it is this intense state of helplessness which is apt to be reactivated by the separation from parents. One version of this was described by a medical student, chronically depressed and failing in his studies, who complained: "I've got to understand the chapter. I never had to do that much all on my own. So much anger at this way of doing it. Here so much on your own. In the sixth grade, I'd do it for the teacher. Here, it's up to you; nobody to please, they don't care. I'm used to the person-to-person basis. They want me to learn, I learn. If I have trouble with a course, get a nice tutor, I learn beautifully. I can't give this to myself. I can't be happy with my accomplishment. I'm only happy about someone else being happy with my accomplishment."

If the identity is not securely enough established, there is more or less insufficiency of the necessary psychic gratification to be derived from ego activity. Herein, in the lack of this gratification, of narcissistic supplies, in the lowered self-esteem, we find the important source of the depression associated with disturbances in identity formation, with failures in the developmental task of adolescence. This depressive consequence of failure, while implicit in many presentations, is not sufficiently elucidated. It is, however, important to stress for its therapeutic implications and I believe it indicates the treatment requirements. Depression is here recognized as a reaction to narcissistic frustration which the ego is unable to prevent and as a reactivation of an infantile ego state of helplessness. The clinical phenomena of late adolescence, with its particular stresses testing to the limits the strength of ego functions, expose with special clarity the relation of affective state and ego adequacy.

The significance of ego deficiency, for depressive states in general, has not had sufficient consideration in analytic studies. Psychoanalytic formulations have, rather, emphasized the depression derived from an attitude in which hatred predominates—i.e., that the problem is one of disposing of hate. The paradigm is: "I cannot love people. I have to hate them. Therefore, people do not love me. They hate me, so I am unhappy and depressed."

This dynamic was recognized particularly in those depressions which can well be referred to generically as the melancholias of later life. In these, however, there is a comparatively well-developed psychic structure. Aggression is directed against the self with relentlessly vindictive self-reproach and persistent suicidal drive. In individual cases, more or less of this attitude may complicate an adolescent's problem. The more intense his archaic hostility, the more difficulty he will have in separating from parents. Sadistic rage, constantly pressing for discharge, was a prominent component in the case of our student, Jason.

A conceptual distinction needs to be kept clear between such depressive states as the melancholias, on the one hand, and the depressions associated with the defective ego organization and the relative deficiencies and failure of the ego in adolescence. In depression stemming from ego deficiency, helplessness is outstanding. It is more indicative of giving up, to die, and does not include as a major component marked guilt and aggression turned on the self.

True enough, the adolescent has a wish to remain forever dependent and to punish parents, but this used as interpretation can remain an empty intellectual notion and miss the point in therapy. Also, rebellion for self-determination is not all unhealthy. We know the little child blames parents for his falls and mishaps. We should be able to see the adolescent begin to react in the same way without taking this to be the whole problem.

In this light, the particular therapeutic requirements of adolescence are comprehensible. It calls for the effort to overcome our own resistance against the adolescent forms of aggression, the reactive and defensive use of hostility, to focus our own and the patient's attention upon his hidden ideals and the fantasies of his parents' omnipotence, to support the patient in ending his narcissistic hurts and the deprivation trauma of separation, and to give him a working concept of his behavior as meaningful in its context.

Many times, and at different phases of adolescence, more can be done, but in general, therapy needs to be actively sustained by the therapist. The responsibility clearly is on the therapist to establish an empathic contact with the patient. For this, what the analyst genuinely and fundamentally is matters more than what he rationally decides to be in regard to his patient. The adolescent patient, above all others, must be able to discern a genuine benevolence which is free, as far as possible, of the eternal ambivalence of man, the ambivalence of love and hate. The psychoanalytic ideal of neutrality is superseded by presence, the presence of the analyst. It is necessary that the patient sense a watchful presence which really exists and is helpful. If the physician's attitude is one of strict neutrality, a frustrating remoteness, it will not do. He who is sparing with the commitment of his person will never become a therapist of adolescents.

Our inquiries meet the student during a particular developmental phase. Thus, we speak today of identity crisis and adolescent diffusion. When the crisis is not resolved, there results identity diffusion, with diffusion of industry and at times the assumption of a negative identity. Here the adolescent, feeling unequal to the demands of parents or of his own ego ideal—e.g., to be "superboy"—finds it easier to identify with what he is least supposed to be.

The language of this conceptualization captures and expresses very aptly the state of affairs for the beleaguered ego of the adolescent. This theoretical framework deserves, I believe, an even broader application. I would urge that it is then, in late or prolonged adolescence, already late in the game and particularly so for those students with the more severe disturbances in functioning. Not infrequently, when such difficulties as diffusion of industry are present urgently at the time of college dropout, they can, in retrospect, be realized to have been symptomatically manifested much earlier, even in childhood, and to have persisted through adolescence.

The self-description of our patient, Jason, may illustrate the point more graphically: "For years, I've not really been doing the work. Managed to pass. I'm the same way. I've always been this way. Had this in me. In the third grade, I wouldn't do the work. I memorized. I refused to understand it. I can't get myself to read. It's out of my control. It's always been. I like to give the opposite answers. I do it all the time. It's a real effort to give the correct one. I want to pull myself together. I'm so dissatisfied with myself." Again, "Solving a problem, I have to do it by an alternative procedure." (Alternative, that is, to the one being taught.) Later, regaining humor, he remarked: "I could have dropped out of kindergarten."

The acquisition of identity is, of course, a lifelong process whose roots go back to the first self-recognition. This concept of identity diffusion which serves so well for understanding the predicament of the late, older adolescent, can very usefully be extended by application to the pre-adolescent and his earlier difficulties can be recognized as a persistent identity diffusion. A general acceptance of such an explicit application would help to bring the more severe difficulties of identity formation earlier to recognition and the possibility of treatment.

It is an incomplete and less effective therapy which appreciates anger and frustrating rage but not the impotent helplessness, and at times hopelessness, arising from contradictions within the ego. It would be an incomplete and inaccurate view which saw the manifestations of trouble in the setting of adolescence and not the origins in infancy and childhood. Indeed, the adolescent is not so far removed from childhood. He is emerging.

In the late adolescent and post-adolescent predicament, an awareness of the importance still of the parental neurosis and of the reciprocal relationships of family members brings attention to the aspects of the here and now, to what keeps the pathology going rather than how it got that way. The multiplicity of ways of continuing and current interaction between family members and an identified patient—which are painful, unsatisfactory to all, provocative of symptoms in at least one, and yet are powerfully reinforcing—can swamp the efforts of a therapist. Interest in the interpersonal in this sense (and even active intervention) need not compete with our interest in the intra-psychic or lead us to underestimate the significance of unconscious identifications, of unresolved unconscious conflict and the damage to the patient's ego by the operation of defensive mechanisms brought into play as a result. The timely vantage point of adolescence is aptly useful for underlining and enlarging our understanding that every inter-psychic event is accompanied by an intra-psychic event. This understanding, indispensably necessary for treatment or management, will lead also to a truer overall perspective on the implications of neurotic involvement in the college dropout.[2]

[2] Papers relevant to the ideas presented in this chapter include the following: K. Abraham, "Notes on the psychoanalytical investigation of manic-depressive insanity and allied conditions," in *Selected papers of Karl Abraham*, London: Hogarth Press, 1927; E. Bibring, "The mechanism of depression," in Phyllis Greenacre (ed.), *Affective disorders*, New York: International Universities Press, 1953; S. Freud, "Mourning and melancholia" (1917), *Standard edition, Complete psychological works*, London: Hogarth Press, 1957, 14, pp. 237-258; S. Freud, "Outline of psychoanalysis," *ibid.*, 1964, 23, p. 175; H. Guntrip, "The manic-depressive problem," *International Journal of Psychoanalysis*, 1962, 43, pp. 98-112; E. H. Erikson, "Identity and the life cycle," *Psychological issues*, New York: International

Universities Press, 1959; K. R. Eissler, "Notes on problems of technique in the psychoanalytic treatment of adolescents," *Psychoanalytic study of the child,* New York: International Universities Press, 1958, 13, pp. 223-253; A. M. Johnson and S. Szurek, "The genesis of anti-social acting out in children and adults," *Psychoanalytic Quarterly,* 1952, 21, pp. 323-343; Jeanne Lample De Groot, "On the development of the ego and superego," *International Journal of Psychoanalysis,* 1947, 28, pp. 7-11.

# CONCLUSION

## THE EDITORS

THE RISING WAVE of college applicants during the past decade has inevitably brought with it mounting nation-wide interest in the 50 percent of the college students who drop out, especially those students with seemingly excellent potential. This interest also pertains to the related problem of how to recognize and promote the development and use of talent. Students confront powerful social pressures to make optimal use of their opportunity for higher education; similarly, colleges are subject to the need to make optimal use of facilities. The growing interest in these problems provided the stimulus for the Princeton University Conference held in October 1964 on "The College Dropout and the Utilization of Talent," and for compiling this book, in which various points of view are brought together with the object of clarifying rather than simplifying the complex phenomena involved.

The conclusions that emerge from the essays in this volume seem to fit into two categories, one of a general nature, concerning overall important considerations related to dropping out and the use of talent, and the other of a specific kind.

In the former category, one of the most obvious and striking conclusions to be drawn is that the phenomena are multifaceted and therefore need to be studied broadly as well as in concentrated detail ordinarily reserved for specialists. To put the matter in another way, the various chapters in this volume suggest that the study of dropouts and development of talent cuts across the lines that mark off various specialists. Research in this field must involve not only census-type studies, but also studies based on theories of growth during the late adolescent period and of the processes of learning and education. While this book has emphasized inhibitions in the utilization of talent, it is clear that many students are successful in actualizing their potential. For a complete understanding of development during the college years, research must constantly work back and forth between the successful and the unsuccessful, between those who are free to "love and work" and those who experience their impulses and talents as burdens or dangers.

Therefore, not the least of the major general conclusions reached here is that adolescence, normally a time of upheaval and rapid change, as Anna Freud and other students of this period point out, has much to do with dropout phenomena as well as with the use of talent. The wishful view of the older generation that adolescence should be a time of smooth and uninterrupted growth not only is challenged by psychoanalysts and students of personality development but also goes against an impressive mass of testimony to the contrary recorded in autobiography, history, and philosophy. Norman Kiell's volume on *The Universal Experience of Adolescence* brings together a great deal of this testimony, stretching back to ancient times, when Aristotle observed of the young that they are "prone to desire and ready to carry any desire they may have formed into action. . . . They are changeful too, and fickle in their desires, which are as transitory as they are vehement."[1]

Another major general conclusion emerges, particularly from the chapters by Dorothy Knoell, and Ford and Urban—namely, that the causes of dropping out lie not only in the student but also in the institution and in the interaction between the two. This view challenges those in the colleges who have been content with the simpler assumption that the trouble is always to be sought in the dropout himself. The intricacies of the turbulent period of adolescence are such that it is often easy to make out a case showing the dropout to be unstable, immature, or the victim of psychopathology. In addition, the combined authority and prestige of faculty and administration tend to reinforce the traditions and ideals peculiar to each college, so that they are seldom brought openly into question even by dropouts or by parents. Instead, the college confronts the student everywhere with pressures to conform at a time of life when he is geared biologically and psychologically to learn to develop and assert his unique characteristics. The question of the desirability of these pressures becomes of par-

[1] N. Kiell (ed.), *The universal experience of adolescence,* New York: International Universities Press, 1964, p. 18.

ticular importance in the case of the student with talent who finds himself unhappy with his college, but who is constantly reminded that the fault may lie with him. Henry James, himself a dropout, defined talent as "the art of being completely whatever it was that one happened to be."

In some respects, the college manifestly must have interests that seem far removed from those of individual students. Dropping out and the necessity for teachers to address themselves largely to groups of students rather than to individuals are, from the college's point of view, practical matters that involve such important problems as the efficient and maximal use of plant facilities and staff, problems about which the late adolescent, caught up in troubles of a far different kind, has little, if any, conception.

The tendency for both the colleges and the students to give first priority to their own problems is an all too natural one. The fact that this tendency is often unwittingly present underscores the need for the difficult feat of self-examination on the part of the colleges as well as of individual students. Projects to meet this need, such as the study that Benson Snyder and his associates are conducting at the Massachusetts Institute of Technology, are already under way at various colleges throughout the country, and the findings should be instructive. In addition, there is a growing tendency for groups of colleges to pool their findings and to exchange ideas with sister-institutions, thus providing another way in which anachronistic policies and procedures can be detected and modified. A third alternative, such as that suggested by Lawrence Kubie, of an agency independent of the colleges to study the problems they have separately and in common has the advantage of making up in objectivity for whatever pain would be inflicted on institutional sensitivities.

But if, on the one hand, the colleges must be governed by policies and interests that do not always coincide with those of individual students and must therefore insist on conformity to standards in the authoritarian manner of the father, they also find themselves inescapably cast in the nurturing role of *alma mater*. Faculty and fellow-students appear to be the leading actors in this latter role, which calls for encouraging a student's attempts to find successful expression for unique abilities, disturbing and futile though these experiments may often be. Here the interest of the individual student and the college coincides.

What the perennial complaint of students about student-faculty relations appears to imply is their tacit need for support and understanding from persons older and wiser than themselves, as well as from their peers. Douglas H. Heath has underscored the importance of interaction on the campus in its permissive as well as its restrictive aspects if the maturing process is to proceed in healthy fashion.[2] He mentions the noteworthy finding that students at Haverford whose academic performance declined had little to say about the influence of any faculty member or course, in contrast to those successfully graduating, who attributed "much of their achievement to such an influence." In addition, he finds that there appears to be a perhaps equally important contribution toward healthy growth deriving from the interaction between the student and his fellows.

As discussed in the chapter on "Personal Determinants and Their Interaction with the Environment," relations between the student and those with whom he comes into daily contact seem to play an immensely important part in his development. When these relations go well, they stimulate expansion and growth; when they go poorly, they lead to withdrawal and constriction. That they are strongly conditioned by the student's past experience with parents and other important persons in his life has been amply confirmed by both the observations of perceptive teachers who take the trouble of inquiring into the meaning of apparently inexplicable behavior and by psychotherapists. Edgar Levenson's chapter, concerning itself especially with college dropouts in psychotherapy, finds major sources of disharmony in the student-family relationship and explores the possibility of improving unfavorable elements by working with both student and parents. The presupposition that the parties concerned will remain sufficiently

[2] D. H. Heath, "Youth in transition: Psychological readiness for college," paper presented at the colloquium on "The Challenge of Curricular Change," Skytop, Pa., April 11-14, 1965.

flexible and open to change to achieve mutual benefit from this approach cannot, of course, always be entertained. The experience of college staff members supports what William A. Harvey's paper points out from the clinical side—namely, that sometimes the parents themselves have become so fixed and incapable of change that it is better to confine attention to the student, who theoretically should have greater flexibility.

We are confronted, then, with the need for greater flexibility on the part of students, parents, and institutions. In a recent address delivered upon receipt of an award for distinguished psychological contributions to education, Sidney Pressey raised the following question as a basic neglected problem in the field: How early, rapidly, and long should formal education be undertaken? He cited evidence from the Fund for the Advancement of Education that students allowed to enter college at a median age of 16, instead of the usual 18, did much better than the average college freshman or freshmen paired with them as to ability. He noted that outstanding contributions in physics and chemistry were made most often at ages 25-29 and concluded: "Might it conceivably be desirable that the law require not only the beginning of full-time schooling at 6, but its ending, say, not later than 26?"[3]

Yet other educators, such as Heath, argue that our entering college students may be better prepared academically than formerly but less educable, less psychologically ready for college: "One effect of the current curricular changes, particularly in the sciences, is the overdevelopment of some skills and attitudes at the expense of both general skill and social development. . . . Culturally induced and rewarded over-specialization too early may eventually limit its own development by interfering with the maturing of all the person. I wager the dangers of too early specialization far outweigh the mythical benefits alleged to accrue from such early concentration."[4] We cannot set one rate and duration of education for students and expect this to be of maximum benefit to all. Perhaps some college students become aware of this and use dropping out

[3] S. L. Pressey, "Two basic neglected psychoeducational problems," *American Psychologist*, 1965, 20, p. 392.

[4] Heath, *op.cit.*, p. 2.

as a means of changing the rate and producing flexibility in the educational system.[5]

In addition to the general conclusions discussed above, certain others with more immediate relevancy should be specially noted.

One of them is our need to reexamine the common assumption that the college dropout suffers from ominous character or psychiatric disturbance, or that outstandingly high grades can be taken as signs that all is well. Certainly the study of the long-range fate of dropouts from Princeton, together with the similar findings reported from the University of Illinois, suggests the need for avoiding an alarmist view, especially if the finding is confirmed that a rather surprising percentage of dropouts later go on to obtain degrees. The present volume does not include comparable statistical studies of the progress over a period of years of students in the high academic achievement category during their college years. But the chapter by Roy Schafer, who is not only an experienced clinician but also a teacher thoroughly familiar with the academic milieu, points out how talent may actually hamper development in the personal-social respects, or be suppressed because the possessor views it as undesirable or even dangerous in the context of adolescence.

Even in the case of the more homogeneous group of students studied at Yale whose withdrawal was provoked by marked

[5] Another area requiring administrative flexibility may be education for minority groups. This volume has not dealt with problems specific to college dropouts who are members of such groups. In some ways the problem may be more critical at the high-school level. On the other hand, it will likely become increasingly important at the college level and needs investigation. A significant study in this area was made by Kenneth B. Clark and Lawrence Plotkin (*The Negro student at integrated colleges*, New York: National Scholarship Service and Fund for Negro Students, 1963). This study indicated that Negro students who had contact with NSSFNS and went on to integrated colleges had a gross dropout rate of one-half the national rate. They suggested that the low dropout rate might be due to high motivation—to drop out means that they will fall back into the ranks of the non-specialized labor force where their race ensures the permanence of low status. Financial need was felt to play a more prominent role in the Negro population than the white. Finally, the report indicated that scholastic aptitude test scores are not closely associated with college grades and that they do not predict college success for Negro students in the same way they do for whites.

psychological decompensation, Arnstein points out the need for open-mindedness and careful consideration of differences among individuals and in their interaction with the environment. It is, of course, now widely believed that roughly the same so-called classical symptoms of depression or of schizophrenia may appear in a variety of students without necessarily implying the same gloomy outcome for all, and that variations in the balance between personality strength and weakness and between the individual and his environment play an important role in prognosis.

Another noteworthy conclusion is touched on in every essay in this book and is discussed at some length in the introduction: dropping out, on the one hand, and academic success, on the other, tend to evoke such strong responses of disapproval or approval in parents, faculty, and others that the student's performance rather than the student himself becomes the focus of attention. His motives, what he is, and what he may be receive secondary consideration. Initially at least, emotionalism, especially on the part of parents, tends to obscure the fact that there may be good logic behind the student's decision to drop out. For many, the decision is merely the termination of a period of stalemate and waste, marked not only by academic inefficiency but also by general inability to profit from the campus interaction, so that to the student these conditions seem more deplorable than the cessation of formal education, whether that be temporary or permanent.

An additional conclusion can be drawn that from the student's point of view, just as there are influences favoring dropping out, there are also counter-influences against it, even when it might be beneficial from a long-range point of view. Similarly, as Roy Schafer's essay brings out, various counter-influences, particularly in the psychological sphere, work against change in students who devote themselves to the single-minded exploitation of talents to the exclusion of balance in the personal and social spheres, where they can remain immature. For the potential dropout, there appear to be two other sets of counter-influences in addition to the disapproval the dropout is apt to encounter, whether from parents, prospective employers, colleges, or others who tend to regard it as a sign of instability. As described in the editors' chapter, there are also counter-influences stemming from such personal considerations as reluctance to give up extracurricular interests and the opportunities the campus provides for development in the social sphere, as well as persisting indecision or perplexity about the self. Or they may largely stem from the absence of any acceptable realistic alternative to remain in college. The experience at Princeton suggests that the decision to drop out voluntarily seldom seems to be lightly made.

A final conclusion is that dropping out may actually be beneficial for students who otherwise would be routinely marking time on the campus without any personal benefit, and particularly for those with various kinds of emotional handicap. Although such a handicap may be temporary, viewed in the perspective of a lifetime, its duration, like the maturing process itself, is not so apt to be measured in days or weeks as in the case of acute physical disorder, but in months or even years. Apart from problems in the more strictly personal sphere, such handicaps may include learning- and writing-blocks, paralyzing fear of examinations even when the material has been conscientiously learned, the kind of perfectionism that centers on grades rather than on subject-matter, and inability to tolerate the give and take of everyday campus interaction through feelings of inadequacy or hypersensitivity. Witnesses on the campus to the intensity of the feelings of frustration and despair that these handicaps evoke in students, who in addition to showing signs of physical impairment tell of entertaining ideas of rash or even harmful action, are inclined to view them as more serious than mere figments of the imagination or deliberate dramatic display. Particularly for students of this kind, dropping out can provide a constructive alternative to the all but impossible dilemma of remaining in college. Relief from the pressure of academic demands, the opportunity to obtain professional help if it is needed, time to catch up in areas of life where development has lagged can, in an informal way, make a substantial contribution to the maturing process and, in a broad sense, to education as well.

## *The Editors*

### *Summary*

Two sets of conclusions seem to emerge from the present volume, one having to do with general considerations pertaining to dropping out of college and the development of talent, and the other with more specific aspects.

In the first category, it seems especially important to note the following: (1) These problems cut across the lines that mark off various specialties and so require attention and understanding of all those concerned with the educational process, whether they be faculty members, coaches, counselors, psychiatrists, or parents. (2) The reasons for dropping out or failing to utilize talent can be found not only in the student himself but also in the conflicting interests of the student, on the one hand, and the college, on the other, as well as in faulty interaction between the two. (3) The nature of the interaction between student and college in both the academic and personal spheres appears to be of high importance in determining whether students withdraw or develop their abilities. (4) The vicissitudes of adolescence, with its dual task of discarding the tendencies of childhood and coming to terms with the responsibilities of adult life, have by no means been left behind by students of college age.

Conclusions in the second category that deserve special notice and thought are the following: (1) The common assumption must be reexamined that the college dropout necessarily suffers from ominous character or psychiatric disturbance, or that the student with outstandingly high grades is well on the road to maturity. (2) The college student's performance, whether he drops out or is seemingly highly successful, tends to evoke in himself and others a response that, being colored by emotions of disapproval or approval, often makes it difficult to see the student in clear and broad perspective. (3) Just as there are influences that from the student's point of view favor dropping out or devoting himself to the single-minded exploitation of his talents to the exclusion of balance in other areas of his life, there are also counterinfluences that resist change, even when it might be beneficial from a long-range point of view. (4) Dropping out may be beneficial, for it may provide a constructive alternative to stalemate or even serious psychological disequilibrium, at a time when the student is still in a stage of development in which remaining in college represents an impossible dilemma. It need not be interpreted as a sign that a student's education has been halted for life.

# *APPENDIX*

## PROGRAMS AND SELECTED PUBLICATIONS RELATED TO COLLEGE DROPOUTS

JAMES MONTGOMERY AND JOHN HILLS

### STUDENT EXPECTATIONS

A student's expectations of his college determine in large measure the satisfaction he obtains from the experience, at least initially.

M. Bundy. *An atmosphere to breathe*. New York: Woodrow Wilson Foundation, 1959.

L. A. Pervin. *Reality and nonreality in student expectations of college*. Report of a project on student-environment interaction under a grant from the National Institute of Mental Health, Princeton University, 1965.

C. W. Taylor, ed. *Research conference on the identification of creative scientific talent*. Salt Lake City: University of Utah Press, 1959.

D. T. Thistlewaite. *Recruitment and retention of talented college student*. Report of a Cooperative Research Program under a grant from the U.S. Office of Education, Vanderbilt University, 1963; and "College Press and Student Achievement." *Journal of Educational Psychology*, 50 (1959), pp. 183-191.

### EARLY WARNING SIGNS

Many students who are potential dropouts show behaviors (difficulty concentrating, boredom, irregular eating and sleeping) and attitudes which warn of coming events.

*Georgetown University*. Residence hall staff meets regularly with the psychiatric division of the health service and the counseling service.

## *Appendix*

### FINANCIAL NEED

Studies are inconclusive as to whether financial need causes many students to leave college.

R. E. Iffert. *Retention and withdrawal of college students.* Bulletin No. 1, U.S. Department of Health, Education and Welfare, Washington, D.C.: U.S. Government Printing Office, 1957.

F. Jex and R. Merrill. "A Study in persistence: withdrawal and graduation rates at the University of Utah," *Personnel and Guidance Journal,* 401 (1962) pp. 762-768.

A number of programs exist to give special scholarships to disadvantaged youth.

*Expanding opportunities.* Washington, D.C.: American Council on Education, 2 (1965), pp. 1-8.

*For your information.* Office of Institutional Research, Association of State and Land-Grant Colleges, Circular No. 67, January 14, 1965.

National Achievement Scholarship Program for Outstanding Negro Students.

Rockefeller Foundation Scholarship Aid for Negro Students.

### STUDENT-FACULTY RELATIONSHIPS

The nature of student complaints about student-faculty relationships needs to be explored. Several programs aimed at combating the isolation of faculty from student body exist.

*University of Tennessee.* Students meet with faculty members in "Apple Polishing Sessions."

### PEER GROUP RELATIONSHIPS

There may be non-academic satisfactions or peer group structures which can reduce dropouts. For example, a University of Minnesota study shows that athletes withdraw less frequently than other comparable students.

J. R. Montgomery, L. C. Lewis, G. H. Whitlock, and J. M.

Porter. "Place of residence and academic persistence." Unpublished study, University of Tennessee, 1965.

J. Stecklein and L. Dameron. *Intercollegiate athletics and academic progress: comparison of academic progress of athletes and non-athletes at the University of Minnesota.* Report Series No. 3, Bureau of Institutional Research, University of Minnesota, 1965.

*University of California at Riverside.* Language groups are brought together in residence halls, increasing the sense of group belonging.

*University of California at Santa Cruz, Grand Valley State College and Monteith College of Wayne State University.* These institutions have created small college-within-large-university designs.

#### COUNSELING AND ORIENTATION PROGRAMS

Counseling programs are useful in getting information to the student at the right time and in helping with psychological difficulties.

*Gonzaga University.* An orientation program in the summer before matriculation is being evaluated.

C. D. Spielberger and H. Weitz. Improving the academic performance of anxious college freshmen: a group-counseling approach to the prevention of underachievement. *Psychological Monographs* Vol. 78 (1964), No. 13.

*University of Maryland.* Experimental use of machines in the College of Home Economics which give information on various college majors.

*University System of Georgia.* Publishes tables with which high-school guidance counselors can predict the performance of their students.

#### REMEDIAL WORK

Some Institutions give remedial course work to selected entering students to bring them up to acceptable standards for the institution.

*Parsons College, Knoxville College,* and many public colleges in Georgia. The *University of Maryland* has a special program for students not academically qualified for entrance, consisting of two college-level courses, special counseling on study habits and attitudes, and a voluntary reading improvement course. Those who complete this program and enroll in the regular program perform as well as other students.

GRADING PRACTICES

Often grading practices remain stable though admissions standards have risen considerably, but sometimes grading standards float with admissions standards.

*California Institute of Technology.* This school moved to give only pass or fail grades to freshmen to encourage learning of material rather than working for grades. The experiment will run through the 1965-67 school years and then be subject to review and evaluation.

E. J. Fisher. *Report on ACT program for freshmen.* Faculty Research Series, University of Tennessee, Winter 1965.

J. Hills. The effect of admissions policy on college grading standards. *Journal of Education Measurement,* 1 (1964), pp. 115-118; and *Housing and grading practices.* Research Bulletin 65-3, Board of Regents, University System of Georgia, 1965.

*Princeton University.* A new program allows students to take up to four courses in which they will receive only a pass or fail mark.

S. C. Webb, "Measured changes in college grading standards." *College Board Review,* 34 (Fall 1959), pp. 27-30.

TRANSFER

Efforts need to be made to assist the dropout in continuing his education.

*Catholic College Admission Center.* This Center corresponds with students who have left college to interest them in preparing for reentering college. It also helps the student to find a college for continuation of his studies.

*Pennsylvania State University.* This university has a flexible system under which a student may transfer from one college to another.

*University of Maryland.* This university allows students transferring from one college to another within the university to drop grades out of their average which do not apply to the new curriculum. A previous "F" remains on the record but is eliminated from the cumulative grade-point average.

*University of Wisconsin at Madison.* A student must be eligible to continue in his present college if he wants to transfer into another college.

*University of Wisconsin—Milwaukee* and *Milwaukee Institute of Technology.* A cooperative program between these two schools enables a student doing poorly at the University to transfer to the other institution. If he performs well at Milwaukee Tech, he may transfer back if he so desires.

### EDUCATIONAL CONDITIONS

Various attempts are being made to make college more interesting and rewarding.

*Allegheny College, Colorado College,* and *Lake Forest College.* Ford Foundation Funds have enabled them to develop independent study by releasing 25 outstanding students from all course work. Each student engages in independent study under a faculty adviser.

*Harvard College* and *Antioch College.* Both of these colleges hold small freshman seminars.

Lanora G. Lewis. "Talent and tomorrow's teachers—the honors approach." *New dimension in higher education.* U.S. Department of Health, Education and Welfare, Washington, D.C.: U.S. Government Printing Office, 1963.

## *CONTRIBUTORS*

ROBERT L. ARNSTEIN, M.D.

Psychiatrist-in-Chief, Department of University Health, Yale University

WILLARD DALRYMPLE, M.D.

Director, University Health Services, Princeton University

DONALD H. FORD, PH.D.

Director, Division of Counseling, Pennsylvania State University

WILLIAM A. HARVEY, M.D.

Assistant Professor of Psychiatry, University of Pennsylvania Medical School

Director of Resident Education, Institute of the Pennsylvania Hospital

JOHN HILLS, PH.D.

Director, Testing and Guidance, University System of Georgia

DOROTHY M. KNOELL, PH.D.

Center for the Study of Higher Education, University of California, Berkeley

LAWRENCE S. KUBIE, M.D.

Consultant on Research and Training, The Sheppard and Enoch Pratt Hospital

Editor-in-Chief, *The Journal of Nervous and Mental Disease*

Visiting Professor of Psychiatry, Jefferson Medical College

Clinical Professor of Psychiatry, University of Maryland

EDGAR A. LEVENSON, M.D.

Director, Young Adult Treatment Service, William Alanson White Institute

JAMES R. MONTGOMERY, PH.D.

Director, Institutional Research, University of Tennessee

LAWRENCE A. PERVIN, PH.D.

Clinical Psychologist, University Health Services

Assistant Professor of Psychology, Princeton University

MICHAEL A. PESZKE, M.D.

Assistant Professor of Psychiatry, University of Chicago Medical School

*Contributors*

Louis E. Reik, M.D.
Chief Psychiatrist, University Health Services, Princeton University

Roy Schafer, Ph.D.
Clinical Psychologist, Department of University Health
Associate Clinical Professor of Psychiatry and Psychology, Yale University

Benson R. Snyder, M.D.
Psychiatrist-in-Chief, Medical Department, Massachusetts Institute of Technology

Hugh B. Urban, Ph.D.
Coordinator, Psychotherapy Program, Division of Counseling, Pennsylvania State University

# INDEX

# Index

# Index

# Index

# Index

# Index